Foresight in Action

EARTHSCAN RISK IN SOCIETY SERIES

Series editor: Ragnar E. Löfstedt

Calculating Political Risk
Catherine Althaus

The Earthscan Reader on Risk
Edited by Ragnar E. Löfstedt and Åsa Boholm

The Ethics of Technological Risk
Edited by Lotte Asveld and Sabine Roeser

Facility Siting
Risk, Power and Identity in Land-Use Planning
Edited by Åsa Boholm and Ragnar E. Löfstedt

The Feeling of Risk
New Perspectives on Risk Perception
Paul Slovic

Foresight in Action
The Practice of Dealing with Uncertainty in Public Policy
Marjolein B. A. van Asselt, Susan A. van 't Klooster, Philip W. F. van Notten
and Livia A. Smits

Hazards, Vulnerability and Environmental Justice
Susan L. Cutter

The Perception of Risk
Paul Slovic

Risk Governance
Coping with Uncertainty in a Complex World
Ortwin Renn

Risk Management in Post-Trust Societies
Ragnar E. Löfstedt

Risk, Media and Stigma
Understanding Public Challenges to Modern Science and Technology
Edited by James Flynn, Paul Slovic and Howard Kunreuther

Risk, Uncertainty and Rational Action
Carlo C. Jaeger, Ortwin Renn, Eugene A. Rosa and Thomas Webler

The Social Contours of Risk (Volumes 1 & 2)
Jeanne X. Kasperson and Roger E. Kasperson

Social Trust and the Management of Risk
Edited by George Cvetkovich and Ragnar E. Löfstedt

The Tolerability of Risk
A New Framework for Risk Management
Edited by Frédéric Bouder, David Slavin and Ragnar E. Löfstedt

Transboundary Risk Governance
Rolf Lidskog, Linda Soneryd and Ylva Uggla

Transboundary Risk Management
Edited by Joanne Linnerooth-Bayer, Ragnar E. Löfstedt and Gunnar Sjöstedt

Trust in Risk Management
Uncertainty and Scepticism in the Public Mind
Edited by Michael Siegrist, Timothy C. Earle and Heinz Gutscher

Uncertainty and Risk
Multidisciplinary Perspectives
Edited by Gabriele Bammer and Michael Smithson

Foresight in Action

Developing Policy-Oriented Scenarios

Marjolein B. A. van Asselt,
Susan A. van 't Klooster, Philip W. F. van Notten
and Livia A. Smits

earthscan
from Routledge

First published by Earthscan in the UK and USA in 2010

For a full list of publications please contact:
Earthscan
2 Park Square, Milton Park, Abingdon, Oxfordshire OX14 4RN
711 Third Avenue, New York, NY 10017

First issued in paperback 2015

Earthscan is an imprint of the Taylor & Francis Group, an informa business

ISBN 13: 978-1-138-86699-7 (pbk)
ISBN 13: 978-1-8440-7677-2 (hbk)

Typeset by MapSet Ltd, Gateshead, UK
Cover design by Benjamin Youd

A catalogue record for this book is available from the British Library

Library of Congress Cataloging-in-Publication Data

Foresight in action : developing policy-oriented scenarios / Marjolein van Asselt ...
[et al.].
        p. cm.
    Includes bibliographical references and index.
    ISBN 978-1-84407-677-2 (hardback)
    1. Public policy. 2. Research methods. 3. Risk management. 4. Political planning. I.
Asselt, M. B. A. van
    H97.F666 2010
    320.6—dc22
                                                          2010004461

To our children:

Damiaan (2002)
Matthijs (2005)
Jasper (2008)
Laura (2008)
Eline (2009)

Contents

List of Figures, Tables and Boxes   ix
Acknowledgements   xi
List of Acronyms and Abbreviations   xiii

1   Researching Policy-Oriented Foresight in Action   1
    Aims   2
    Introduction to foresight   3
    Dutch foresight   8
    Research questions   11
    Research approach   12
    Audience   17
    Structure of the book   19

2   First Impressions of Foresight Practice   23
    Forecasting and foresight   23
    Preparing the journey   25
    Conclusions   38

3   Dealing with Policy   41
    Introduction   41
    Policy-free scenarios   41
    Policy-free and policy-oriented foresight   43
    The no (significant) policy change principle   47
    Struggling with policy   50
    Policy at the framing level   57
    Conclusions   58

4   Practising the Scenario Matrix   61
    Attending to the scenario matrix   61
    Textbook descriptions: The backbone functional meaning   62
    Getting started: Backbone and foundation   65
    Analysing multiple representations   67
    Multiplicity continues to reign: The scaffold functional meaning   70

More functional meanings: The showcase 73
Conclusions 74

5 **Dealing with Prospective Uncertainty** 79
Prospective uncertainty 79
Uncertainty awareness 80
Uncertainty manners 82
The danger of 'certainification' 97
Conclusions 100

6 **The Past, the Present and the Future** 105
Introduction 105
Meantime 106
Temporal repertoires 106
A case in time 108
Discontinuity in foresight 119
Conclusions 133

7 **Reflection on Action** 137
Summary of findings 137
Discussion 140
From reflection on action to reflection in action 142
Lessons for policy audiences 144

References 147
Appendix 163
Index 167

List of Figures, Tables and Boxes

Figures

1.1   Futurist in action   5
2.1   The scenario cartwheel   28
2.2   Policy-oriented scenario studies mapped in the scenario cartwheel   31
2.3   Scenario families   35
4.1   The scenario matrix   63
4.2   Selection of axes   63
4.3   Visualization of one of our observations   64
4.4   The SCENE scenario matrix   66
4.5   Scenario matrix used as foundation   67
4.6   A scenario matrix representation that figured in the SCENE project   68
4.7   Scenario matrix as two-dimensional possibility space   69
4.8   Scenario matrix used as scaffold   69
4.9   Enactment that sits comfortably with multiple functional meanings   72
4.10 Scenario matrix used as showcase   73

Tables

2.1   Dutch policy-oriented scenario studies   33
2.2   Themes of Dutch scenario studies   34
4.1   Functional meanings of the scenario matrix   75
5.1   Uncertainty manners observed in foresight practice   98
6.1   Empirically informed description of temporal repertoires
employed in foresight   114
6.2   Summary of foresights that included discontinuity   128

Boxes

1.1   Future   1
1.2   History of Dutch policy-oriented foresight   9
1.3   Triangulation   14
2.1   Forecasting   24
2.2   Example of snapshot scenario   26

2.3 Example of chain scenario 27
2.4 Backcasting 27
2.5 The Flight of the Flamingos 30
2.6 Description of scenario studies mapped in the scenario cartwheel 32
2.7 Long-term themes in Dutch scenario studies 34
3.1 Minimally differentiated trend policy 48
6.1 Quotes from the *Welvaart en Leefomgeving* (WLO) final report 119
6.2 Relevant observations in other endeavours 120

Acknowledgements

In 2001, Marjolein van Asselt received a career grant (*Vernieuwingsimpuls*) from the Dutch Science Foundation (NWO) to carry out research on foresight practice. Philip van Notten and Susan van 't Klooster participated in the project as PhD researchers. During the grant period (2001 to 2006), we investigated how experts explore the long term for policy audiences. Our observations and analysis have been published in journal articles, book chapters, two PhD theses and several popular scientific writings. Various peers and practitioners have urged us to write a synthesis book, which integrates the most important insights, scattered over various publications, in one volume. Fortunately, NWO provided another grant to support writing such a book. In addition, we benefited from some smaller grants from De Jonge Akademie (DJA) of the Dutch Royal Academy of Arts and Sciences (KNAW).

Our home institutes, Maastricht University and the Institute for Environmental Studies (VU Amsterdam University), are kindly thanked for their continuing support in all senses. We also benefited from stays at other institutes – for example, Oxford University (with a special word of thanks to Steve Woolgar, Jerry Ravetz and Steve Rayner), the King's Centre for Risk Management in London (with a special word of thanks to Ragnar Löfstedt) and the Centre for Science, Technology and Society at Santa Clara University, California (with a special word of thanks to Geoffrey Bowker and Susan Leigh Star).

We are particularly grateful to our contributors in foresight practice; we thank them for their openness and trust and for allowing us to participate in their daily professional lives. Over the years, we also benefited from all kinds of formal and informal peer review. We thank all peers who reviewed our work. The PhD projects were co-supervised by Jan Rotmans (Philip van Notten) and Wiebe Bijker (Susan van 't Klooster), who are thanked for their high-level input and for thinking along. Am Sleegers and Dale Rothman, who co-authored papers related to the PhD project of Philip van Notten, also deserve a special word of thanks. Furthermore, we would like to thank Jessica Mesman, with whom we collaborated on the issue of prospective uncertainty, Jan-Willem van der Pas and Rein de Wilde, who co-authored a report on Dutch foresight practice, and Karin van der Ven, who provided feedback on earlier drafts of some chapters. In the final stage of writing the book, we benefited from the foresight project of the Scientific Council for Government Policy (WRR), for which Marjolein van Asselt is the responsible council member. More specifically, we benefited from literature research and discussions within the project team (with a special word of thanks to Sietske Veenman, Franke van der Molen, Nina Faas and Wouter van der Torre), within the council, with experts and with policy audiences. We also warmly thank a number of colleagues and friends who have taken the time and effort to read and comment on the manuscript: Arnim Wiek, Ragnar Löfstedt, Frederic Bouder, Tessa Fox and Antal Sanders. Finally, we thank Annet Butink for her help with the graphics and Andreas Lachenmaier and Lidwien Hollanders for their work concerning indexing.

List of Acronyms and Abbreviations

BEPA	Bureau for European Policy Advisers
CO_2	carbon dioxide
CPB	Centraal Planbureau (The Netherlands Bureau for Economic Policy Analysis)
DATAR	Délégation à l'Aménagement du Territoire et à l'Action Régionale (French ministry of spatial planning)
DJA	De Jonge Akademie (The Young Academy, part of the KNAW)
EASST	European Association for the Study of Science and Technology
ECN	Energieonderzoek Centrum Nederland (Energy Research Centre of The Netherlands)
EEA	European Environment Agency
EU	European Union
GDP	gross domestic product
GHG	greenhouse gas
IPCC	Intergovernmental Panel on Climate Change
KNAW	Koninklijke Nederlandse Akademie van Wetenschap (Dutch Royal Academy of Arts and Sciences)
MNP	Milieu en Natuur Planbureau (The Netherlands Environmental Assessment Agency)
NWO	Nederlandse Organisatie voor Wetenschappelijk Onderzoek (Dutch Science Foundation)
OECD	Organisation for Economic Co-operation and Development
PBL	Planbureau voor de Leefomgeving (The Netherlands Environmental Assessment Agency)
R&D	research and development
RIVM	Rijksinstituut voor Volksgezondheid en Milieu
RPB	Ruimtelijk Planbureau (Institute for Spatial Research)
RPD	Rijksplanologische Dienst (predecessor of RPB)
4S	Society for Social Studies of Science
SCP	Sociaal en Cultureel Planbureau (Social and Cultural Planning Office)

SME	small- and medium-sized enterprise
SRA	Society for Risk Analysis
SRES	IPCC Special Report on Emissions Scenarios
STS	science and technology studies
TNO	Nederlandse Organisatie voor Toegepast-Natuurwetenschappelijk Onderzoek (The Netherlands Organization for Applied Scientific Research)
UK	United Kingdom
UN	United Nations
UNEP	United Nations Environment Programme
US	United States
VROM	Ministerie van Volksgezondheid, Ruimtelijke Ordening en Milieubeheer (Dutch Ministry of Spatial Planning and Environment)
VVR	*Verkenning van de Ruimte* (Spatial foresight)
WBCSD	World Business Council for Sustainable Development
WFS	World Futurists Society
WFSF	World Futures Studies Federation
WLO	Welvaart en Leefomgeving (The future of the Dutch natural and built environment)
WRR	Wetenschappelijke Raad voor het Regeringsbeleid (Scientific Council for Government Policy)

1

Researching Policy-Oriented Foresight in Action

Scientific research is grounded in data-gathering and analysis. Data about the future (see Box 1.1), however, cannot be gathered or analysed in classical ways. Nevertheless, society demands systematic assessments of the future, and in scholarly circles calls are made for serious study of the future (e.g. Sardar, 1999a; Slaughter, 2002; van der Duin et al, 2004; see also the peer-reviewed journals *Futures, Foresight* and *Technological Forecasting & Social Change*). H. G. Wells's article 'The discovery of the future' in *Nature* (1902), in which he explored the possibilities of the study of the future as a scientific activity, can be considered an early point of reference. Nowadays, different national and international, public and private organizations around the world have the assignment or ambition to explore the long term. Numerous professionals employed by these organizations produce statements about prospective conditions, actions that have not yet occurred, events that have not yet happened, processes that are not yet manifest, states not yet in existence and policies not yet in force. The intriguing question is: how do these experts produce such assessments of the future?

Policy-oriented foresight came into vogue during the 1960s and 1970s. With the term 'policy-oriented foresight', we refer to assessments of the

---

BOX 1.1 FUTURE

The use of 'future' in the English language dates back to the 14th century. It derives from the Latin notion *'futūrus'*, meaning 'about to be', which became assimilated in French as 'futur'. Broadly speaking, future and its translations refer to the time that is to be or come hereafter. It is not clearly delineated in terms of time horizon: it may mean tomorrow, next year, the coming decade, the next 20, 30 or 50 years, or even forthcoming centuries (Brier, 2005). In the context of foresight, future usually refers to the long term – namely, beyond the next ten years.

future in a public policy context.[1] Early studies sketched long-term societal developments, with the aim of raising awareness among politicians and the general public. Famous examples involve *The Year 2000* by Kahn and Wiener (1967) and the Club of Rome's *Limits to Growth* report (Meadows et al, 1972). The French governmental organization for spatial planning, Délégation à l'Aménagement du Territoire et à l'Action Régionale (DATAR), founded in 1963, is another early example of an institute engaged in policy-oriented foresight. Recent renowned examples of policy-oriented foresight endeavours (see also Ringland, 2002b) involve the UK foresight programme (www.foresight.gov.uk) (Berkhout et al, 2001; Berkhout and Hertin, 2002; Department of Trade and Industry, 2002), the UN's Global Environment Outlooks (UNEP, 1997, 1999, 2002, 2007), the climate change scenarios produced by the Intergovernmental Panel on Climate Change (www.ipcc.ch), the activities of the Forward Studies Unit of the European Commission (established in 1989 and incorporated in the Bureau for European Policy Advisers (BEPA) in 2001) and the Organisation for Economic Co-operation and Development (OECD) future trends reports and foresight activities in areas as diverse as education, transport, agriculture, technology and creative society (www.oecd.org). The famous Shell scenarios (www.shell.com/scenarios) are examples of scenarios developed in business contexts; but at the same time, they aim at influencing public policy. So they can be considered a special case.

Aims

In this book, we describe how experts assess the future in the practice of policy-oriented foresight. To that end, we conducted empirical research in foresight practice. Our observations enable us to understand how policy-oriented foresight is carried out. As a result, this book is about policy-oriented foresight in action. Different authors (see, for example, van der Staal and van Vught, 1987a,b; Ester et al, 1997; Bell, 2000; Brown et al, 2000; Dammers, 2000; WRR, 2000; van der Meulen, 2002; and Adam and Groves, 2007) have argued that reflection on foresight in action is both lacking and needed. Ester et al (1997) explicitly advise gaining more insights into the 'logics in use'. A similar plea is made by Brown et al (2000, p4), who argue that it is necessary to look at 'the "real time" activities of actors' in order to understand 'how the future … is constructed … by whom and under what conditions'.

We describe foresight in action. We explain what people actually *do* when they explore the future. We aim to 'inscribe'[2] real-time mechanisms at work[3] by means of so-called thick descriptions, which are informative stories attentive to details. What does it mean to inscribe? The researcher 'writes it down. In so doing, he turns it from a passing event, which exists only in its own moment of occurrence, into an account, which exists in its inscriptions and can be reconsulted' (Geertz, 1973/1999, p19). Empirical research in foresight practice enabled us to produce detailed descriptions of what futurists active in the context of public policy do. Through the stories told in this book, we aim to inscribe and explicate how professional futurists tell the future.

The stories themselves do not answer the question of how to do foresight. First and foremost, they present to a broader audience how practitioners do foresight. With this book we aim to provide an account of foresight practice that is new to futurists and that is of interest to newcomers and to policy actors, as targeted users of policy-oriented foresight. This book is an attempt to provide a *re-consultable*, empirically informed reflection on foresight practice in order to enable futurists to look in the mirror. We aim to disclose manners, activities, pitfalls and challenges that usually become concealed or overlooked in stylized self-accounts and methodological-epistemological discussions.[4] Our empirically informed reflection on action aims to help futurists better reflect in action. It is supposed to be a resource for self-reflexivity. To that end, in each of the core chapters, we compare what textbooks say with what we saw futurists doing in practice. We describe how futurists struggle with policy (Chapter 3), how they employ a particular tool (the scenario matrix) (Chapter 4), how they cope with uncertainty (Chapter 5) and how they deal with time (Chapter 6). By confronting theory and practice we aim to provide insights into problems, practical solutions, lessons to be learned and leads for quality improvement (Chapter 7). With our examination of foresight in action we want to contribute to a quality improvement, both in the practice of policy-oriented foresight and in the actual use of foresights for policy purposes.

Introduction to foresight

Humankind did not always contemplate the future as a realm of action (for a comprehensive treatment, see Adam and Groves, 2007; see also, Morgan, 2002, with reference to Bury, 1932, and Polak, 1971). In early times, the future was considered a sacred domain ruled by the gods. Only in modern times did the idea arise that humans could influence or even shape the future (Adam and Groves, 2007; Nowotny, 2008). This view of the future as a realm of action encouraged interest in contemplating the future. This has been and is done in a variety of ways, including:

- *Utopian novels*, such as *Utopia* (1516) by Thomas Moore, *New Atlantis* (1627) by Francis Bacon, *Walden* (1854) by Henry David Thoreau and *Island* (1962) by Aldous Huxley, and their counterparts, the dystopian novels – for example, *The Time Machine* (1895) by H. G. Wells, *Brave New World* (1932) by Aldous Huxley and *1984* (1949) by George Orwell, constitute a particular literary genre in which possible, preferable or dreaded futures are explored.
- *Science fiction* (Clute et al, 1993) can be portrayed as laboratories for exploring alternative futures (Rose, 2000).[5] Classics include Mary Shelley's *Frankenstein* (1818) and the work of Jules Verne (1828 to 1905) and Isaac Asimov (1920 to 1992).

- The future is also explored in popular *trend-watching* endeavours, such as Marshall McLuhan's *Understanding Media* (1964), Alvin Toffler's *Future Shock* (1970), John Naisbitt's *Megatrends* books (1982, 1990, 1992, 1996) and the trend-watching by Faith Popcorn (www.faithpopcorn.com). The images of the future drawn by trend watchers usually promise technology-driven prosperity (de Wilde, 2000).

In such a broader perspective, foresight is just another attempt to make sense of the time ahead. Most experts involved in foresight whom we encountered, however, do not want to be associated with utopian and dystopian novel writing, science fiction and trend-watching, arguably to avoid a 'pulp image' (Miles, 1993) and with the aim of constructing or sustaining a status as 'authorised experts' (Galtung, 2003). Scholars and practitioners involved in foresight assume that the foresight approach to exploration of the future is different.

To a certain extent, the aspiration of foresight resembles the ambition of scholarly historians. Like historians, futurists[6] try to portray a spirit of a different time through systematic inquiry, but with different means, as they lack the equivalent of sources and traces of previous civilizations that provide the resources for historians. Futurists present foresight in different ways: as the skill of making meaning in looking ahead (Fuller, 1999), as 'the process of developing a range of ... possible ways in which the future could develop and understanding these sufficiently well to be able to decide what decisions can be taken today' (Horton, 1999, p5), and as the act of inventing, examining, evaluating and proposing possible, probable and preferable futures (Bell, 2003, p73). The aim of foresight is presented as the ambition to reframe the familiar and to anticipate events before they occur (Burt and Wright, 2006, with reference to Shepherd and Tsoukas, 2004). Instead of attempting to define foresight, we prefer to introduce policy-oriented foresight by means of three scenes: two stories and one picture from Dutch policy-oriented foresight practice.

Scene 1

Two men and three computers in an office. Both men are working on a computer. One of them, let's call him John, turns to his roommate and asks: 'Martin, shall we do another iteration with Paulus?' Paulus is a computer model. Martin answers: 'That's of no use because Rick (another person in the office next door) is busy with sustainable technology.' Martin assumes that they have to wait until Tuesday before they can 'iterate with Paulus'. John asks whether it would nevertheless be 'illustrative' to do an iteration. Martin doesn't agree: 'I can't do it before Tuesday.' John is concerned about the time schedule for the calculations: 'That'll be cutting things too fine.' Martin reacts: 'If Rick would've given me something, but he is still busy puzzling. We should've done this months ago, but ...'. John interrupts. Martin responds: 'I agree that Rick has probably done it more thoroughly than Steve (another colleague who used to be involved in their endeavour), who didn't have time either. Let's assume that Rick will deliver something on Monday. Wind is most important. I'll try to extrapolate biomass. So if you want to see it, I may be able to do some iterations on Monday.' Martin turns to the stranger in the room: 'The last time, we were also delayed by months due to maternity leave, a world trip and because the client changed his mind with regard to transport.' Martin talks to John again: 'OK, John, we'll do it Monday morning, unless Sam (another collaborator) says that he wants it now.'

Scene 2

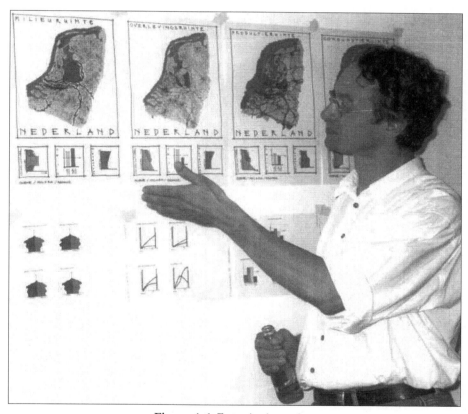

Figure 1.1 *Futurist in action*

Source: Susan van 't Klooster

Scene 3

Seven people, three men and four women, of different ages between 30 and 50 years, have gathered together in a meeting room. They have an 'agenda' and a 'script'. Both have been distributed in advance by email. The agenda of this so-called 'integration session' reads:

10.00 am	*Opening*
10.05 am	*Announcements*
10.15 am	*Report of the previous meeting*
10.30 am	*Balance and knowledge questions*
13.00 pm	*Lunch break*
13.30 pm	*Balance and knowledge questions*
16.30 pm	*Appointments*
17.00 pm	*Closure*

It turns out that the label 'balance and knowledge questions' refers to an activity to be carried out in two subgroups. In the 'script', the subgroups' assignment is described in more detail. Before breaking into subgroups, the participants discuss how to feed the results of the subgroup discussions back to the plenary session. The 'script' author proposes that they write down a lot on flip-over sheets and that they read each other's sheets. Informed by the exchange, the chairperson decides to reserve an hour for feedback and allocation of tasks.

The subgroup that needs to discuss the themes 'international' and 'national' issues interprets the 'script' as a starting point, not as a road map. The three people start their work by reading another document – namely, 'Conclusions of the subprojects'. During the encounter, they browse through other documents, which turn out to be reports of 'subprojects'. One of the women especially wants to look up the documents again and again. The subsequent discussion doesn't develop smoothly. Another woman explicitly invites and challenges the other two with remarks such as 'You don't dare to ...'. At some point in the exchange, she presents what she announces as 'an example' (i.e. 'nature nationally fragmented and internationally joined together'). During the exchange, the three talk about 'ranges', 'knowledge questions' and 'levers for policy'. After some deliberation they draw their conclusions, stating that in all 'scenarios' the most important nature areas are kept, but the outlooks in the scenarios differ in terms of quality. At some point, the leading woman decides to visit the other subgroup in order to draw some inspiration.

End of scenes

The scenes described above can be considered as snapshot images taken on our journey in policy-oriented foresight practice. We, as researchers, are the 'stranger in the room' featured in the first scene. What do these scenes reveal about foresight? The settings sketched, the descriptions of what the people involved are doing, the kind of exchanges between them, the sorts of non-human actors (such as computer models), the variety of stage props (documents, agenda, flip-over sheets) and vocabulary used, indicate that the stage where the scenes are taking place is a professional context in which colleagues are engaged in some group assignment. Notions such as 'subprojects' and 'iterations', the apparent dependence on colleagues' work and expertise, and references to previous meetings and new appointments suggest that the assignment is a socially intricate and lengthy collaborative endeavour. It is obvious that the professionals are not engaged in routine work. For example, it is clear from the subgroup dynamics that the 'script' featuring in the third scene is not a standardized manual. One of the professionals is constantly glancing through documents as if she is hoping for clues and hooks. The visit to the other subgroup for inspiration also indicates that what to do and how to do it is neither self-evident nor easy. Their self-descriptions of 'busy puzzling' and facing 'delay' also indicate that the activity is a demanding team endeavour. Although all people who feature in the scenes are experienced professionals, they seem to seek assurance about how to progress, notwithstanding their experience. It is not a straightforward familiar project that can be easily structured and strictly planned.

The posters in the second scene present maps with labels. These Dutch labels read 'socio-cultural', 'environment' and 'demography'. A number of issues feature in the first and the third scene – namely, sustainable technology, transport, national issues, international issues and nature. 'National' and 'international' issues are references to the geographical scope(s) to be considered in the endeavour. Notions such as sustainable technology, transport, environment/nature, demography and socio-cultural refer to broad societal issues. The scenes reveal that policy-oriented foresight involves addressing a wide range of complex issues and different geographical scales.

The scenes not only shed some light on the kind of endeavour, the type of subjects considered and the kind of people involved, but also provide some indications about the kind of activities these futurists are involved in. Terms such as 'extrapolate', 'scenarios', 'ranges', 'calculations', and 'levers for policy' are references to the kind of actions performed (extrapolation, calculation, exploration) and the kind of output (scenarios, range, levers for policy) produced. The aim seems to be to construct prospective stories which support policy-relevant claims set and staged in future times.

Futurists, who are regarded as experts specialized in anticipating the future, consider foresight to be a process of systematic inquiry. But systematic inquiry of the future appears to be a mission impossible. This problem has always been recognized by those involved in foresight:

- 'A statement about the future cannot be uttered with the claim that it is true; we can always imagine that the contrary will happen, and we have no guarantee that future experience will not present to us as real what is imagination today' (Reichenbach, 1951, p241).
- 'Knowledge of the future is a contradiction in terms' (de Jouvenel, 1967, p5).
- 'How can we study the future and make justified statements about that which does not exist?' (Bell, 2003, p148).

The future is a construct made possible through the human sense of time (compare Nowotny et al, 2001, and Koselleck, 1985). The future resides in the mind. It does not exist in a material or concrete sense, although at the same time the future is not just imagined, but also made and, in a way, precluded in our past and present actions (Adam and Groves, 2007). Standard scientific methods fail, as the future cannot be known or studied empirically. Adam and Groves (2007) even argue that 'mechanistic science' and associated approaches curtail the capacity to engage with the future. So familiar research methods are not sufficient or are even dead weight.

Foresight is thus a conceptual practice in the sense that stories told by futurists are imaginations and social constructions. In fact, enquiry implies envisioning, inventing and constructing futures. In the context of contemporary foresight, it is accepted practice to argue that it is all about social constructions. Hardly any of the futurists portrayed in this book would be upset. Foresight is about processes, events and actions that have not (yet) taken place. So, even futurists who still prefer to adhere to positivistic ideals[7] about 'science', in general, will quite easily accept that foresight is a social construction process. The constructivist thesis[8] (Kuhn, 1970; Latour and Woolgar, 1979; Bijker et al, 1987; Searle, 1995; Hacking, 1999) is thus hardly controversial in this context.

Dutch foresight

Generally, The Netherlands is considered a pioneer and one of the most active countries in the field of foresight, in general, and policy-oriented foresight, in particular. In The Netherlands, policy-oriented foresight is highly institutionalized (Hoppe, 1980; van Vught, 1985; van der Staal and van Vught, 1987a,b). It is hardly possible to imagine the Dutch public policy landscape without foresight (Schooneboom, 2003; Halffman and Hoppe, 2005). The high level of institutionalization implies that there is a web of institutes with the attributed or self-assigned role, task or assignment to assess the future. These institutes, commonly referred to as 'planning agencies'[9] or 'research centres', are non-academic knowledge-producing institutes working in what is usually described as the interface between 'science' and 'policy'. The following institutes are considered to constitute the core of this Dutch foresight network:

- The Netherlands Bureau for Economic Policy Analysis (Centraal Planbureau – CPB);
- The Netherlands Environmental Assessment Agency (Milieu en Natuur Planbureau – MNP, which used to be part of the Rijksinstituut voor Volksgezondheid en Milieu – RIVM); RIVM's foresight activities are reviewed in van Asselt (2000) and van Asselt et al (2001a);
- the Social and Cultural Planning Office (Sociaal en Cultureel Planbureau – SCP);
- the Institute for Spatial Research (Ruimtelijk Planbureau – RPB) and its predecessor Rijksplanologische Dienst (RPD); the RPB recently (2008)

merged with MNP into The Netherlands Environmental Assessment Agency (Planbureau voor de Leefomgeving – PBL);

- the Scientific Council for Government Policy (Wetenschappelijke Raad voor het Regeringsbeleid – WRR);
- Energy Research Centre of The Netherlands (Energieonderzoek Centrum Nederland – ECN);
- The Netherlands Organization for Applied Scientific Research (Nederlandse Organisatie voor Toegepast-Natuurwetenschappelijk Onderzoek – TNO).

Foresight is practised in these institutes. Interestingly, though, even if foresight is a major activity, the professionals whom we encountered do not view themselves as 'futurists'. These professionals instead have the self-image of being a 'researcher', an 'expert' on a particular topic or a 'policy analyst'.

Policy-oriented foresight endeavours to encourage a long-term orientation in policy and politics. The target audience is 'policy', which is conceptualized, in practice, as a specific minister or ministry, or more vaguely as 'policy-makers in The Hague'[10] or 'the government'. Foresights can be initiated by the institutes themselves or are carried out at the request of, or even commissioned by, specific policy-makers.

BOX 1.2 HISTORY OF DUTCH POLICY-ORIENTED FORESIGHT

The Scientific Council for Government Policy (WRR) was founded in 1972 and received the explicit task to conduct foresight and to improve, stimulate and coordinate policy-oriented foresight in The Netherlands (Royal Decree, 6 November 1972). In 1977 the WRR published its first broad assessment, *The Next 25 Years*, also referred to as the general foresight endeavour ('*algemene toekomstverkenning*' in Dutch, abbreviated to ATV) (for a retrospective assessment, see van der Duin et al, 2004). This report is generally considered to be the first Dutch example of policy-oriented foresight. In 1980 and 1983, the WRR published two reports under the heading 'policy-oriented foresight' (in Dutch 'beleidsgerichte toekomstverkenning', abbreviated to BTV). At the same time, other policy-oriented agencies began to get involved in foresight. In 1975, urban planning scenarios were published by the Rijksplanologische Dienst (RPD). The Netherlands Bureau for Economic Policy Analysis (CPB) and the Social and Cultural Planning Office (SCP) published their first long-term assessments in 1985. The Energy Research Centre of The Netherlands (ECN) also engaged in foresight: it issued its first energy outlook in 1987. In 1988, the environmental agency RIVM produced the first environmental outlook, entitled *Concern for Tomorrow*, which received much political and public attention. Ever since these first long-term assessments, institutes have begun to engage in policy-oriented foresight on a regular basis, ranging from very specific sector-oriented studies to broad, rather holistic, analyses.

In addition, individual authors (e.g. Rademaker, 2001; Das and Das, 2004;) also produce policy-oriented foresights. Furthermore, ministries (Ministerie van Verkeer en Waterstaat, 1998), local authorities in larger cities (e.g. Gemeente Amsterdam, 1999; Gemeente Leiden, 2004) and provinces are now involved in foresight, usually supported by consultancy agencies (van Twist et al, 2002; de Baak Management et al, 2005). The Netherlands is host to several consultancy agencies specialized in foresight – namely, Futureconsult and de Ruijter Strategie BV. For an up-to-date overview of Dutch foresight (which also includes private-sector foresights where reports are publicly available), see www.toekomstverkenning.nl (in Dutch).

Policy-oriented foresight is serious business in the Netherlands. Brown et al (2000) even argue that universally (or at least in the Western world):

> ... *by all measures, the future has become a big business. Witness in this regard the importance of the future in contemporary fiction and film, the need for public policy dealing with the environment to justify itself in terms of long-term sustainability, the growing market for scenarios ... and horizon scanning in organizations, and even the emergence of books such as this one.* (Brown et al, 2000, p5; see also Adam and Groves, 2007)

In this perspective, The Netherlands is part of a larger international trend. Taking into account its rich history, The Netherlands is an important site to study foresight in action. The majority of Dutch foresight endeavours is only public domain for those who understand Dutch. This book therefore discloses, in English, a particular foresight tradition to a broader audience.

There are a number of reasons why Dutch practice is a particularly interesting case study in foresight. We already indicated that foresight is big and highly institutionalized in The Netherlands. Furthermore, Dutch experiences serve as a source of inspiration for foresight endeavours elsewhere. For example, the *Environmental Outlooks* of the Dutch environmental agency RIVM (RIVM, 1988, 1991/1992, 1993, 1997, 2000) inspired the United Nations to produce the *Global Environment Outlook* series and served as a benchmark for foresight activities of the European Environment Agency (EEA). The Dutch environment agency is actively involved in international environmental foresight, such as in the Intergovernmental Panel on Climate Change (IPCC) scenario endeavours. Some Dutch studies are available in English, such as the *Scanning the Future* and *Four Futures of Europe* reports produced by The Netherlands Bureau for Economic Policy Analysis (CPB) (CPB, 1992; de Mooij and Tang, 2003). The first report is cited in English, French and Spanish publications, involving articles in peer-reviewed journals (ranging from *Ecological Economics* to *Journal of Business Ethics*, and from *Transportation Planning and Technology* to the *Journal of Housing and Built Environment*) and various scenario studies and foresight endeavours, such as Bertrand et al (1999), Gallopín (2004), Raskin (2005), and the IPCC *Fourth Assessment Report* (IPCC, 2007). This illustrates the role of Dutch foresight in the international scene.

Due to the wealth of foresight endeavours, the high level of institutionalization of Dutch policy-oriented foresight, and the impact of Dutch foresight and involvement of Dutch futurists outside The Netherlands, Dutch policy-oriented practice is an attractive area for studying foresight in action. In a five-year research endeavour, we have observed futurists in action in two Dutch institutes – namely, the spatial planning agency, RPB and the energy research centre, ECN. For each institute, we included three foresight endeavours in our fieldwork. One of the foresight endeavours concerned a collaborative project with The Netherlands Bureau for Economic Policy Analysis (CPB) and The Netherlands Environmental Assessment Agency (then MNP, now PBL). We furthermore benefited from revisiting earlier empirical research in Dutch foresight practice (van Asselt, 2000, and van Asselt et al, 2001a). This fieldwork constitutes the core of our empirical study of foresight practice.

Research questions

In this book, we turn the analytical gaze to practices through and in which 'futures' are produced.[11] How, for example, do futurists construct stories and future claims? How do they sort things out? What methodologies, approaches and tools are used in constructing futures? How do futurists deal with uncertainty, complexity and the possibility of discontinuity? How do they deal with the fact that a multitude of assessments of the future may be equally legitimate? In sum, how do they produce 'knowledge' about the future?

New and original empirical research is needed to address these questions, as reliable and valid answers cannot be derived from so-called *self-accounts* (Latour and Woolgar, 1979) – namely, reports by futurists in which the foresight approach is described and justified. We observed that methodological accounts are often lacking and, if available, are stylized. Notwithstanding the recognition, also among futurists, that foresight presents an extraordinary challenge in intellectual and methodological terms, methodological accounts are usually (very) short descriptions of some main steps or are confined to a simple scheme. As a result, a linear and step-wise process is suggested: choices, considerations, discussions, struggles, compromises, unproductive steps, flaws, practical adjustments, experiments, difficulties, challenges and local solutions are concealed. Van der Staal and van Vught (1987a,b) explicitly qualified futurists' self-accounts as constructions that do not reflect the construction process. Foresight practice is messier and more complex than is suggested in futurists' accounts. Furthermore, self-accounts are usually produced in hindsight. As a rule, they are not informed by structured notes, observations and analysis of the actual process, but are rooted in the original plans and/or the highly subjective impressions and evaluations of the process. A further disadvantage is that retrospective process descriptions might be coloured by how the foresight is evaluated by target audiences. In case the foresight was positively received and used, the retrospective self-account may be of a different tone and emphasis than in situations in which the foresight turned out to be ignored. A retrospective attitude is likely to enhance linearization – namely, a straightforward and 'clean' representation of a much messier process. We want to counter such idealized portrayals as they do not provide us with a basis for understanding foresight in action. Even worse, linear accounts are likely to uncritically or unconsciously mobilize and strengthen methodological myths. This actually obscures how foresight is practised. In order to capture how futurists produce statements about the uncertain future, it is necessary to empirically research foresight practice.

Research approach

We aim to achieve an understanding of the detailed activities that futurists perform in their effort to assess the future. For this type of interest in actual practice, studying practitioners while they are working is recommended (Schön, 1983; Latour and Woolgar, 1986; Knorr-Cetina, 1995). Such *in situ* monitoring or 'participant observation' as a research approach is generally associated with ethnography, a research style that is rooted in anthropology (see Hammersley and Atkinson, 1995, for a well-referenced introduction). Participant observation involves close attention, with some exactness, to the daily doings, deliberations and social processes in action. This means that the researcher 'takes notes, makes tape recordings (both video and audio), conducts interviews and amasses all the relevant documents ... for example, draft calculations ... computer print-outs, [internal] memos ... their correspondence ... the articles, books and reports which are being read and/or referred to and otherwise used' (Woolgar, 1988, p84). A preference for participant observation as a research approach typically stems from dissatisfaction with the available self-accounts (see, for example, Latour and Woolgar, 1986, and Woolgar, 1988).

As far as our knowledge extends, Dobbinga (2001) has been the first to perform participant observation in foresight practice. During 1996 to 1999, she studied a scenario project that was conducted at the Dutch Ministry of Transport and Water. Her observation and analysis focused on organizational dynamics. She roughly described the scenario approach used (Dobbinga, 2001, pp47–51), but was particularly interested in the use of scenarios as a management tool to challenge traditional views and routines within an organization. Brooks (2004) conducted participant observation (1998 to 2001) in the US Institute for the Future, a non-profit organization that advises private, public and non-governmental sectors about long-term strategies for innovation. His PhD thesis provides some insight into how these particular futurists assess the future. Brooks planned to write a book about this research, which, when finished, might be used to systematically compare his observations with ours.

From 2001 till 2005, we pursued extensive participant observation among practitioners involved in actual foresight endeavours in The Netherlands. We noted what we saw happening, what we saw futurists doing and what we heard them say, in meetings and workshops, but also in phone calls or bilateral chats. We talked with them and asked questions, both informally and in arranged open interview settings. We collected documents produced by the futurists, and other texts which featured in the futurists' activities. We retrieved and received e-mails, took pictures, audio recorded many meetings and transcribed the tapes. We shared some observations with the futurists and recorded their feedback. The following field note excerpt indicates that capturing what is going on is easier said than done:

This was a very complicated session. On the one hand, there is repetition compared to previous sessions... The futurists themselves seem not to understand what is going on, and express that they have difficulty in following the discussions. They repeatedly acknowledge that it goes everywhere and nowhere and that they need structure. There is hardly any direction, although the project leaders try to chair and other participants attempt to contribute through process remarks. A report of what has been said in this meeting doesn't provide any insight into the process of foresight. For this particular field report, we have therefore chosen ... a different kind of reporting. I have tried to use my notes to provide a kind of impressionistic report as a context for the literal observations. It was difficult to structure the literal observations [based on notes and transcribing the tape] or to break it down into topics, as so much jumbles together, that only chronological order provides a little sense. The consequence is long text pieces. I have tried to mark some sections in those lengthy texts in bold text. I have also tried to characterize the discussion in terms of phases, but that didn't give solace either. Finally, with catchwords (between brackets and underlined) I have tried to somewhat 'code' the extracts. (Field notes, August 2004)

Our participant observation took place in a number of places – namely, in offices, meeting rooms, secretariats, canteens, coffee corners, kitchens, corridors and elevators, but also in other places outside the walls of the institutes where the observed futurists practised foresight, including trains, a football stadium and a beach tent. We thus studied futurists in action in different places and settings, an approach usually characterized as 'multi-sited'.

We made an honest effort to design our research appropriately (research proposal in 2001 and an extended research plan in 2003 discussed in a peer review workshop); but nevertheless it was only in retrospect that we really made sense of what we have been doing or trying to do. We read Geertz (1973/1999) rather late, but it went the way he 'foretold':

We [the researchers] then, in fact, look into them [general notions considered to be interesting] ... (or, often enough, look instead into others that turn out to be more interesting), and after doing so we return to sort through our notes and memories, both of them defective, to see what we might have uncovered that clarifies anything or leads on to useful revisions of received ideas... The writing this produces is ... shaped more by the occasions of its production than its post-hoc organization into chaptered books and thematic monographs might suggest. (Geertz, 1999, pvi)

Nevertheless, we hope to provide readers with enough insight in our research methodology to allow them to judge the quality of our way of researching foresight practice as well as the stories we tell about foresight in action.

Multi-method

With a liberal idea of triangulation in mind (see Box 1.3), we employed a *multi-method* approach. In addition to the participant observation in two Dutch institutes, we investigated other foresight practices. As relative insiders (see the following section), it was natural to continue to be active in national and international foresight communities. Through this active involvement, we gained some insight in foresight practices elsewhere, which enabled us to reflect on our findings. Furthermore, we scrutinized a large number and a wide range of foresight reports, carried out a retrospective case study on a particular European foresight endeavour, and ran an experiment to explore particular foresight approaches in practice.[12] We do not claim that this multi-method approach enables us to generalize. However, it helps to put our observations into context. The additional research activities enabled us to evaluate which of our observations are typically Dutch, and which reveal more general insights into foresight practices. Those observations we considered of general relevance constitute the core of this book.

Natives stepping out

Notwithstanding the multi-method approach, a particular type of participant observation constituted the core of our empirical study. In our participant observation, we took an unconventional approach, as we were not strangers to the tribe of futurists. We were natives: all members of the core research team

---

BOX 1.3 TRIANGULATION

The notion of 'triangulation' is used in social scientific research to refer to the use of various sources and various methods in the study of the same phenomenon in order to increase the quality of findings (Jick, 1979; Swanborn, 1981/1994; Flick, 1992; Seale, 2004). As Woolgar (1988) elucidated, historically the notion of triangulation is derived from navigation and entails the message that certainty about a phenomenon is enhanced when the same object is viewed from different positions. As he did not agree with the positivistic idea of scientific certainty, Woolgar (1988) went as far as declaring the defeat of the triangulation principle.

Being aware of its methodological history, we nevertheless dare to employ the term triangulation. We use it to denote the use of different research methods and various empirical sources. However, contrary to many triangulation adepts, we do not claim that triangulation increases the validity of our research. For us, the various ways of researching foresight practice have challenged us to play around with ideas and insights and to turn them upside down, to mirror them and to mingle them. The notion of a triangle is quite helpful in conveying what we aimed for and what we did. Even if a triangle is equilateral, if you turn it, it looks different: ▲▶▼◀. Combining various triangles of different shapes (equilateral, isosceles or scalene) yields quite a broad drawing repertoire. It is in this spirit that we would like to continue to entertain the notion of 'triangulation'.

(Marjolein van Asselt, Susan van 't Klooster and Philip van Notten) had practical experience in foresight prior to the research reported in this book. We participated in different foresight endeavours and developed various methodological proposals.[13] In our experience, futurists, including ourselves, find it hard to explain how the foresight was carried out and how methodology impacted upon the stories told (compare van der Helm, 2007, who critically reviewed one of our self-accounts). At the same time, we also agreed with Hines's appeal: 'How did you arrive at this vision of the future? As professional futurists, shouldn't we be able to answer these questions in our sleep?' (Hines, 2000, p533).

How can we come to grips with all kinds of tacit or taken-for-granted methodological issues while actively practising foresight? We thought about ways to question what futurists, including ourselves, take for granted in order to gain both sufficient depth in our reflection and to produce insights that would challenge futurists. We concluded that we had to distance ourselves from foresight practice in order to be able to understand how futurists assess the future. Hence, we chose to adopt the stance of an ethnographer and to practise participant observation in policy-oriented foresight.

The idea of ethnography is developed from the traditional version of anthropology – namely, a Western researcher going to remote, exotic cultures. Nowadays, ethnography is increasingly practised 'at home' – namely, in Western societies. Famous examples involve Knorr-Cetina (1981); Gilbert and Mulkay (1984); Lynch (1985); Latour and Woolgar (1986) and Traweek (1988). Nevertheless, the analogy of a stranger is still important as a role model. The art of ethnography is to make the familiar seem strange in order to see what is taken for granted by the natives themselves. Especially when practised 'at home', participant observers need to bracket their familiarity (Woolgar, 1988) – namely, to question what they take for granted and consider self-evident. Bracketing familiarity requires that participant observers put themselves in the shoes of a stranger. The general conviction is that the more familiar a researcher is at the onset of the research, the more difficult it is to maintain the stance of a 'stranger': the participant observer will be inclined to qualify what is going on as 'normal' and 'natural' as he/she is already a (quasi-) believer, who tends to (unconsciously) mobilize preconceived views. Therefore, ethnographers are usually outsiders to the practice of interest and some even argue that they have to be (relative) outsiders in order to produce insights of interest. So the usual trajectory of participant observation is to shift from being an outsider to someone who is accepted by the natives, without becoming one themselves.

Our approach had to be different, as we were insiders who wanted to bracket our familiarity in order to examine what is taken for granted. Our approach of 'natives stepping out' can be characterized as 'outside insider' as opposed to the classical 'inside outsider' position. Although we realized that we embarked on the most extreme variant of ethnography at home, we were nevertheless convinced that to be able to address our research interests, we needed to conduct participant observation. We had no better alternative for two reasons:

1 Self-accounts in the reports did not suffice to address the questions we were interested in. The same holds for *ex-post* interviews with practitioners. We needed detailed descriptions of actual practice, including activities which usually remain unnoticed. Ethnographers refer to this kind of data as 'thick descriptions'. In order to be able to address the issues of interest, we needed to observe futurists in action.
2 Precisely because of our familiarity with the practice, we were convinced that we had to distance ourselves from foresight practice in order to be able to see things differently. In other words, we needed the ethnographic idea of making the familiar strange as a research attitude and as a research principle.

The outside-insider position required that we had to divert from some conventions, just as Miller and Slater (2000), Hine (2000) and Constable (2003) had to rethink ethnography while exploring its use for studying 'virtual culture'. What work did we do to bracket our familiarity? We made three choices that we consider significant:

1 We decided to work with two participant observers, with the advantage that we could blow the whistle on each other's way of participant observation.
2 Where usually participant observers immerse themselves in practice in order to increase familiarity, we decided to refrain from doing any foresight work.
3 We chose to work with what we came to call 'ethnographic moments' over the course of four years instead of a shorter period of a couple of weeks or months of full-time participant observation. In this way it would be easier to refrain from doing any foresight, enabling us to endorse a fresh view on the practice.

The latter choice had another advantage. Through our prior experience with foresight practice, we knew that many foresight endeavours usually take one to two years, whether planned or unplanned. For our research interest in the development process, it was important that we could be involved over the full course of a foresight project. The ethnographic moment approach enabled us to cover six foresight endeavours in action during five years.

Like Steve Woolgar,[14] we treat participant (namely, immersed as a quasi-member) and observer (namely, a kind of fly on the wall) as a continuum. In this view, participant observation is not just simply choosing a position on this continuum and then sticking to it over the course of the study. The challenge resides in consciously moving back and forth over time between being more of an observer and adopting more of a participant style. For example, in many meetings we did not verbally participate in the discussions (observer style), but often were asked to provide some feedback on what had been going on (participant style). Sometimes we were asked permission to use our field reports in the foresight project that we were investigating. In some cases, we agreed to share parts of our field reports which were then used as a kind of minutes of the meeting (participant style). On other occasions we refused permission (observer style). In some meetings, we were explicitly invited to actively participate. In one such a case, we were even appointed to report subgroup work back to the plenary (participant style). In this reporting back, we juggled with the use of the prepositions 'we' and 'you': 'we should, uh, I mean you should …'. This juggling nicely illustrates the double identity of a participant observer. The different modes yield different observations, views and experiences, and its diversity enriches our understanding of actual practice.

Notwithstanding the fact that at some observation moments we adopted a participant style, we refrained from taking over foresight work. In that sense, our approach is fundamentally different from the classical approach adopted by Dobbinga (2001): she served as a full-time member of the foresight team. Taking into account our previous experience, if we had participated through doing foresight work, we would just have been full insiders, implying that our 'ethnography' would degenerate into mere self-reporting.

Critical to our approach is what we describe as 'reflexive looping'.[15] Schön (1983) argues that professions can develop through reflection. He argues for reflection in action – namely, practitioners who self-critically wonder about what they are doing and how they are doing it. The claim is that through such reflection in action, practitioners improve their practice. Our detailed descriptions of foresight in action can be characterized as reflection *on* action. This empirically informed reflection on action aims to help futurists better reflect *in* action.[16] To that end, we decided to cast our stories in ways that are of interest to futurists. The natives who stepped out thus return home in the end. Through such reflexive looping, we aim to contribute to the further development of foresight practice.

Audience

Our research can be characterized as interdisciplinary, which necessitates explanation as to the academic communities for which this book is supposed to be of relevance.

The first community of interest involves practitioners and scholars involved in foresight. This includes authors and readers of the journals *Futures, Foresight* and *Technological Forecasting and Social Change*, as well as the World Futures Studies Federation (WFSF) and the World Futurists Society (WFS), which among others serve as platforms of exchange among futurists. Although these scholars endorse critical reflection on actual practice, publications rooted in participant observation are rare. Through the reflexive looping practised in our research on foresight in action, we contribute to a more empirically informed understanding of challenges and pitfalls characteristic of foresight. We believe that it can also help newcomers get to work.[17]

The field usually referred to as science and technology studies (STS) is another community of interest. Our research builds upon the constructivist tradition and employs approaches and concepts developed in STS. Key journals include *Science, Technology and Human Values*, *Social Studies of Science* and *Public Understanding of Science*. The major societies are the Society for Social Studies of Science (4S) and the European Association for the Study of Science and Technology (EASST). With roots in technology assessment, STS has a history of active involvement in foresight. A number of futurists featured in this book have a background in STS; in some cases even a PhD. Social processes of knowledge construction and 'boundary work'[18] between the realms of expertise and policy are central subjects of study in STS. Researching foresight practice can be considered a particular specialization. In the STS community, interest in foresight practice is growing; witness, for example, the book on *Contested Futures* (Brown et al, 2000) and the 2007 Negotiating the Future seminar organized at the STS centre TIK at Oslo University.

The third community of interest is the risk research community. Key journals include *Risk Analysis* and the *Journal of Risk Research*. The Society for Risk Analysis (SRA) (with its regional chapters) is the main society in this field. The interest of risk researchers in foresight is rather limited, notwithstanding a special issue of the *Journal of Risk Research* devoted to a particular foresight endeavour (Wilkinson et al, 2003, vol 6, no 4–6), the use of scenario analysis in particular risk domains (e.g. earthquakes, nuclear energy and climate change) and foresight endeavours with an expressed interest in risk (such as the UK Foresight Future Flooding project; Evans et al, 2004a,b). Risk researchers recognized as early as 25 years ago that 'risk analysis is essentially a listing of scenarios' (Kaplan and Garrick, 1981, p14), especially in situations of high uncertainty: 'the risk assessment process inevitably leads to a scenario approach (often implicit rather than explicit)' (Rogers, 2001, p5). Giddens (1991, p29) also argued that foresight is 'not an eccentric preoccupation, the contemporary equivalent of the fortune tellers of old'. He emphasized that foresight, described as 'the consideration of the counterfactual possibilities', 'is intrinsic to reflexivity in the context of risk assessment and evaluation' (Giddens, 1991, p29). Nevertheless, it seems that foresight is not an issue that receives serious attention in the risk community. In case risk researchers want to engage in the assessment of uncertain risks, they need to engage with foresight in one way or another. This book enables them to learn how futurists attempt to assess the future and the kind of challenges involved in practising foresight.

Finally, this book is not just relevant to futurists and scholars in various communities. It also aims to be relevant to policy actors, who are supposed to be the target group of policy-oriented foresight. The idea of policy-oriented foresight is that it attempts to help policy actors take responsibility for the long term. In many cases, policy actors decide about commissioning or initiating a foresight endeavour. Insight into foresight in action will enable them to fairly evaluate a particular foresight endeavour and to participate in discussions about the value of policy-oriented foresight. It will help policy actors to properly judge and use scenarios presented by futurists. And it will provide a basis for deciding about participation in a foresight activity. In this way, we also hope this book will contribute to a quality improvement in the actual use of policy-oriented foresights for policy purposes.

Structure of the book

Like professional futurists, we offer stories. This book is, in the first place, a storytelling book. Our stories are about foresight practice. We could have written, and may write, different stories on foresight practice. However, the stories in the following chapters are the ones we considered most illustrative and insightful. In each of the stories, we confronted textbook ideas with what we saw futurists doing. In this way, we were able to draft new answers to the questions on how experts assess the future and what can be learned from such foresight in action.

In Chapter 2 we report some first impressions of foresight practice. Readers familiar with the idea of scenarios could skip this chapter. In Chapter 3, we examine how futurists struggle with policy. Textbook ideas turn out to be of little help. This struggling with policy seems typical for policy-oriented foresight. In Chapter 4, we attend in detail to how the scenario matrix, broadly presented as a standard tool, is used. We report that in foresight in action the scenario matrix is used in different ways that also differ from how it is presented in textbooks. In Chapter 5, we describe manners that futurists employ in the face of prospective uncertainty. Although foresight is often presented in textbooks as the art of managing uncertainty, we show that dealing with uncertainty is a tough challenge. In Chapter 6, we focus on the meaning of time. We report on how futurists in foresight endeavours understand time. We describe how the futurists, in practice, depart from foresight ambitions outlined in textbooks. In Chapter 7, we summarize and discuss our findings. What lessons can be learned from foresight in action?

Reflection pages

We hope that scholars in the fields of foresight, STS and risk research, foresight practitioners and (potential) foresight users will actively translate the insights they gained through this book to their own practice. For this reason, the final page in every chapter provides space for the reader to write down ideas, insights and thoughts about how to use them.

Note about style

We have been careful with observations that we thought may have social or political repercussions for individual futurists or the institutes involved. For this reason, we prefer anonymity as much as possible.[19]

Notes

1 The basic assumption guiding this book is that policy contexts differ sufficiently from the private sector to consider policy-oriented foresight a special category. For those interested in foresight in business contexts, we refer to Schwartz (1991), van der Heijden (1996), Ringland (2002a, 2002b), van der Duin (2006), Leemhuis (1985), Wack (1985a, 1985b), Godet (2001), Lindgren and Bandhold (2003), Wright et al (2008), and the special issue of *Futures* on organizational foresight ('Coping with the future: Developing organizational foresightfulness, 2004, vol 36, no 2).

2 The notion of 'inscribe' is introduced to the ethnography literature by Geertz (1973/1999).

3 The description 'real time mechanisms at work' is taken from Knorr-Cetina (1995).

4 Well-referenced contributions on methodology-epistemology of futures studies include Inayatullah (1990), Schwartz (1991), van der Heijden (1996), Sardar (1999a,b), Slaughter (1999), Bell (2003) and the Slaughter (1984) article series 'Towards a critical futurism'.

5 For a discussion on differences between Western and non-Western science fiction traditions, see Miljovevic and Inayatulla (2003).

6 We do realize that the use of the term 'futurist' as shorthand for experts engaged in foresight activities could be questioned, but we did not come across a better term. Van Lente (2000) used the notion 'experts of promises', but he employed it in the context of the particular use of foresight products in creating and sustaining expectations about new technologies.

7 The term positivism was first coined during the 19th century by the social scientist Auguste Comte (1798 to 1857), who rejected metaphysics in favour of the belief that only science could reveal the truth about reality. The idea that the natural laws governing nature could be 'revealed' or 'discovered' by means of empirical observation and rational explanation ('logical positivism') was formally established as the dominant scientific method in the early 1930s (Hess, 1999; Seale, 2004). In those days, the positivist notion of science also held sway in what is now demarcated as the 'social sciences', asserting that not only nature but also social reality was governed by causal laws, which scientists could logically deduce by means of empirical observation and rational explanation. An example of this approach is Emile Durkheim's sociological study on suicide (1897). Nowadays, the term 'positivism' is often used pejoratively by academics in the humanities and the social sciences, who favour a social constructivist outlook on the relationship between science and reality (Hess, 1999). In the context of foresight we also use positivism as the antonym of a social constructivist outlook on science.

8 The social constructivist thesis boils down to the general notion that scientific knowledge is socially constructed. Scholars who subscribe to a constructivist notion of science pay tribute to the epistemological position that scientific facts are not 'ready-made' entities 'out there in reality', waiting to be 'discovered' and 'collected' by scientists. As they argue, scientific knowledge is the result of negotiation among scientists. Science is thus seen as an inherently social enterprise.

9 Planning agency is the literal translation of '*planbureau*'. Even agencies recently established, such as the Planbureau voor de Leefomgeving (2008), are called '*planbureaus*'. However, internationally the agencies prefer not to be associated

with planning and present themselves as 'bureau', 'assessment agency', 'office' or 'institute'. This ambivalence towards planning is noteworthy.

10 Although Amsterdam is the Dutch capital, the Dutch government has its seat in The Hague.

11 A similar starting point has been employed in Brown et al (2000). This edited book focused on technological foresight (to which they refer as 'prospective technoscience'). In the various contributions, the authors addressed, among other issues, the structure of promises (van Lente), the shared familiarity in future narratives (Deuten and Rip), the breakthrough motif (Brown), the power of future-oriented metaphors (Wyatt), science fiction (Rose), failed futures (Geels and Smit), scripts (de Laat) and configurations of future-oriented networks (Nelis).

12 For a detailed description of this experiment, see van Notten (2005, Chapter 6).

13 From 1993 to 2000, Marjolein van Asselt has been involved in various scenario endeavours in policy contexts, ranging from computer simulation modelling exercises (Rotmans, 1997; Rotmans and van Asselt, 1999) and participatory scenario endeavours (Kasemir et al, 2003), to endeavours in which both participatory and quantitative approaches were used (Middelkoop et al, 2004; van Asselt et al, 2001b) and various foresight consultancy activities for municipalities, provinces and ministries. Susan van 't Klooster was involved in the Visions project as well as the NOP-Irma project. Philip van Notten had experience as a consultant with scenario planning in the private sector.

14 As visiting scholar at Oxford University in 2005, Marjolein van Asselt attended Steve Woolgar's course on qualitative research methods, in which he presented participant observation in this way.

15 We owe this phrasing to Professor Rein de Wilde (Maastricht University).

16 The distinction between reflection in action and reflection on action is inspired by Schön (1983).

17 Apart from some courses and programmes (see, for example, Slaughter, 2004), in many countries there is no academic or vocational training for futurists.

18 The notion of 'boundary work' was coined and developed by Gieryn (1983 and 1995). This STS body of literature emphasizes new sites of knowledge production which blur classic and comfortable boundaries, such as between science and policy. The number of STS studies examining such boundary work is increasing (Wynne, 1982; Jasanoff, 1990; Jasanoff and Wynne, 1998; Hilgartner, 2000; Hoppe, 2002; Halffman, 2003; Dunsby, 2004; Schmid, 2004; Halffman and Hoppe, 2005; Jasanoff, 2005; Lahsen, 2005; Bijker et al, 2009).

19 See Neyland (2006) for a reflexive discussion on anonymity.

Reflections

2

First Impressions of Foresight Practice

Forecasting and foresight

In the scholarly literature on long-term assessment, foresight is usually distinguished from forecasting (see, for example, van der Duin, 2006; van der Steen, 2009). In such literature forecasting is portrayed as the attempt to predict the future. Foresight, on the other hand, is presented as the attempt to explore the future. In this book we will, for that reason, also refer to forecasting as the predictive style of assessing the future and foresight as the exploratory style.

The predictive style is usually associated with trend extrapolation and the establishment of time series and point estimates. Forecasting aims to produce very specific statements about the value of a particular indicator on a specified moment in the future, such as a country's gross domestic product (GDP) in five years time. This approach to the future is very data intensive and involves quantitative analysis and modelling as a dominant means of predicting the future. The main assumption employed in forecasting is the idea of continuity. It is assumed that the future will be shaped by processes, mechanisms and factors that shaped the past. It is furthermore assumed that these processes, mechanisms and factors are sufficiently known and understood to support prediction. In the predictive style, the product is a forecast – namely, a clear picture of what the future will look like (see, for example, Armstrong, 2001, p2).

While the predictive style aims at *one* future forecast, the exploratory style aims at surveying *multiple* futures. In foresight, the basic assumption is that the future is inherently uncertain. Therefore, it makes much more sense to develop various scenarios of how the future may develop. The aim is to explore the 'possibility space' (Berkhout and Hertin, 2002) – namely, the wealth of thinkable options for the future, including the most radical outlooks. Foresight is usually associated with the notion of scenarios. The word scenario is derived

BOX 2.1 FORECASTING

The reader with an interest in forecasting is referred to the *Principles of Forecasting* handbook (and the support website: www.forecastingprinciples.com) edited by Armstrong (2001), qualified as a 'known expert with an impressive track record in forecasting research' (De Menezes, 2004), and to the *Journal of Forecasting* (published since 1982). A content analysis of the articles published in this journal during the period of 1996 to 2008 (titles, selected abstracts, selected full texts) reveals that the field of forecasting is dominated by business economics and macro-economics, which is illustrated by the main issues assessed: sales, interest and exchange rates, (un)employment, prices, GDP, inflation, recession, return on investment, market developments, industrial production and consumption patterns. Only a handful of articles concerned non-economic forecasting, such as weather forecasting, forecasting in the field of transport, forecasting of coastal wave heights and population projections. Methodological papers deal with model approaches, model comparisons, mathematical algorithms, model testing, data issues, indicators and forecast accuracy. A limited number of papers reported psychological research (surveys, experiments) on judgement and bias in forecasting practice. From the articles collected in the *Journal of Forecasting*, another feature of the predictive style can be observed: time horizons are usually short – namely, several months to two to four years.

from the Latin '*scaena*', meaning 'scene', and was originally used in the context of performing arts (theatre, film) (Kleiner, 1996; Ringland, 1998). Herman Kahn, one of the best-known scholars in the field of foresight and broadly considered the founding father of the scenario idea, adopted the term in the context of foresight because of its emphasis on storytelling (Aligica, 2004). Kahn defined scenarios as 'hypothetical sequences of events constructed for the purpose of focusing attention on causal processes and decision-points' (cited in Aligica, 2004, p75). Van Notten (2005) observed that among futurists, numerous definitions of scenario are employed. Notwithstanding differences, it is agreed that a scenario is not a prediction, but a description of a hypothetical situation, a story about a possible future. The scenario approach combines analysis with imagination. In the context of foresight, scenarios are also referred to as 'thought experiments' and 'what if' analysis.

Herman Kahn's scenario approach is broadly considered one of the first foresight endeavours. His technique of 'future-now thinking', introduced at the RAND Corporation (Kleiner, 1996), a US-based policy advisory organization, drew from the field of military strategic planning (van der Heijden et al, 2002). Inspired by Kahn and others, Royal Dutch Shell established its Group Planning Unit in 1964 (Kleiner, 1996; Schwartz, 1991; van der Heijden, 1996; Shell International, 2008). Since then, Shell has become a key reference for the scenario approach. Although not explicitly presented as a scenario study, the famous Club of Rome report (Meadows et al, 1972) can be considered as one of the early examples of applying the scenario idea in policy-oriented foresight. Nowadays, scenario approaches are widely used in policy contexts (see, for example, Ringland, 2002b).

Within the futurist community, it is argued that the predictive style (forecasting) was dominant during 1950 to 1970 (see, for example, van der

Duin, 2006; van 't Klooster, 2007). Futurists state that during the last decades a shift can be observed from a dominance of the predictive style (forecasting) to a preference for the exploratory style (foresight). This shift has been attributed to a broader societal recognition of the limitations inherent to prediction in view of complexity, uncertainty and discontinuity. We observed, both in reports and at the meetings we attended (various field notes), that futurists 'testify' that they are not in the prediction business. For example:

- [C]ontemporary long-term studies do not pretend to predict the future course' (CPB, 1992).
- '*The Netherlands 2030* is not a prediction' (de Jong, 1997).
- Foresight is 'by definition no prediction of the future' (RIVM, 2000).
- Foresight is 'not about predictions' (Pálsdóttir et al, 2002).

We started our investigation in foresight practice by adopting this state-of-the-art picture drawn by futurists. This means that we assumed that foresight is the dominant approach in assessing the future and that foresight generally entails the development of various scenarios.

Preparing the journey

Just as many travellers prepare for a journey by reading books about the country they aim to visit, we prepared for our journey in foresight practice with surveying reports in which scenarios are presented. We thus used futurists' self-accounts as a means to get some first impressions. In this chapter, we share the first impressions on foresight in action, which we developed through the analysis of a wide variety of publicly available scenario studies. The aim of this chapter is to provide a first-order answer to the question 'How do experts assess the future?'. Through analysis of similarities and differences between scenarios and scenario studies, we aim to provide a basis for constructing such an answer.

Scenario studies

Only few scholars present a collection of case studies, such as Ringland (1998, 2002a, 2002b) and Fahey and Randall (1998), and they do not compare scenario studies. The only comparative studies that we are aware of are those by Greeuw et al (2000), Heinzen (1994), the WRR (2000) and a discussion in a *Futures* special issue (April 2002, vol 34, no 3–4). These comparative studies generally focus on particular aspects of scenario development.

We collected approximately 100 scenario studies produced around the globe during the period of 1985 to 2003 (van Notten et al, 2003; van Notten, 2005). About 30 scenario studies were selected for further analysis based on the adequacy of the available documentation (see Box 2.6 and the Appendix). They were drawn from a wide variety of contexts ranging from studies produced in the governmental sector[1] as well as intergovernmental scenario studies,[2] to scenarios produced by the business sector[3], civic scenario studies[4], as well as academic endeavours. The studies covered a variety of topics, including a regional study; sectoral studies for transport, telecom and nutrition; country studies; and issue-based studies addressing gender equality, the labour market, climate change and leadership. From these 30 studies, 22 can be qualified as policy-oriented foresight. Information about the studies was drawn from primary and secondary sources, ranging from reviews of recent scenario processes to interviews with people involved in those studies.

As background for our empirical study, we also tried to gain an overview of policy-oriented scenario studies produced in The Netherlands (1997 to 2005) (van Asselt et al, 2005b; www.toekomstverkenning.nl). We found about 200 studies, which is, on average, 25 studies per year. We do not claim that this overview is comprehensive, but it surely indicates that policy-oriented foresight is serious business in The Netherlands. We selected about 20 studies for further analysis. We aimed to create a set which could be considered sufficiently representative in terms of topics addressed, the importance of the scenarios in the Dutch policy context and the variety of outlooks (see Box 2.7). This set of studies yielded well over 80 scenarios.

The studies that informed our first impressions constitute a biased set since we only included studies available in English or Dutch.[5] Not all scenario studies carried out are written down in publicly available media, which also biased our selection. Nevertheless, we considered the scenario studies we looked at to be a useful basis for constructing a first idea of contemporary foresight practice.

Snapshot and chain scenarios

A closer look at the various scenarios reveals that some scenarios describe a future end state – namely, a conceivable state of affairs at a particular future moment (see Box 2.2). Jungermann and Thuring (1987) refer to this type of scenarios as 'snapshot scenarios'.

BOX 2.2 EXAMPLE OF SNAPSHOT SCENARIO

Example of snapshot scenario (end state)
Fragment from the scenario 'Old leaves us cold' (Futureconsult, 2006)
5 December 2016. Good morning diary: I really dread the idea of moving house. Next week I have to move to The Styx nursing home in Valkenburg,[6] after 65 years here in Wittevrouwenveld.[7] The neighbourhood is empty and depraved, but it is nevertheless my little Maastricht neighbourhood... The thing I fear the most is the 'senior wash' in The Styx: a human car wash. One push on the button and ten oldies are washed simultaneously... You don't have privacy... Everything goes automatically, except getting dressed. You have to do that yourself because there is no staff... I do understand that. Who would want to work for a pittance with those sore-head old people?... That's why only people above the age of 55 still work in healthcare. Nowadays, it's all about the money. And that is exactly the thing I don't have!

BOX 2.3 EXAMPLE OF CHAIN SCENARIO

Example of chain scenario (plot)
Fragment from the scenario 'Strong Europe' (de Mooij and Tang, 2003)
An institutional crisis is looming after EU enlargement in 2004. In this scenario, European member states are willing to sacrifice their national sovereignty in order to obtain a solution to this crisis... Countries that initially remain outside the core group step in at a later date... Turkey becomes a member of the European Union and, although Ukraine and Russia do not become full members, they become more integrated with Europe... The outward orientation of Europe, the deepening of the internal market, and rapid growth in Central and Eastern Europe contribute to productivity growth in the European Union... Population growth does not change much during the coming decades. In light of ageing, however, employment growth falls, especially after 2020. Annual GDP growth will be 1.8 per cent between 2000 and 2020, and ... 1.3 per cent between 2020 and 2040.

Other scenarios concentrate on pathways into the future (see Box 2.3). Such scenarios portray events connecting the present with imaginable future states. These types of scenarios involve a plot in the sense of stories about causes and possible effects. Such scenarios are referred to as 'chain scenarios' (Jungermann and Thuring, 1987) or as 'a causal tapestry' (Schoemaker, 1993). Snapshot scenarios can be compared to a photograph, while chain scenarios are more like a movie.

Not all scenarios take the present as the starting point of storytelling. Some scenarios tell a story about the sequences of events as if the future is already history. In so-called backcasting endeavours, a future point in time is taken as the starting point for the analysis (see Box 2.4)

BOX 2.4 BACKCASTING

Backcasting dates back to the 1970s, when Lovins (1976) used 'backwards-looking analysis' to explore long-term energy policy for the US. Later, Elmore (1980) developed the 'backward mapping' approach. Robinson (1982) eventually coined the term 'backcasting' as an alternative to traditional planning and forecasting methods. Defining what is desirable or undesirable is central in backcasting. One or several images of the future are painted as the starting point for the analysis. The next step is working backwards to the present situation to explore which interventions are needed to attain the desirable future or to avoid undesirable ones (van de Kerkhof et al, 2002). For recent applications of the backcasting approach to foresight, see Banister et al (2000), Weaver et al (2000), Robinson (2003), Tansey et al (2004), van de Kerkhof (2006) and Quist (2007).

Scenario cartwheel

In order to develop an overview of contemporary foresight practice, we considered it useful to further explore differences and similarities between the scenarios that we studied. Iterative analysis of the scenarios suggested that it was productive to use three very basic questions:

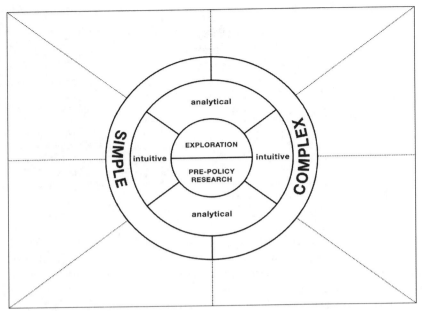

Figure 2.1 *The scenario cartwheel*

Source: adapted from van Notten et al (2003); van Notten (2005)

1 Why were the scenarios developed?
2 How were the scenarios developed?
3 What kinds of scenarios were developed?

In short, these questions addressed the goal of a foresight endeavour, the process design and the content of the scenarios produced.

For each question we aimed to identify two poles of a spectrum, instead of trying to do justice to all kinds of nuances. These three-dimensional poles (goal, process design, scenario content) enabled us to draw a three-dimensional scheme, which we refer to as the scenario cartwheel (see Figure 2.1; van Notten et al, 2003; van Notten, 2005). It should be noted that with regard to the goal and the development process, we were dependent on information provided by the futurists themselves. So in this first encounter with scenario practice, we had to rely on self-accounts, the 'official historical narrative', described in the available reports.

Detailed attention to the aims of actual scenario studies reveals that scenario studies differ in their approach to exploration. A number of scenario studies – for example, Hammond (1998), Department of Trade and Industry (2002), Bruun et al (2002), de Mooij and Tang (2003) and McCorduck and Ramsey (1996) – use exploration as a means to raise awareness and to encourage out-of-the-box thinking. As Hammond (1998, p16) states: 'to be useful … a scenario must jar us out of familiar assumptions and challenge us to think about how the world might be different'. Studies in this vein 'just' present alternative futures. Hammond (1998, p7) presents scenarios 'that lead to radically different worlds and that may shed light on the social choices that might distinguish one path into the future from another'. Three sharply contrasting scenarios from the world in 2050 are drawn. In the first one, 'Market World', a powerful global market (also including developing regions) emerges, driven by technological innovation. This scenario is marked by 'widespread prosperity, peace, and stability' (Hammond, 1998, p23). The second scenario, 'Fortress World', provides a gloomy alternative to the first one, assuming that market-led economic growth will not only fail to solve, but in the long term may actually exacerbate social and environmental problems. Indeed, global capitalism will only increase the contrasts between rich and poor. The third scenario, 'Transformed World', creates the image of a world which is changed fundamentally, both socially and politically. In this world, solidarity and deliberate social choices are valued as much as economic progress due to market forces. These three fundamentally different visions of the future provide an opportunity to think through and explore the meaning, the feasibility and the actual desirability of these possible futures. Often, in this kind of foresight endeavour, the development process is deemed as important as the scenarios developed. The scenario development process is valued in terms of its contribution to learning and communication (also referred to as 'strategic conversation' among the people involved in the foresight activity; see van der Heijden, 1996).

Other scenario studies also examine various alternative futures, but aim to arrive at normative evaluations (e.g. in terms of probability or desirability) and/or aim to use the scenarios as a basis for generating policy options or even providing policy recommendations. The famous 'Mont Fleur' study (Le Roux et al, 1992;[8] see also Nekkers, 2006, p71) provides an illustrative example of a scenario study in this vein. The 'Flight of the Flamingos' scenario, however, is presented as the most desirable. This scenario describes a South Africa successfully negotiating the post-apartheid transition period (see Box 2.5). This scenario can be seen as providing a promising direction for South African development.

We presented these poles pertaining to the goal of scenario studies as 'exploration' versus 'pre-policy research' (van Notten et al, 2003; van Notten, 2005), although it can be debated whether these labels best capture the differences observed. We also discovered that some scenario studies involve a first round in which broad scenarios are developed along the lines of exploration, while a second set of scenarios is subsequently developed to zoom in on particular aspects as input to strategy development. The aim of this second set of scenarios fits more in the pre-policy style. The scenario study *Four Futures of Europe* (de Mooij and Tang, 2003) is an illustrative example as it builds on the more exploratory long-term scenario study *Scanning the Future* (CPB, 1992). In *Four Futures of Europe*, 'policy challenges that the European Union and the member states will be facing during the coming decades in light of a number of trends' are addressed (de Mooij and Tang, 2003, p13).

BOX 2.5 THE FLIGHT OF THE FLAMINGOS

The 'Flight of the Flamingos' scenario is one of the four scenarios developed in the 'Mont Fleur' scenario exercise, undertaken by a group of 22 prominent South Africans in 1991 and 1992. The scenario served to stimulate debate about how to shape the political system of South Africa in the coming decade, the year 2002 being the end-point of the scenarios. The 'Flight of the Flamingos' scenario was deemed the most desirable.

Fragment of the 'Flight of the Flamingos' scenario:

> *This is the scenario of inclusive democracy and growth. Flamingos characteristically take off slowly, fly high and fly together.*
>
> *A decisive political settlement, followed by good government, creates conditions in which an initially slow but sustainable economic and social take-off becomes possible. The key to the government's success is its ability to combine strategies that lead to significant improvements in social delivery with policies that create confidence in the economy.*
>
> *Access to world markets and relative regional stability facilitates the flamingos, but South Africa does not receive massive overseas investments or aid on the scale of a Marshall Plan. The government adopts sound social and economic policies and observes macro-economic constraints. It succeeds in curbing corruption in government and raises efficiency levels.* (Le Roux et al, 1992, p17)

As argued in Chapter 1, self-accounts are only of limited value in providing insight in the production process. Nevertheless, it is interesting to see what differences in approach can be inferred from an analysis of self-accounts. On the one hand, we identified scenario studies that aim to use approaches designed to achieve analytical rigour. In such so-called 'analytical' (van Notten et al, 2003; van Notten, 2005) endeavours, models, either computer simulations or qualitative models, are used as a means to systematically explore the future. The scenario study *Which World?* (Hammond, 1998), for example, bases its three global scenarios of 2050 on quantitative data and analyses of the World Resources Institute, and as such exemplifies this type of 'desk-researched studies' (van Notten, 2005, p40). The same goes for 'Possum' (Banister et al, 2000), a model-based foresight project aiming to achieve a sustainable European transport system in 2020. This study uses a modified backcasting technique to create three scenarios, which serve to explore several potential policy paths to the desired end-state; a sustainable European transport system. Another example of an 'analytical' foresight endeavour is the third *Global Environmental Outlook* (UNEP, 2002), which draws on a large variety of quantitative models and analyses to develop and illustrate its four scenarios about the global environment.

At the other pole, we find accounts of scenario development processes that we decided to characterize as 'intuitive' (van Notten et al, 2003; van Notten, 2005). This type of foresight practice often uses creative techniques and participatory workshops involving a wide variety of participants. In the 'Mont Fleur' (Le Roux et al, 1992) and 'Destino Colombia' studies (Global Business

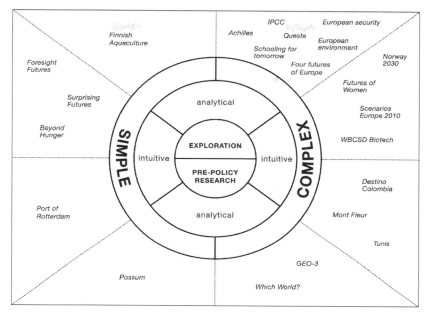

Figure 2.2 *Policy-oriented scenario studies mapped in the scenario cartwheel*

Source: adapted from van Notten et al (2003); van Notten (2005)

Network, 1998), wide sections of South African and Colombian society were involved in the development of scenarios. They even included guerrillas, clergymen and trade unionists.

An examination of the various scenarios suggested that they also differ in their complexity. In so-called 'complex' (van Notten et al, 2003; van Notten, 2005) scenarios, the storylines are composed of an intricate web of many interwoven events and processes. The level of heterogeneity of the factors/variables included is very high. An example of complex scenarios is the scenarios described in the Organisation for Economic Development and Co-operation (OECD) study *Schooling for Tomorrow* (OECD, 2001). In so-called 'simple' (van Notten et al, 2003; van Notten, 2005) scenarios, the number of variables included is rather low and the set of factors is homogenous, while the level of integration across domain, sector or geographical scale is also rather limited. The scenarios from the 'Possum' study (2000) are simple, in the sense of being very particular and exclusive in focus on the transport sector. It should be noted that 'simple' is not a quality judgement. Simple scenarios are not necessarily easy to develop, and in some contexts simple scenarios may be more appropriate than complex ones.

In Figure 2.2, 22 policy-oriented scenario studies (for a short description, see Box 2.6) are mapped in the scenario cartwheel.

The cartwheel mapping demonstrates that in current scenario practice, all goal (process design) scenario content combinations are practised. Although

Box 2.6 Description of scenario studies mapped in the scenario cartwheel

The following policy-oriented scenario studies were included in our analysis (see the Appendix for full references):

1 *Surprising Futures* (1987): a scenario exercise designed to experiment with methodology for developing 'surprise-rich' scenarios.
2 *Beyond Hunger in Africa* (1990): a study that aimed to look beyond the conventional image of Africa as a 'hungry' continent by experimenting with methods for creating surprising scenarios.
3 *European Security beyond the Cold War* (1991): four scenarios that explore the possible outcomes of change and disorder in European security at the end of the 1980s.
4 *Mont Fleur* (1992): a scenario study designed to stimulate debate about the shape of post-apartheid South African society.
5 *Port of Rotterdam scenarios* (1996): scenarios and strategic options for the Port of Rotterdam.
6 *The Futures of Women* (1996): the question of whether men and women will be equal by the year 2015 is addressed, as well as what the implications of success or failure to achieve equality will be.
7 *Destino Colombia* (1998): a scenario study with the aim of defining alternative routes for Colombia as a basis for developing a shared vision for the drafting of long-range policies.
8 *Questa* (1998): a study by The Netherlands Ministry of Transport and Public Works on the future of The Netherlands with a focus on mobility issues.
9 *Scenarios Europe 2010* (1999): a study on possible futures for Europe developed within the European Commission.
10 *The European Environment at the Turn of the Century* (1999): a scenario describing the future of the environment in Europe, developed by the European Environment Agency.
11 *Which World?* (1998): three global scenarios from the perspective of 2050.
12 *WBCSD Biotech* (2000): a study by the World Business Council for Sustainable Development in which three scenarios were developed on the role of biotechnology in society.
13 *IPCC SRES* (2000): a scenario study by the Intergovernmental Panel on Climate Change that addressed greenhouse gas emissions' impact upon climate change on a global and a regional level.
14 *Norway 2030* (2000): a scenario study describing possible futures for Norway.
15 *Possum* (2000): scenarios for achieving sustainable development and to assist the European Commission in future decisions about the Common Transport Policy.
16 *Schooling for Tomorrow* (2001): an OECD study that included the development of six scenarios for the future of schooling.
17 *Finnish Aquaculture* (2002): four scenarios for Finnish aquaculture that aim to illustrate the importance of contingent developments.
18 *Foresight Futures* (2002): four scenarios that were developed in the UK National Foresight Programme to identify potential opportunities from new science and technologies, and to establish which actions could help to realize those opportunities.
19 *GEO-3* (2002): a *Global Environment Outlook* developed by the United Nations Environment Programme that outlined four global scenarios and their implications on a continental scale.
20 *Achilles* (2002): a study on the history and possible futures of the 'market state' with a focus on security, culture and economics.
21 *Tunis* (2002): scenarios for the future of the Tunisian capital.
22 *Four Futures of Europe* (2003): a study by The Netherlands Bureau for Economic Policy Analysis (CPB) that focuses on the issues of international cooperation and pressure on European public sectors.

Table 2.1 *Dutch policy-oriented scenario studies*

Title	Year	Developed by
Broad studies		
Beleef 2030; 4 toekomstscenario's voor de energiewereld	2003	Essent
Sociaal en Cultureel Rapport 2004; In het zicht van de toekomst.	2004	SCP
Kwaliteit en Toekomst	2004	RIVM
Energie en Samenleving in 2050	2000	Ministerie EZ
Economie en fysieke omgeving; Beleidsopgaven en oplossingsrichtingen	1997	CPB
Vier gezichten op Nederland: Productie, arbeid en sectorstructuur in vier 1995–2020 scenario's tot 2040	2004	CPB
Mobility		
Questa; Verplaatsen in de Toekomst	1998	Ministerie van V&W
Big cities and provinces		
Leiden Stad van Ontdekkingen; Profiel Leiden 2030	2004	Gemeente Leiden
Limburg uitstekend in Europa	1998	TNO
Stadsmanifest Almere 2030	2004	Gemeente Almere
Healthcare		
Gezondheid op Koers? Volksgezondheid Toekomst Verkenning 2002	2002	RIVM
Technology		
Burger en overheid in de informatie samenleving: De noodzaak van institutionele innovatie	2001	Commissie ICT en Overheid
Trendanalyse biotechnologie 2004	2004	COGEM
Potentiële risico's van bio-nanotechnologie voor mens en milieu	2004	COGEM
Toekomstflitsen, visies op onze waterplaneet	2004	Robbert en Rudolf Das
Environmental issues		
De ongekende ruimte verkend	2003	RPB
Nationale Milieuverkenning 2000–2030	2000	RIVM
Demography		
Bevolking en Scenario's: Werelden te winnen?	2004	RIVM
Lange-termijn bevolkingsscenario's voor Nederland	2004	RIVM
European studies		
Four futures of Europe	2003	CPB
Policy and politics		
Representatief en Participatief, Dubbele Democratie	2002	Xpin (Inter-departementaal expertisebureau voor innovatieve beleidsvorming)
Beelden van bestuur: Berenschot trendstudie	2002	Berenschot

Source: for full references, see van Asselt et al (2005a, 2005b) and www.toekomstverkenning.nl, which also includes pdf files of the reports of most of these studies

Box 2.7 Long-term themes in Dutch scenario studies

These themes, presented in random order, are derived from our analysis of about 80 scenarios taken from 20 Dutch foresights. In foresight, political, economic, social, technological and environmental categories (abbreviated to PESTE or SEPTE) are often used to refer to categories of themes. For this reason, we have tried to categorize the themes that we derived from Dutch scenario studies into these categories. We added a 'various' category to denote themes that could not be unequivocally assigned.

Table 2.2 *Themes of Dutch scenario studies*

Theme	Issues
POLITICAL	
Geopolitical stability	
The future of Europe	Development of the EU (expansion, political reforms, functioning European institutions) and position of The Netherlands in Europe
Government	Deregulation, privatization, liberalization, decentralization, citizen participation, role of civic society, type of government and the level of power
ECONOMIC	Economic growth; type of economy
SOCIAL AND/OR CULTURAL	
Demographics	Population growth/decrease, ageing population, migration and integration of migrants
Social dynamics	Individualization, social cohesion, levels of solidarity, social responsibility and care, type of social contacts
Individual development and values	Level of education, information, articulation, competition and involvement, type of ideals (among others, hedonism and environmental awareness)
Public order and safety	'Ghettoization', crime and terrorism
Social security	Type of social system, role of EU, healthcare
Social inequality	Decrease/increase, on different scales (global, European, national)
TECHNOLOGICAL	Innovation, efficiency
ENVIRONMENTAL	Environmental quality, spatial claims and type and quality of landscapes
Natural resources	Energy use, use of raw material, water issues, climate
VARIOUS	
International dynamics	Globalization, international and intercontinental cooperation, collaboration and organization
Mobility	Transportation, fuel choice, emissions and congestion
Disasters	

we decided to disregard nuances, this analysis nevertheless already reveals eight clusters of scenario approaches. If the 22 studies included in our sample can be taken as sufficiently representative, our analysis suggests that the majority of policy-oriented foresight aims at the construction of complex scenarios. Both the analytical and the intuitive style are employed in contemporary policy-

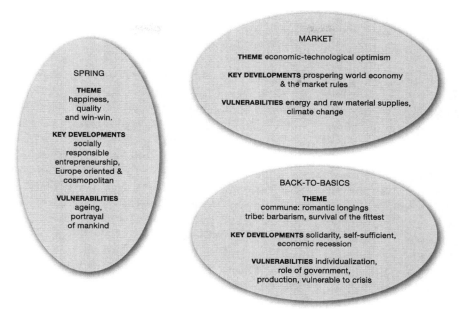

Figure 2.3 *Scenario families*

Source: adapted from van Asselt et al (2005c)

oriented foresight. Finally, policy-oriented foresight involves scenario studies aimed at exploration for the sake of awareness-raising, creative thinking and strategic conversation, as well as scenario studies that aim to provide normative judgements about and/or options for the future.

Scenario families

A set of about 20 Dutch policy-oriented scenario studies (see Table 2.1) was used to explore contemporary scenario practice in The Netherlands in more detail. We examined some 80 scenarios that could be distilled from these studies (van Asselt et al, 2005a, 2005b).

Analysis of these scenarios enabled us to draft a list of the kind of issues examined in Dutch policy-oriented foresight (see Box 2.7).

We also evaluated whether the scenarios could be grouped in what is referred to as 'scenario families' (compare IPCC, 2000). For each family, we identified the main themes, key developments and vulnerabilities (see Figure 2.3). We also explored vulnerabilities within each family in terms of developments, events or system dynamics that would challenge the scenarios' basic assumptions. This analysis suggested that three themes regularly feature as the main storyline in Dutch scenarios:

1   economic-technological optimism;
2   back to basics, in two variants:

- romantic longing;
- fear of bullying and barbarism;

3 sustainable development: adaptation and learning from past failures.

The large majority of the 80 scenarios could be grouped into four scenario families. We identified only 12 scenarios that sketched alternative futures which significantly deviate from the main themes of the scenario families. The 'Netherlands Polderland' scenario, which is part of the Questa scenario exercise (Ministerie van Verkeer en Waterstaat, 1998) is an example of such a so-called '*einzelgänger* scenario'. This scenario pictures The Netherlands in 2030 as peaceful, tranquil and marked by a culture of communication and consensus. Not much happens: developments are referred to in terms of 'evolution' instead of 'revolution'. An important event, however, is the abolishment of political parties, which are replaced by public, apolitical and interactive governance structures, responsible for developing, implementing and maintaining laws and policies. These official bodies are supervised by the Ministry of General Affairs, and usually discuss electronically with citizens and relevant societal organizations. Sometimes they do not succeed in making decisions, which is then accepted as a sacrifice to a precise societal decision-making process. Despite the fact that world trade has become increasingly global, Europe is primarily self-centred. The economic centre of gravity has shifted from the west to the north, east and south of Europe. Even Africa has become involved. The Netherlands has therefore become less attractive to immigrants. With respect to the market of technological developments, The Netherlands remains a 'passive follower'. Nevertheless, the level of knowledge remains high: universities have a good reputation, not because of research quality but because of teaching excellence. Employment numbers are relatively high and so is the quality of healthcare.

Another *einzelgänger* scenario is the 're-ideologizing' scenario from the scenario study 'Representative and participative' (van der Heijden and Schrijver, 2002) on the future of Dutch democracy. The point of departure of this scenario is the assumption that the Dutch representative democracy will be seriously threatened by individualization, de-ideologization and globalization. With the explicit ideal of upholding representative democracy, the authors explore how these societal trends could be transformed or even turned around.

In summary, we analysed 20 Dutch foresight studies to explore contemporary scenario practices in more detail. The 80 scenarios identified in these studies were grouped into four scenario families representing key themes explored in Dutch foresight. In addition, we identified some so-called '*einzelgänger* scenarios' – namely, scenarios that present futures which diverge significantly from the outlooks covered by the scenario families.

Reuse

We also observed from the scenario studies' reports, as well as from our first visits in Dutch foresight practice, that futurists tend to build on previous scenario studies. Such reuse of scenarios was, for example, observed in policy-oriented foresight for Dutch water management (van Asselt et al, 2001b; Middelkoop et al, 2004) where one foresight study served as a key point of reference. In one of the ECN foresights, Shell scenarios were used as a point of reference (various field notes). The environmental foresights regularly produced by RIVM (RIVM, 1988, 1991/1992, 1993, 1997, 2000, and Milieu en Natuur Planbureau, 2006) constitute a series. The second *Environmental Outlook* (RIVM, 1991/1992), for example, was an update of the foresight *Concern for Tomorrow* (RIVM, 1988; van Asselt, 2000). The CPB scenario study *Four Futures of Europe* explicitly acknowledges that the scenarios 'have some overlap with scenarios that have been developed before' (de Mooij and Tang, 2003, p173). In addition, these 'four futures' are themselves used as points of departure for other foresight endeavours, such as the *Welvaart en Leefomgeving* (WLO) study (Janssen et al, 2006). A futurist involved in the WLO foresight explicitly stated that he considered the earlier CPB foresights 'as a coat hanger' or 'umbrella' for their exercise, while another argued that WLO is 'of the same kind' (various field notes). In one of the observed foresight endeavours, the tables and graphs used in a previous CPB scenario study were used as a template: the tables and graphs were emptied and refilled according to the new foresight. Scenarios produced by CPB are also used in these RIVM foresights. Schooneboom (2003) goes as far as stating that almost all Dutch scenario studies make use of CPB scenarios. Foreign scenario studies are also used as building blocks, such as the IPCC SRES scenarios (IPCC, 2000; RIVM, 2000) (SRES is the abbreviation of the report title in which the scenarios were presented, namely IPCC Special Report on Emission Scenarios).

Notwithstanding this reuse, in some cases Dutch futurists explicitly disassociate themselves from earlier policy-oriented foresights. For example, the SCENE foresight (Dammers et al, 2003) was portrayed as radically different from other earlier spatial planning scenarios. In the disassociation mood, earlier foresights also serve as a point of reference for positioning and characterizing a particular futures study.

We observed that Dutch futurists reuse previous scenarios – Dutch (especially the CPB), but also foreign ones. This observed use of preceding assessments of the future as a basis for new foresight endeavours provides some explanation for the strong clustering of scenarios sketched above. On the other hand, in other cases, futurists also explicitly disassociate themselves from previous scenario studies.

Conclusions

This chapter has described our first impressions of foresight practice. Foresight should be distinguished from forecasting. Forecasting, as we understand it, aims to predict the future, while foresight aims to explore the possibility space – namely, the wealth of thinkable options for the future, including the most radical outlooks. To that end, foresight involves surveying multiple scenarios. A scenario is a description of a hypothetical situation. Foresight is also referred to as what-if analysis. In the scholarly literature, it is argued that a shift can be observed from a dominance of forecasting to a preference for foresight.

We further prepared our journey through an analysis of publicly available policy-oriented scenario studies. The scenarios differ. We came across snapshot and chain scenarios as well as simple and complex scenarios. Scenario studies differ in goal and process design. Nevertheless, we also observed that with regard to the main themes, characteristic values and key developments, many scenarios could be grouped into three scenario families: economic-technological optimism (market family), back to basics and spring families. But there are also 'einzelgänger scenarios' – namely, scenarios that present futures that diverge significantly from the outlooks covered by the scenario families. Not all scenarios are developed from scratch: preceding assessments of the future are reused. In sum, the picture that can be derived from the first impressions of foresight practice involves elements of variety (types of scenarios, goal, process design, einzelgänger scenarios) and elements of convergence (scenario families, reuse of preceding assessments of the future).

What do the first impressions suggest about foresight in action? It is to be expected that in foresight practice, futurists are busy constructing scenarios. They accept uncertainty and their aim is to include even rather radical outlooks. To this end, they combine analysis with imagination. For our first impressions, we have relied on self-accounts. In the following chapters, we describe patterns and mechanisms in policy-oriented foresight in action. We detail how futurists deal with policy (Chapter 3), how they develop scenarios (Chapter 4), how they deal with uncertainty (Chapter 5) and how they understand time (Chapter 6). In this way, we reflect on the first-order answer to how experts assess the future.

Notes

1 Broad national foresights and studies produced by local governments, particular ministries and agencies.
2 Such as those produced by the Organisation for Economic Co-operation and Development (OECD), the United Nations Environment Programme (UNEP), the World Bank and the Intergovernmental Panel on Climate Change (IPCC).
3 Usually done by multinationals; but we also found studies for small- and medium-sized enterprises (SMEs) and inter-company endeavours.
4 Such as conducted in South Africa and Colombia (Achebe et al, 1990; Le Roux et al, 1992; Global Business Network, 1998).

5   Nevertheless, in the core set of studies, we included foresights conducted in/about the Europe Union and European countries – namely, The Netherlands, the UK, Sweden, Norway and Finland; but also studies conducted in/about the US, Africa as well as African countries – namely, South Africa and Tunis, and Colombia.

6   A village in The Netherlands, about 15km from Maastricht.

7   A neighbourhood in Maastricht.

8   The scenario team of the Mont Fleur scenarios consisted of 22 individuals – too many to mention in a reference list. Therefore, we chose to only mention the first author.

Reflections

3

Dealing with Policy

Introduction

In this book, we distinguish policy-oriented foresight from foresight in business based on our research approach. We studied foresight in action in practices that are policy oriented. We did not want to assume *a priori* that our findings could be extended to foresight in business, without studying such practices. The question is, however, whether it is, indeed, necessary to distinguish policy-oriented foresight from foresight in business. Through the story which we share in this chapter, we hope to make a case that the distinction makes sense or is even needed. In this chapter, we show that futurists involved in policy-oriented foresight are confronted with typical challenges dealing with policy.

In scenario theory rooted in foresight experiences in business, scenarios should be policy free. In the foresight endeavours which we studied, we observed that futurists struggle with this policy-free principle (compare Girod et al, 2009, who demonstrated comparable tensions in the Intergovernmental Panel on Climate Change (IPCC) scenario practice between the policy-free principle, which Girod et al refer to as 'non-intervention', and the actual scenarios). In this chapter, we describe the struggles as well as the strategies that futurists developed to deal with policy in policy-oriented foresight. In order to provide background, we first discuss the idea of policy-free scenarios.

Policy-free scenarios

What we propose to refer to as the policy-free principle is rooted in the use of scenarios in business contexts, also referred to as organizational foresight. Thinking about policy, generally referred to in terms of strategy and strategic options, is distinct from assessing the future through scenarios. We have the impression that this idea of policy-free scenarios, usually referred to as 'contextual scenarios', developed from the way in which Shell assessed the future (Schwartz, 1991; van der Heijden, 1996; Grant, 2003; Sharpe and van der Heijden, 2007). These books serve as standard references in the literature on organizational foresight. The policy-free principle implies that scenarios describe possible futures which are the upshot of interplays between various driving forces in which it is assumed that the client of the foresight would not act. As the driving forces and the interplays are uncertain, it is possible to construct a set of scenarios that differ significantly. In this way, the foresight client is confronted with various ideas for the future context of the organization.

The idea of assessing the future in the form of policy-free scenarios is, implicitly or explicitly, endorsed in various foresight textbooks (see, for example, Ringland, 1998, 2002a, 2002b; Nekkers, 2006). We also found that the idea is prominent among foresight practitioners. We witnessed how a policy-oriented scenario study – namely, *Four Futures of Europe* developed by The Netherlands Bureau for Economic Policy Analysis (CPB) – was disqualified with reference to the policy-free principle. In a meeting of futurists, one of the participants literally stated that the foresight was not a scenario study, because policy was included in the scenarios (Field notes, 6 February 2004). Building upon our reading of the literature as well as our experiences in foresight practice, we conclude that it is generally assumed that experts assess the future through the development of policy-free scenarios.

This policy-free principle seems to be associated with a particular mode of use for which the scenarios are arguably developed. This mode of use is routinely referred to as 'wind tunnelling' or 'robustness testing' (van der Heijden, 1996; Ringland, 1998; Grant, 2003; Nekkers, 2006; Sharpe and van der Heijden, 2007): the scenarios serve as a means to test policies in order to figure out whether a particular policy is 'robust' (i.e. policies 'that appear to trigger a favourable future, that seem to avoid highly undesirable ones, and that are flexible enough to be changed or reversed if new insights emerge' (van Asselt, 2000, p5)). In other words, a set of policies is confronted with a range of scenarios in order to test their robustness. The idea is that scenarios in which policy is integrated cannot be used to this end.

We witnessed that the idea of wind tunnelling/robustness testing is also prominent in Dutch foresight practice (e.g. field notes, 13 November 2003):[1]

> *In my view, you use the scenario approach if you want to formulate robust policy in the face of uncertainty. To that end, it is good, I think, that the scenarios sufficiently vary... If you decrease the variety a priori, you cover less uncertainty.* (Field notes, 14 December 2004)

> *I want the people from VROM [the Ministry of Environment and Spatial Planning] to use our scenarios to analyse policies. If you already incorporate policy [in the scenarios], you cannot use the scenarios to that end.* (Field notes, 23 March 2004)

Both quotes illustrate that the policy-free ideas expressed in foresight literature are obviously part of the practitioner's frame of reference.

The policy-free principle is therefore connected with a presumed mode of use – namely, wind tunnelling/robustness testing. A relevant question is to what extent robustness testing is a practised mode of use in policy contexts. A quick scan of how scenarios are used in Dutch policy contexts (van der Duin et al, 2008) suggests that robustness testing is not very popular in these contexts. Much foresight embraces the policy-free principle (Ringland, 2002a, 2002b; Nekkers, 2006; Ramírez and van der Heijden, 2007).

Recently, the policy-free principle has been questioned in the literature on organizational foresight, even by van der Heijden himself (Ramírez and van der Heijden, 2007). Ramírez and van der Heijden (2007, p97) contend that policy-free foresight ends up 'overemphasizing how far the context limits the scope for ... action'. They qualify this approach to the future as 'reactive'. Although van der Heijden is definitely to 'blame' for the popularity of the policy-free principle, in this recent reflection, Ramírez and van der Heijden (2007, pp97–98) wonder how it is possible that 'scenarios have ended up lodged in this rationalist positivist corner, while its origins were of a more exploratory nature'. In this context they refer to the original idea of foresight phrased by Herman Kahn as 'to think the unthinkable'. So the question is whether the policy-free principle, routinely referred to in descriptions of how to do foresight, is well grounded and well thought out.

We have the impression that, notwithstanding conceivable critique, the policy-free principle is part of the majority view in contemporary foresight literature on how to assess the future. What about foresight in action? Is the policy-free principle practised? We witnessed that in policy-oriented foresight, the policy-free principle served as an ambition, while concurrently, as we will show below, it was also clear that the futurists agreed that a policy-oriented policy-free foresight is not defendable. In the following section we detail how this ambivalent attitude was played out in practice.

Policy-free and policy-oriented foresight

We witnessed various occasions in which policy-free was, implicitly or explicitly, presented as the supreme approach to assessing the future. At the same time, we noticed that often in one and the same breath, policy-free was considered an unachievable or undesirable ideal in foresight endeavour. We heard futurists arguing that 'Fully policy-free is impossible'; 'We cannot assume that in the future policy-makers are blind. That is not realistic'; and 'The [future] world is not without policy' (Field notes, 23 March 2004). In another meeting, a futurist warned: 'We should not define policy away' (Field notes, 11 May 2004). When there will be new circumstances (e.g. 'huge economic growth') or 'bottlenecks' (e.g. with regard to mobility), 'policy-makers will respond. That is what policy-makers do.' Or in other words: 'It is not realistic [to assume] that from today onwards no policy will be pursued' (Field notes, 23 March 2004).

So, in practice, futurists diverted from the policy-free principle and included policy in their outlooks in one way or another. To illustrate this claim, we present two scenes in which departure from the policy-free principle is clearly visible.

Scene 1

In a work session in one of the foresight endeavours (SCENE) (Field notes, 14 December 2001), the explicit assignment was 'to forget policy as much as possible', which was in line with the policy-free principle. At the same time the addition 'as much as possible' already indicated that entirely policy-free was considered difficult or even impossible to achieve. The policy-free principle was also explicitly questioned. One of the participants in this spatial planning foresight argued that 'there is policy behind use of space and the preferences for particular spatial functions'. In his opinion, policy cannot be disconnected, as is assumed in the policy-free assignment. Notwithstanding the implicit and explicit recognition that policy-free is a difficult, if not unattainable, ideal, the 'forget policy' assignment was apparently upheld and further concretized as 'VROM neutral' – that is, assuming no change in the policies of the Ministry of Spatial Planning and Environment (in Dutch abbreviated to VROM). At first glance, the VROM neutral starting point appeared to be in line with the policy-free principle. However, it actually assumed that current policy will extend into the future and/or that policies currently proposed will be implemented. Therefore, this interpretation actually meant a shift: neutral signified no policy change instead of no policy. The VROM neutral principle thus prompted the inclusion of policy in the scenarios.

Scene 2

In one of the other foresight endeavours (VVR), futurists discussed future housing demand, types of houses and types of quarters in one of their meetings (Field notes, 3 December 2002). One of the futurists involved argued that in their assessment of the future, the so-called 'building and removal programmes' (i.e. particular government initiatives) should not be included. The futurist carried on: 'Ideally, we should not incorporate what is not yet built'[2] but is foreseen in long-term policy plans. In this foresight endeavour, various computer models were used. The same futurist continued that, however, 'in case you exclude policy, the model doesn't run... That is how the model works.' A senior futurist concluded: 'So it is almost impossible to rule out policy.' The group of futurists accepted that policy-free in their case was practically impossible in light of assumptions that drive the models.

In the second scene, it is also obvious that the futurists, on the one hand, subscribed to the policy-free principle as the supreme approach to the assessment of the future, while, at the same time, they easily accepted that it is an unattainable ideal. At face value, the reason why they diverted from the policy-free ambition – namely, because of assumptions in the models – may seem very pragmatic. They could have discarded the models and searched for another approach to assess the future. However, they did not even consider this option. Over the course of our observations, it became clear to us that the models were considered embodiments of their understanding of the future world, or a particular subsystem. So the fact that policy assumptions are deep seated in the models means that the futurists cannot imagine how it would work in a policy-free way. Therefore, it is not surprising that the futurists did not consider discarding the models; but it is all the more astonishing that the policy-free principle was still presented as the ideal approach to assessing the future.

Why do the futurists continue to perceive the unattainable policy-free principle as the supreme ambition? Policy-free is associated with the apolitical, which is considered the preferred stance for experts:

> In one of the meetings a typical Dutch practice featured: political parties can ask (and many do so) the planning agencies to assess the political programmes of political parties (see Huitema and Turnhout, 2009). A senior futurist reframed this practice in foresight terms: political programmes are 'actually desired futures' and in assessing them, the planning agencies treat them as 'realistic scenarios': 'In fact, we assess them as scenarios in terms of robustness, environmental consequences, etc.' Triggered by this image, another senior futurist objected that there is a big difference between the party programmes and their WLO scenarios: 'We develop value-free, scientific scenarios.' (Field notes, 13 November 2003; emphasis added)

This view is also expressed in another meeting: 'Our work is to refer to what actually happens and to base our assumptions [on that knowledge] instead of reasoning from desired futures' (Field notes, 23 March 2004). Such exchanges and statements nicely illustrate what we have witnessed and sensed during our field work: it is important for futurists to be apolitical, a stance that is interpreted as being more 'academic'. The apolitical preference is also evidenced as follows:

> Futurist N emphasized that he wanted 'to prevent that in this foresight political choices are made'. In his view, the key question for policy is 'what to want' and 'we should not choose for them... We have to clarify pros and cons. But we should not choose.' He was challenged by another futurist: 'Do you think building in the Green Heart [a relatively rural area in the urban western part of The Netherlands] is acceptable?' Futurist N responded right away: 'I don't want to think about that. As researcher, I want to assess pros and cons ... to present that to policy-makers and then it is up to them to choose.' (Field notes, 23 March 2004)

> *We cannot prioritize, because we don't have a normative frame.*
> *That means that we cannot say anything about what would be*
> *better ... worse or nicer ... because that is a political choice.*
> (Field notes, 18 November 2004)

It is not surprising that the policy-free principle resonated in such a context, notwithstanding the fact that at the same time it was, implicitly or explicitly, considered unattainable. This ambivalent position is exemplified in the following scene:

> *Some futurists discussed how to deal with policy in their scenar-*
> *ios. One of them, futurist N, stated: 'Entirely policy free is*
> *impossible, but including policy is also difficult... If you assume*
> *a particular policy, the scenarios cannot be used for testing that*
> *policy against the scenarios.' He referred to an earlier foresight*
> *experience: 'We experienced that disadvantage in 1992. The*
> *Betuwe-route [a contested railway plan] was taken up in one of*
> *the scenarios. So how, then, to evaluate the Betuwe-route?'*
> *Another futurist replied: 'You actually mean that all scenarios*
> *have to be policy free?' Futurist N agreed: 'Yes: that was what we*
> *were struggling with'; and he concluded: 'You have to exercise*
> *restraint with regard to fleshing out policy.' Elsewhere in the*
> *same meeting, futurist N stated that he considered it 'better' to*
> *include 'how policy works' (i.e. the government as endogenous*
> *actor, but 'in my view', it is 'too difficult, too complex, too*
> *complicated, to build that into the scenarios, so we won't do*
> *that'). (Field notes, 23 March 2004)*

The following excerpt illustrates the ambivalence with regards to dealing with policy in policy-oriented foresight. Furthermore, another motivation for policy-free is brought to the fore. The story told here is that the audience of policy-oriented foresight prefers policy-free, while it is suggested that the futurists' ideal is that government is an actor in the scenarios:

> *According to senior futurist P, the question 'How active do you*
> *assume the government will behave in the scenarios' is elemental.*
> *He explained that in previous foresight endeavours, government*
> *policy changed over time in line with the scenarios. In other*
> *words, the Dutch government was 'assumed as endogenous' (i.e.*
> *part of the system) and 'responded accordingly'. He narrated that*
> *the ministries asked them recently to assess those scenarios*
> *without policy because with policy the scenarios were arguably*
> *considered less useful by the ministries. So they did an exercise in*
> *which policy was kept constant. However, this yielded 'trivial*
> *outcomes'. He explained that informed by these experiences, in*

the WLO foresight they have chosen to work with what they refer to as 'minimally differentiated trend policy'.[3] (Field notes, 13 November 2003)

The various observations discussed above indicate that futurists on the shop floor search for a kind of compromise with regard to dealing with policy: both policy-free and government as an endogenous actor are considered unachievable or undesirable ideals. Another extreme that the futurists worried about in dealing with policy in policy-oriented foresight is that it erodes into presenting 'futures desired by policy', also referred to as 'desired futures' (e.g. Field notes, 23 March 2004). In the last scene the ambition of finding a middle ground is most obvious. The compromise is even explicitly presented: 'minimally differentiated trend policy'.

In sum, in foresight in action, the working attitudes with regards to the policy-free principle are ambivalent. On the one hand, the policy-free principle is still cast as the supreme or desired approach to assessing the future. In our view, this preference is sustained because of the aim of conducting apolitical policy-oriented foresight. The apolitical stance is interpreted as 'scientific', which is the kind of qualification that the futurists on the shop floor aim at. On the other hand, policy-free is considered an unattainable or undesirable ideal. The futurists regard the assumption that in the future no policy is pursued as unrealistic. In their view, this yields trivial outcomes. Furthermore, policy is considered an essential driving force in society's development. The futurists cannot imagine how it would work in a policy-free way: governments are crucial actors, who respond to changes and bring about change. As a result, they fear that policy-free policy-oriented foresight is either of bad quality or useless for policy. In this situation of ambivalence, futurists attempt to find a middle ground between policy-free assessment, including government as an endogenous actor. In the next section, we detail whether and how these compromises were practised in our case studies.

The no (significant) policy change principle

In all foresight endeavours that we observed, futurists departed from the policy-free principle. Policy was, in one way or another, and to a greater or lesser extent, a component of assessing the future. Informed by our observations in various policy-oriented foresight endeavours, we conclude that futurists on the shop floor preferred a stance in between the unattainable policy-free ideal, on the one hand, and policy as a fully endogenous part of the outlooks, on the other. This stance, which futurists referred to as 'neutral', 'policy poor' and 'minimally differentiated trend policy' (see Box 3.1), can be characterized as *no (significant) policy change* compared to current policy. This stance means that the futurists use current policy as a basis to construct future policy. This construction involves a kind of extrapolation of current policy over the time period covered in the foresight. Futurists themselves also

---

BOX 3.1 MINIMALLY DIFFERENTIATED TREND POLICY

Each project adopted, implicitly or explicitly, the no (significant) policy change stance as its point of departure. This was most explicit in the *Welvaart en Leefomgeving* (WLO) endeavour. In this foresight practice, the futurists proposed the 'minimally differentiated trend policy' principle as their compromise between policy-free and endogenous government. This concept was the upshot of earlier experiences, serious thoughts and discussions.

How was minimally differentiated trend policy conceptualized? The basic ideas behind 'trend policy' and 'minimally differentiated' were introduced as follows:

> *In presenting the WLO endeavour to other colleagues, one of the project leaders explained that 'minimally differentiated trend policy' is an important attribute of the scenarios. Futurist T explicitly admitted that the scenarios will not be 'fully policy free'. Trends in policy will be extrapolated. However, because the futurists consider this extrapolation of policy 'not so realistic', some room for manoeuvre is incorporated. For each scenario, especially after 2020, policy will be assumed that is in line with the scenario, while it minimally differs from the extrapolation of current policy (Field notes, 21 August 2003). This approach was also described in another session as 'we are not groping in the dark with regard to [future] policy'. There will be changes in policy, but we assume 'adjustments in the spirit of current policy. That needs to be consistent' (Field notes, 23 March 2004)*

---

referred to this approach in terms of 'extrapolating policy' and 'extrapolating the developments [in policy] of the last years' (e.g. Field notes, 23 March 2004). This also entails that constructed future policy is ideally kept constant over the different scenarios, although we witnessed that slight adjustments in the spirit of the scenario are considered acceptable. In this way, futurists tried to balance apolitical academic ambitions, on the one hand, with ideas about relevant content.

So the policy-free principle was not implemented in the policy-oriented foresights in action which we observed. Although the policy-free principle obviously resonated on the level of ambitions, in none of the foresight endeavours observed did the futurists seriously attempt to apply the principle. In practice, the no (significant) policy change principle served as a starting point.

Doubts

Notwithstanding the prevailing consensus with regard to the no (significant) policy change principle, this starting point continued to be critiqued at the same time. The overall question 'what is current policy?' was raised in a critical sense in various meetings (e.g. 13 November 2003). Such contributions questioned whether the idea of reasoning from current policy assumed in the no (significant) policy change principle was actually feasible. For example, in the following exchange the no (significant) policy change starting point was openly put into question:

One of the futurists asked: 'How are you going to do that [extrapolate policy] when there is no policy? In that case, you put policy in the scenarios.' On the other hand, in extrapolating policy: 'It is assumed that the current government will be 40 years in power. We should not assume that. It is possible to reverse, to adjust policy and laws. Also, today's policy impulses do not necessarily define the future. (Field notes, 23 March 2004)

Futurist J stated: 'A trend break [in government policy] is not what we want.' Futurist C objected: 'It is not about what we want. The question is what the scenarios tell us.' In his view, the foresight should be about possibilities: 'I just want to understand how it could work.' As a consequence: 'in the one scenario the government wants to do something and the government doesn't want to act in another scenario'. (Field notes, 18 November 2004)

In the latter scene, the prescription that future policy is the same in each of the scenarios is also questioned. We occasionally witnessed this. For example, we heard a futurist suggesting: 'Couldn't we formulate ... policy per scenario?... I don't think it [policies] has to be similar in all scenarios. That is the other extreme' (Field notes, 23 March 2004).

Both kinds of doubts, pertaining to whether it is possible to extrapolate policy and whether it is needed to keep the constructed policy constant in all scenarios, are expressed in the following contribution:

Is trend policy still defendable?... Shouldn't we differentiate per scenario?... Wouldn't it be better if we incorporate different perspectives on government in the different scenarios? (Field notes, 23 March 2004)

The most fundamental criticism voiced pertained to whether the no (significant) policy change is as apolitical as the futurists wanted it to be. Policy is, by definition, political. Current policy is also the upshot of a particular political process. Assuming that current policy is implemented and extended into the future favours a particular set of political choices. In a discussion in the SCENE project (Field notes, 14 December 2001), the participants signalled that there are different normative opinions on 'what is considered good in current policy', indicating that a 'neutral' position in a normative sense with regard to current policy is impossible. The normative problem is also visible in the next excerpt, which highlights the views of a futurist who is obviously unhappy with current policy:

'If you extrapolate [that] ... are you then not just extrapolating ... [a particular] policy of the last year?', with an intonation in his

*speaking and non-verbal behaviour that revealed that this futur-
ist is strongly opposed to that policy.* (Field notes, 11 May 2004)

Elsewhere, it was argued that 'current policy has a clear political colour' (Field notes, 13 November 2003), for which reason it was considered problematic as a starting point for constructing future policy. It was suggested that in order to deal with this political nature of policy, it should be possible, in scenarios, to adjust current policy according to different political positions.

This kind of questioning of the no (significant) policy change principle (and the associated idea of policy kept constant over the scenarios) could be heard now and then. However, in our experience this kind of criticism remained marginal in the sense that the no (significant) policy change principle continued to be endorsed.

Struggling with policy

In all foresight practices observed, the no (significant) policy change principle continued to be the central point of reference in the foresight endeavours. However, we witnessed that this starting point yielded a number of issues that were difficult to solve or address. These issues involved questions such as:

- Which policy documents should one take as the basis for defining current policy?
- How should one deal with policies formulated over the course of the foresight endeavour?
- Who is the policy-maker?
- How can one extrapolate policy?

The first issues refer to taking points of reference for defining current policy. The last issue refers to constructing future policy from the points of reference. We will illustrate the issues pertaining to points of reference and constructing future policy with some salient observations. In some of the observations, doubts about the no (significant) policy change principle discussed in the previous section reappeared as problems in practising the no (significant) policy change principle.

Points of reference

The futurists struggled with the issue of which policy document to take as a basis for defining current policy. In the SCENE project, the no (significant) policy change stance was translated into the 'VROM neutral' principle. In doing so, the issue of which policy documents to take as a basis for defining current policy was narrowed down to the policy documents of the Ministry of Environment and Spatial Planning. But it turned out that this could not solve the issue. In one of the SCENE workshops (Field notes, 14 December 2001), it was argued that there are various memorandums from the ministry that are not all geared to one another. So the question of which documents to take was narrowed down, but not resolved. In the WLO foresight, various policy memorandums from various ministries were listed as relevant for the foresight endeavour (e.g. 21 August 2003). Thus, in this case it did not just involve various competing policy memorandums from one ministry, but concerned policies from various ministries, as well as policies on the national, provincial and local level. The policies were listed without explaining how they would be used and how tensions between the different policies ought to be dealt with.

Against this background, it should come as no surprise that we witnessed intense debates on what to consider current policy. The huge efforts to define current policy are, for example, visible in the following scene:

> *Two futurists got the assignment to write a proposal together about how to define minimally differentiated trend policy. However, each of them wrote a memo individually. Although one futurist joked: 'Two memos for the price of one', it was obvious that there was, as futurist T phrased it, 'a fundamental difference between the two proposals'. Furthermore, futurist S reported that 'other working groups are also busy with similar pieces [i.e. writing down what current policy entails]' and 'they should be warned that there is still discussion about the principle of minimally differentiated trend policy'. Other futurists agreed: they were also aware that the working groups were busy writing down what they consider minimally differentiated trend policy and that in doing so, the working groups encountered similar problems as those visible through the two proposals. It was explicitly stated that 'the different working groups use different definitions of trend policy' – for example: 'The working group Housing could consider building in the floodplains as part of trend policy, while the working group Nature might oppose that'. In this exchange, the basic question [was]: 'Is trend policy still defendable?' One of the project leaders replied: 'Maybe we have overlooked basic issues? Maybe we have to discuss it again?' because of issues that 'we did not realize back then'. Or 'could we still proceed?' Agreement with regard to the approach was considered a necessity and it was clear that [this] could not be reached; but at the same time, it was obvious that the futurists would like to go on. (Field notes, 23 March 2004)*

The question of what to take as current policy also had a temporal dimension. What should one do in the event of recent policy change? This quandary is visible in the following positioning:

> *We take the policy change as starting point. We have said [that] we first look at the last ten years, and then we consider the last*

two years. If something is proposed [in recent policy], we have to include that in a sound way. (Field notes, 23 March 2004)

The question of what to take as the basis for defining current policy was further complicated by the fact that during the foresight endeavours, which usually lasted one to two years or even longer, policy was produced. How one should deal with such new policy was a serious challenge in various foresight endeavours. During the WLO project, the *Nota Ruimte*, the long-term spatial policy plan of the Ministry of Environment and Spatial Planning, was launched:

> *'This memorandum did not exist last year; it has appeared during our process' (Field notes, 23 March 2004). In discussing the issue, one of the project leaders stated explicitly: 'The connection with policy ... is difficult. If we allow trend policy to deviate from new policy, our foresight is difficult to sell.' Also in this discussion, the question [of] what to take as [the] basis is observable: 'Current policy is not the* Nota Ruimte. *I have heard that there are two positions in the Cabinet'. Furthermore, 'the* Nota Luchtvaart *[air transport policy] will follow. Are we sure we have to consider all [new policies]?' Another futurist objected that she perceived the* Nota Ruimte *'as a further implementation of the [policy] change of the last years'. 'To what extent does the* Nota Ruimte *differ from [what we consider] trend policy? How seriously should we take the* Nota Ruimte?', *asked another futurist. Futurist C stated that he takes the past as starting point: 'It has happened that way in the past years, and we take that as our starting point, independent of what has been written down. We extrapolate past policy responses and we don't honour each desired future. One can write down everything in a policy document.' Futurist N reacted: 'In that case, you deviate from the* Nota Ruimte.' *Futurist C admitted [this] and added: 'I don't mind.' Futurist N agreed: 'Neither do I.' One of the project leaders concluded: 'We won't solve this now' and another proposed 'to park this issue'* (Field notes, 23 March 2004)

In this scene, it is clear that the futurists struggled with the question of which policy documents to take as a basis for defining current policy, in general, and dealing with new policies, launched in the course of their foresight. Some preferred to use the newest policy as their point of reference, while others disqualified (particular) policy documents as merely desired futures, which should not provide the basis in their assessment of the future. The issue was not resolved. There is yet another dimension of the struggle with policy in policy-oriented foresight: in this scene, futurists on the shop floor expected that how policy was envisaged in the foresight would be relevant for how well the assessment of the future would be received by their policy audiences.

The discussion of how to deal with the *Nota Ruimte* continued. One of the project leaders stated that he had put the issue of how to deal with the *Nota Ruimte* on the agenda again (Field notes, 11 May 2004). Other futurists agreed that 'we have to do something with it'. In their brainstorm, futurists proposed confronting the *Nota Ruimte* with their images of the future, which could be read as a proposal for wind tunnelling/robustness testing. They also tried to characterize the *Nota Ruimte* in terms of which of their scenarios it would best fit. Although not explicitly acknowledged, the latter approach was actually more in line with considering government as endogenous in the scenarios and with accepting that, as a consequence, future policies differ between different scenarios. In the two proposals on how to deal with the *Nota Ruimte*, the two original opposites – namely, policy-free and government as endogenous actor – reappeared. This retreat seems to suggest that the no (significant) policy change principle, as the compromise between these two extremes, did not provide sufficient guidance for foresight in action.

How did the futurists proceed? Instead of resolving the issue at a strategic level (how to deal with the *Nota Ruimte*), it became a classic hot potato issue that was delegated to other futurists or set aside to deal with later. The question was asked whether and how in the various working groups the *Nota Ruimte* was dealt with. It was also explicitly suggested that dealing with the *Nota Ruimte* should be delegated to the working groups. Another proposal was to organize a 'lunch lecture' about it; but that idea was rejected: 'You can read it. The *Nota* is publicly available.' Another proposed: 'If we are ready, we have to check the *Nota Ruimte* systematically.' Over the course of the discussion, the attitudes diverged from a coping approach to advocating serious consideration in which the project leaders should take the lead:

> We could not let this pass. I can check how in the various text pieces [i.e. their own texts] the Nota Ruimte is treated and propose how we can deal with it. We have to do more than just wait and see what happens [in the working groups]. (Field notes, 11 May 2004)

But the discussion was not settled. It continued to sweep from one immature option to the other. The concluding remark is illustrative of the futurists' struggle with how to deal with new policy: 'I think the problem will vanish in time' (Field notes, 11 May 2004). In an earlier discussion on this issue (Field notes, 23 March 2004), the futurists felt that they were struggling. One of them even ironically proposed 'ignoring [the *Nota Ruimte*]' as the easiest approach. Both this ironic contribution and the fierce response: 'No!! Intelligent dealing [with the *Nota Ruimte*] is not ignoring it', illustrate how tense the futurists' struggle was.

In this context, it was also brought to the fore that the government is not the only actor. This raised other questions about who is the policy-maker, as is visible in the following excerpt:

> *A senior futurist argued: 'Next to government, other actors are active.' In his view, the question 'Who actually chooses and decides?' is not so easy to answer. He took business parks as [an] example to illustrate his concern: 'Is that due to market mechanisms or do we consider that government policy? Who is going to invest? Are new institutions necessary?'* (Field notes, 18 November 2004)

The latter questions pertaining to investments and institutions also bring to the fore the issue of uncertainty with regards to the realization of planned policy. Even in case business parks were attributed to government policy, the question was whether it was realistic to assume that plans would be implemented as originally stipulated in case other actors have to invest or new institutional structures have to be built. In the follow-up discussion, it was concluded that the no (significant) policy change principle implied the assumption that there would not be significant institutional change either. They would not consider the possibility 'of a private actor interested in public transport infrastructure. In fact, we take the current institutional setting as given' (Field notes, 18 November 2004). Another futurist concluded that:

> *The behaviour of the government is captured in trend policy. But the scenarios might differ in how market actors operate within that context... So trend policy only applies to the [Dutch] government.*[4] *We have to realize that other actors can respond with surprises.'* (Field notes, 18 November 2004)

In sum, the futurists struggled profoundly with what to consider current policy. Issues that complicate the matter are competing policy documents, recent policy changes and newly issued policies, which appeared over the course of the foresight endeavour, as well as how to isolate government policies from the actions of other actors. In our view, these struggles, which were not solved at the strategic level, if solved at all, indicate that in foresight in action applying the practitioners' compromise of no (significant) policy change was far from easy.

Constructing future policy

The next issue that appeared on stage was how to construct future policy. Or in the terms used by the futurists themselves: how to extrapolate current policy? Obvious mismatches existed between the time horizons of policies and foresights. It was clear that in constructing future policy, the futurists had to go beyond what was written down in policy documents. Even long-term policy plans used to have time horizons that did not extend as far into the future as the foresights intended:

> *With regard to infrastructure, much is already determined [in policy plans]. Until 2020, not much can be varied [between the scenarios]... We build the same infrastructure in the four scenarios till 2020. Afterwards, we will differentiate slightly, depending on whether more or less budget is available.* (Field notes, 19 October 2004)

In the Verkenning van de Ruimte (VVR, translated as Spatial foresight) endeavour (Field notes, 3 December 2002), it was, for example, argued that 'there are no fixed policy plans for the next 30 years', so they had to assume housing policies. Two other futurists explicitly agreed. One of them explained that in the models, it was assumed that after 2005, in which year the current national spatial planning policy plan would expire, every municipality would build (see endnote 2) according to local demand. This served as an example of the kind of assumptions about government employed in constructing future policy.

With regards to the issue of extending current policies into the future, various difficulties were identified – for example, whether it was realistic, helpful and/or desirable to assume that current policy would be implemented as planned. Most futurists argued that there is considerable uncertainty in realizing planned policy. As a consequence, questions such as 'How certain do we have to be about building policies in order to incorporate them?' (Field notes, 3 December 2002) were raised. The futurists also struggled with the question of how to extrapolate policies without creating friction-free utopian futures (Field notes, 23 March 2004). One of the futurists suggested that he wanted to explore not the policies as such, but the tensions in the housing market that accompanied these policies. He proposed extrapolating the friction between supply and demand, 'which has historically been accepted by the government and [we assume that] it will be accepted in the future'. But this proposal was also debated: 'Let's assume that there is a tension due to shortage of policy. You extrapolate that into the future, while the recent trend is to push back the deficit. What do you take as [the] starting point? The friction or the policy effort of the last two, three years?' (Field notes, 23 March 2004). It was, furthermore, questioned whether the friction idea can be applied to all kind of policies, and the warning was made that they should not 'wrongly introduce bottlenecks in the scenarios'. With regard to infrastructure, it was argued that '[we] can reasonably assume that roads will be built... About mobility, [in the scenarios] we have to respond to bottlenecks, that is what policy-makers do.' One of the other futurists felt lost: 'Which bottlenecks do you want to solve [in the scenarios] by assuming policy, and which not?' The futurists then talked about standing midway between driving blind and eliminating bottlenecks by assuming perfectly adequate future policy.

We read this course of debate – in which a proposal presented as a solution (to counteract friction-free utopian futures) degenerates into an unclear compromise stance – as an example of how the futurists struggle with the, at face value, simple idea of extrapolating policy.

With regards to constructing future policy, we also witnessed intense struggles at the strategic level and very pragmatic ways of dealing with policy at the tactical level, which were not necessarily in accordance with the idea of no (significant) policy change. Although the no (significant) policy change principle was already constructed as a compromise in view of the unattainable and undesirable policy-free ideal, we observed that new intermediate positions had to be constructed and very pragmatic choices had to be made in order to proceed.

Coping with policy

The futurists struggled with applying the no (significant) policy change principle in their actual assessment endeavour. Both with regard to defining the points of reference and constructing future policy from these points of reference, we observed that issues could not be solved at the strategic level. Coping with policy appears to be a more common response than dealing with it, which suggests some kind of coherent strategy. The no (significant) policy change principle did not provide adequate guidance on how to deal with policy in foresight. It was, however, not disregarded. Notwithstanding the fact that criticism was voiced, it remained the common frame of reference.

We conclude that neither the policy-free principle nor the no (significant) policy change principle facilitated the futurists in dealing with policy. Neither of the principles provides sufficient, if any, guidance on what to do at the practical level. In our view, the state of affairs in policy-oriented foresight is adequately described as one of struggling with policy, which, we think, is exemplified in the following scene:

> Futurist T argued that with regard to 'the question how we will deal with policy [in this foresight] ... we need to make a thinking turn'. He concluded [that] informed by the discussion, 'we are now essentially back to the start of this endeavour'. As they obviously wrestled with the issue, the project leader suggested 'parking' the issue of dealing with policy and discussing it in another meeting with other people (referred to as 'the coordinators'), 'both in practical and strategic terms'. Later in the meeting, another futurist tried to return to the issue; but that discussion was immediately kept short with reference to the [fact] that it was delegated to the coordinators. (Field notes, 23 March 2004)

In this exchange, the futurists explicitly admitted that they wrestle with how to deal with policy. Their coping strategy is to delegate it, either to other futurists or in time. We consider this scene exemplary for what we observed in foresight practice with regard to the question of how to deal with policy in the scenarios of the future. The futurists agreed that in one way or another, the scenarios should include future policy, but they struggled with doing so, both on the strategic level of principles and guidelines as well as on the tactical level.

Policy at the framing level

We have earlier described the futurists' struggles with how to accommodate (future) policy in their scenarios. We saw that the policy-free principle was useless in foresight practice and was replaced with what we referred to as the no (significant) policy change principle. We detailed how the futurists struggled with applying this principle.

Between the lines, it was, however, also discernable that the futurists struggled with policy on another level. The aim of policy-oriented foresight is to have an impact upon the policy realm. Among futurists, different ideas circulated about what was needed, and ideas were voiced at various occasions, especially in promoting or defending their own contribution to the collective assessment. We could sense that policy or, better, expectations about the policy realm played a role in framing foresight to a greater or lesser extent. See the following scene which, with comparable observations, gave rise to the idea of the role of policy in policy-oriented foresight at yet another level:

> *In an early meeting of the WLO foresight endeavour, senior futurist T argued that 'if we want to achieve something [i.e. in the policy arena]', it is 'not just about the content of the study', but also about communication in the course of the foresight process. In accordance with that line of thought, in this particular meeting a policy-maker from one of the ministries was invited as an external adviser to think along with the futurists. According to futurist T, it was important that the foresight team establish contacts, the sooner the better, 'with policy-makers on the shop floor'; [in addition], they had to inform 'policy-makers at the highest level' about the WLO endeavour. However, the communication process was not just considered a means in organizing impact; input from policy-makers was also considered highly relevant, if not crucial, for framing the assessment: futurist T argued that it was important to 'assess policy questions' and agendas as a basis to 'chose and prioritize' issues for their foresight endeavour.*
> (Field notes, 13 November 2003)

This refers to another dimension of dealing with policy – namely, the role of policy in framing the foresight endeavour. We believe that this dimension has to be touched upon in this chapter. It is also our impression that, although less obvious than on the level of future policy in the scenarios, the futurists struggled with the question of how and to what extent policy should be a factor in framing foresight. It appears that the role of policy in framing is also an unreflected or at least under-reflected issue, both in foresight practice and in scholarly literature.

Nevertheless, we limit ourselves to agenda-setting because notwithstanding our intensive journey in policy-oriented practice, we did not adequately grasp the role of policy at the framing level. We know that in some of the foresight endeavours, there were regular exchanges between futurists and policy-makers. However, we were not always allowed to attend these meetings. This is one of the reasons that we evaluate our observations as insufficient with regards to the question of whether and how policy framed the foresights. We cannot tell stories at the same level of analytic understanding as we can about using a particular foresight tool (see Chapter 4), dealing with prospective uncertainty (see Chapter 5) and dealing with time (see Chapter 6). These stories enable us to address the research question of how futurists assess the future in sufficient depth, such as the tale in this chapter on how futurists struggled with dealing with policy in the scenarios. Therefore, it is sufficient to indicate that in policy-oriented foresight practice, policy does not just play a role in accommodating policy in the scenarios, but also in framing the assessment.

Conclusions

The aim of this book is to describe how futurists actually examine the long term. To this end, we have studied foresight in action. All of the foresight endeavours observed were policy-oriented – namely, they aim at being relevant to actors in the policy realm and to policy-makers (civil servants and politicians) in particular. We posed the question of whether we had to distinguish this type of practice from foresight in business. Only policy-oriented foresight practice was examined; as a result, we had no empirical basis upon which to examine this issue. Is it possible, however, to extend our empirically informed insights beyond the subcategory of policy-oriented foresight to the broader field of foresight, or would this be immodest?[5]

One way of addressing the issue of categorization is to examine whether there are important issues so typical of policy-oriented foresight that they warrant differentiation. In this chapter, we have reported our findings with regard to the issue of dealing with policy in policy-oriented foresight. We demonstrated that, for valid reasons, the policy-free principle developed in the context of business foresight and put forward in textbooks is considered an unattainable and undesirable approach in policy-oriented foresight. We witnessed that, in contrast to the traditional practice in business contexts, futurists in policy-oriented foresight have to include policy in their scenarios in one way or another. We think that this is an important attribute of policy-oriented foresight. Our observations demonstrated how profoundly futurists struggle with dealing with policy, both on the level of scenarios and on the level of framing. Taking this into account, we consider it necessary to emphasize the distinction between foresight in the context of policy and business. Demarcation is an effective approach to highlighting difference, which we employ here without any reservations. We do so because, informed by our observations, we are convinced that (more) reflection on the challenges associated with policy is needed, in practice as well as in the scholarly literature. Although we have searched thoroughly, we did not find articles or book chapters addressing this issue. We consider this an omission. We hope that our analysis inspires reflection and further research on dealing with policy in policy-oriented foresight.

What, furthermore, does the empirically informed analysis in this chapter yield with regard to the overall research question 'How do experts assess the future?' In this chapter, we have shown that the policy-free principle is of little use and that futurists struggle with how to deal with policy in their scenarios. They try to find a middle ground between two extremes that are considered unattainable and/or undesirable – policy-free and government as an endogenous actor. The favoured compromise can be characterized as no (significant) policy change. Although this principle sounds simple and straightforward at face value, we have indicated that it is not. Our analysis suggests that futurists have managed to proceed not because they have solved issues or agreed on a particular approach, but by muddling through. As a consequence, even for a specific foresight, the question of how they actually dealt with policy is difficult to answer. So, attempting to unravel how they accommodated policy and cataloguing their approaches would suggest a methodical level that does not do justice to actual practice. For this reason, we have decided to confine ourselves to sharing the struggles. So the short version of this chapter with regard to what policy-oriented foresight entails, in practice, could be phrased as struggling with how to deal with policy in assessing the long term.

Notes

1   We observed that in foresight practice, the term 'robust' was also used in a different way as is evidenced in the following quote: '[We have to] identify robust trends – namely, developments which feature in all scenarios and which [policy-makers] have to consider definitely' (Field notes, 18 November 2004). We came across the notion of 'robust trends' several times, for which reason we consider the cited quote representative. We think there is a tension between the use of scenarios to identify robust trends and the original idea of using scenarios to draft robust policies. We will return to this issue in Chapter 7, as we need the stories in the upcoming chapters to further explain the tension in this observation.

2   The Dutch government does not build houses; but national and local governments together heavily regulate house building in a number of ways. Among others, they decide where housing corporations (which used to be state entities, but which were privatized in the 1990s), real estate developers and private individuals may build houses. Furthermore, they set targets for the number of houses to be built and issue permits for actual house-building projects. In The Netherlands, it is not possible to build a house on your own estate without a building permit, which should be in accordance with the overall spatial plan – house building is heavily regulated. Against this background, it is understandable why the Dutch futurists in this particular scene talked about the Dutch national and local governments as house builders. This should be read as a shorthand for the strong regulatory role of Dutch national and local governments.

3   In Dutch: *minimaal gedifferentieerd trendmatig beleid.*

4   Although this futurist explicitly argued that this trend only applied to government policy, we witnessed that it spilled over to how other phenomena and processes were perceived and dealt with in assessing the future (e.g. Field notes, 14 December 2004). We heard a futurist arguing: 'The behaviour of people [with regard to moving to newly built quarters] is a trend' (Field notes, 23 March 2004).

5   Some would argue that it is far from modest to analytically generalize our insights informed by observations primarily in Dutch practice to the broader category of policy-oriented foresight. See Mol (2002) for an enlightening reflection on this issue.

Reflections

4

Practising the Scenario Matrix

Attending to the scenario matrix

The question 'How do experts assess the future?' could be reframed as 'How do futurists construct scenarios?' In the previous chapter, we reported on how futurists struggled with dealing with policy in their scenarios. Neither the policy-free principle endorsed in textbooks nor the no (significant) policy change principle that practitioners themselves proposed as a kind of compromise provided adequate guidance. As a consequence, the story on struggling with policy offered only limited insight into how futurists actually construct scenarios. The aim of the current chapter is to better understand how scenarios are constructed. To that end, we attend in detail to a particular device – namely, the scenario matrix (see Figure 4.1).

The scenario matrix is widely referred to as 'standard' by practitioners and scholars:

- 'The standard tool used to sort out ideas and factors is the two-dimensional matrix' (Ringland, 2002b, p174).
- 'This approach is not uncommon in scenario building ... and has been used convincingly' (Berkhout and Hertin, 2002, p41).
- 'One of the most used techniques to develop scenarios' (Ministerie van Binnenlandse Zaken en Koninkrijksrelaties, 2003, p32).

Although the scenario matrix is referred to as standard, it does not mean that all scenario studies use the scenario matrix. It might, in fact, be deliberately disregarded. Nevertheless, we witnessed that in some of the foresight projects that we observed, the scenario matrix was used as a device in constructing scenarios. Inspired by Bowker and Star (2000),[1] who analysed how classifications assist in sorting things out, we decided to attend to the ways in which futurists employed the scenario matrix in actual foresight endeavours. Relevant questions for this activity are: what kind of assumptions are at work in a scenario study? Which logics and representations are in use and which functions are ascribed to the scenario matrix? We propose the notion of 'functional meaning' as shorthand for the answers to those questions.

We noticed that in foresight practice a multiplicity of various functional meanings can be employed at the same time. The term multiplicity is used here in the same way as in Mol (2002), denoting situations where variety is or cannot be resolved, while at the same time limits exist in terms of what professionals will accept as an 'enactment' (Mol, 2002).[2] Mol used the verb 'enact' in medical practice to affirm the coexistence of many answers to the question of what a particular disease *is*: in each answer a version of the disease is enacted. Likewise, multiplicity in the context of foresight implies that various functional meanings of the scenario matrix are enacted in foresight practice, while limits exist as to what futurists will accept as an enactment of the scenario matrix. 'Multiplicity' can be considered as a theoretical counterpart of 'closure', a notion used to describe courses of social construction in which one enactment is selected as the accepted and acceptable framing (Bijker, 1995).

We propose inscribing the functional meanings we observed as four metaphors: the scenario matrix as *backbone*, *foundation*, *scaffold* and *showcase*. In this chapter, we explain how various functional meanings are introduced and used in foresight practice.

Textbook descriptions:
The backbone functional meaning

The scenario matrix is often treated as the standard ordering device, as can be seen in its frequent use in recent foresight endeavours – see IPCC (2000); Berkhout and Hertin (2002); Ringland (2002); de Mooij and Tang (2003); Bruggink, (2005); and Smith et al (2005). The scenario matrix also features in van der Heijden (1996) and Wack (1985a). Both are widely considered to be standard works on futurist methodology. Furthermore, the scenario matrix is often associated with the highly regarded foresight activities of Shell, which further contributes to the idea of the matrix as a 'golden tool' (van der Heijden, 1996; Bradfield et al, 2005).[3]

In the textbook description, the scenario matrix[4] is composed of two axes (A and B) and four quadrants (see Figure 4.1).

According to textbooks, the most important 'driving forces' serve as the axes of the matrix from which the four stories about the future are told. Schwartz (1991, p102) even argues that 'Without driving forces, there is no way to begin thinking through a scenario'. The scenario axes are composed of the two driving forces that score highest in terms of 'uncertainty' and 'impact', when identifying and prioritizing the driving forces that are relevant to a particular scenario study. This is visualized in Figure 4.2.

We propose the metaphor of a *backbone* as a way of describing the functional meaning that textbooks attach to the scenario matrix. In the same manner that backbones support bodies, it is suggested in the textbooks that the

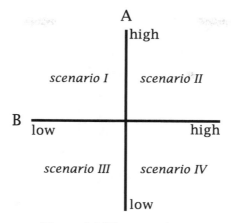

Figure 4.1 *The scenario matrix*

Source: Authors

stories about the future cannot exist without the scenario matrix. In futurists' own words: the axes of the scenario matrix 'determine the story's outcome' (Schwartz, 1991, pp101–102). However, as with many caveats, the warning of van der Heijden (1996, p205) has been forgotten: 'this approach is only practical if two ... overwhelming driving forces can be identified'. In succeeding textbook descriptions, it is no longer a question of *whether* two driving forces can be identified, but of *which* two driving forces to choose. The assumption that there are always two dominant driving forces, is rarely challenged (Berkhout and Hertin, 2002; Ringland, 2002; Ministerie van Binnenlandse Zaken en Koninkrijksrelaties, 2003). Van der Heijden's term 'overwhelming' is

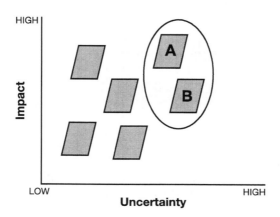

Figure 4.2 *Selection of axes*

Note: A and B refer to the two most important driving forces, which are then used as axes of the scenario matrix in Figure 4.1.
Source: Authors

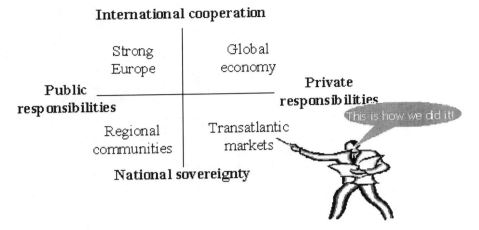

Figure 4.3 *Visualization of one of our observations*

Source: Field notes, 12 February 2004

also relevant here as it conveys an image of something external that engulfs futurists. Similarly, Schwartz (1991) seems to suggest that good futurists will discover the relevant driving forces through the skilled gathering of information. Futurists in a particular endeavour do not just work with *a* scenario matrix. Good futurists work with *the* scenario matrix.

The backbone functional meaning is not just a textbook description. It is practised by futurists in front-stage portrayals.[5] In February 2004, we attended a presentation on a finished foresight endeavour. The futurist who was primarily responsible for the study presented a scenario matrix on a PowerPoint slide. His methodological account was limited to the phrase 'this is how we did it' while pointing to the slide (see Figure 4.3).

Similar *ex-post* stories that are based on the backbone functional meaning can be found in articles in futurists' refereed journals. Smith et al (2005, p9), for example, argue that the scenario matrix 'shows the two axes and the four scenarios which *arise* from them' (emphasis added) and talked about the 'four different scenarios *generated* by these two axes' (emphasis added). These futurists even explicitly refer to the scenario matrix as a 'skeleton', a term very similar to our backbone metaphor.[6]

The backbone functional meaning prescribes how to do foresight: futurists study patterns and dynamics in order to discover the two most important driving forces. Once these are identified, they are plotted on two axes yielding four quadrants. This scenario matrix then determines the four futures to be told.

Informed by science and technology studies (STS) research, we expected that foresight practice would not conform to the backbone functional meaning. STS scholars subscribe to a constructivist notion of science, holding to the epistemological position that scientific facts are not 'ready-made' entities 'out there in reality' waiting to be 'discovered' and 'collected' by scientists. Rather, they contend that scientific facts are the results of negotiation. As argued in Chapter 2, the constructivist thesis is hardly controversial in the context of foresight: futurists do not *discover* the future, but actively *construct* futures. It is thus to be expected that futurists cannot discover the two most important driving forces as axes for the scenario matrix, as is assumed in the backbone functional meaning. But if it does not work according to the backbone functional meaning, how do futurists then employ the scenario matrix?

Getting started:
Backbone and foundation

In one of the foresight endeavours – the SCENE project – the scenario matrix technique was adopted as the way to do foresight. The SCENE project ran from September 2001 to May 2002. We were present at several regular project meetings, workshops, bilateral meetings and lectures related to the project, as well as at informal talks and interviews, both over coffee, lunch and other breaks in the programme, as well as scheduled meetings. We collected relevant project documents, and at the end of the project, we were fortunate enough to receive a CD-ROM containing the project leader's files. This wealth of material enabled us to attend in detail to the practical functional meanings attached to the scenario matrix.

We briefly summarize the amount of work and the kind of activities needed to construct a scenario matrix.[7] In two stakeholder workshops, selection criteria of various kinds were implicitly and explicitly added, emphasized, and further specified in the search for relevant driving forces. Those selected were scored, re-examined and clustered in view of this varying and diverse set of selection criteria, which were again reformulated and clustered. In these ways, the futurists succeeded in reducing the number of driving forces; however, notwithstanding all effort, they did not identify two overwhelming driving forces. They finally succeeded in constructing a scenario matrix by further applying and reinterpreting various selection criteria and transforming the choice between driving forces into a choice between two candidate scenario matrices. The resulting economic growth–environmental awareness scenario matrix (see Figure 4.4) is thus the outcome of this social construction process.

We do not know what the futurists thought. But our experiences in how they staged and continued to stage the scenario matrix suggest that in this phase of the SCENE project, the futurists still believed or pretended to believe in the backbone functional meaning, notwithstanding their own construction endeavours. Until this point, the upholding of the backbone myth, while at the same time actively constructing their scenario matrix, did not obstruct the foresight endeavour. But the futurists' next move, which we detail below, was to shift the functional meaning from the backbone logic to another functional meaning, which we propose to describe as the metaphor of *foundation*.

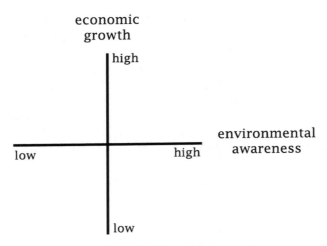

Figure 4.4 *The SCENE scenario matrix*

Source: adapted from van 't Klooster and van Asselt (2006); van 't Klooster (2007)

The futurists organized a stakeholder workshop (16 January 2002), and from its agenda, it was crystal clear that they intended to work from the basis of the economic growth–environmental awareness scenario matrix. However, various participants heavily criticized the proposed scenario matrix. The long and heated discussion derailed the workshop agenda. Although the futurists made some effort to argue in favour of the chosen axes in terms of 'impact' and 'uncertainty', it was clear that the futurists did not want to push it: stakeholder support was deemed more important than the original backbone criteria.

Instead of rescuing the backbone functional meaning by constructing scenario axes supported by the stakeholders, the futurists ascribed a different function to the scenario matrix. This was an interesting move as the criticism was targeted towards the choice of the axes, while the backbone idea was not explicitly questioned. After a break, the futurists presented the scenario matrix as just a 'frame' for the process of foresight instead of a backbone for the futures to be told (Field notes, 16 January 2002). The chair of the workshop used the scenario matrix as portrayed in Figure 4.5 to argue that the workshop participants were to be divided in four groups, each linked to one scenario quadrant. As a result, the scenario matrix was used as a procedural device for creating four groups.

The futurists argued that the scenario matrix could ensure the common ground that was needed to be able to work together, while preventing overlap between groups. In this way, the functional meaning of the scenario matrix was transformed into a procedural device: a *foundation* providing some structure for the process of foresight. Just as numerous buildings can be built on the same foundation, the scenario matrix was presented just as a basis from which

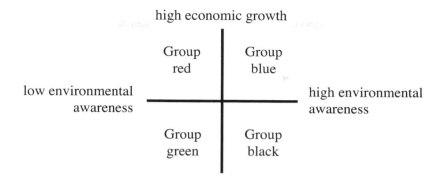

Figure 4.5 *Scenario matrix used as foundation*

Source: adapted from van 't Klooster (2007)

to develop various scenarios. The workshop participants agreed to the use of the contested scenario matrix consistent with this new functional meaning, and the economic growth–environmental awareness scheme was preserved as a result. In the foundation functional meaning, the scenario matrix serves as a way to structure or enable foresight, but it does not determine the contents of the futures (to be) told. It allows for flexibility in the choices of the axes and the meaning of the quadrants. The construction processes needed to select the scenario axes, as summarized above, sit uncomfortably with hardcore backbone futurists. It is not a problem for futurists advancing the foundation functional meaning. For them a scenario matrix is a socially constructed process device.

Notwithstanding the shift in functional meaning, the backbone rhetoric continued to be in use. In the methodology section in one of the final reports (Pálsdóttir et al, 2002), for example, it is still claimed that 'the most important and uncertain driving forces ... were determined' and that these 'were plotted on two axes' so that 'four scenario quadrants appeared' (see also Field notes, 16 January 2002). Some futurists continued to pay tribute to the backbone functional meaning. Notwithstanding the closure around the axes, no closure with regard to functional meaning was established in this phase.

Analysing multiple representations

To improve our understanding of the functional meanings of the scenario matrix, we paid detailed attention to various representations of the scenario matrix in the course of the SCENE project. Figure 4.6 depicts ideal/typical backbone representations: two axes yielding four futures.

The four quadrants are characterized by names such as 'The Netherlands – a consumers' space' (see Figure 4.6). We also came across versions of the scenario matrix that seriously depart from the backbone functional meaning.

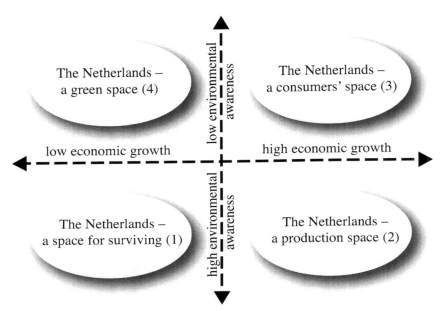

Figure 4.6 *A scenario matrix representation that figured in the SCENE project*

Source: adapted from van 't Klooster and van Asselt (2006); van 't Klooster (2007)

At first sight, Figure 4.6 and 4.7 look very similar, apart from renaming the scenario in the right upper quadrant. However, a closer look reveals that the scenario circles are no longer positioned as centres of the quadrant: the upper left quadrant has been moved on the environmental axis (above), while the lower left quadrant has been moved left on the economic axis. The scenario circles in the right quadrants are no longer centred. As a consequence, in Figure 4.7 the scenario matrix is not conceived as a 2 × 2 matrix yielding four possible futures, but as a two-dimensional possibility space (Berkhout and Hertin, 2002; see also Chapter 2). The scenario matrix is used to map four scenarios in a possibility space. The axes do not present a low–high dichotomy, but they are enacted as a continuum ranging from low to high, allowing many possible futures. The sense of matrix is transformed: it multiplies the number of possible futures and it changes the relationship between the axes and the scenarios. The scenarios are still associated with the two axes, but the relationship is reversed. The quadrant – namely, the position on the axes – does not determine the scenario narrative; rather, the scenario narrative determines the position on the axes. This representation violates the backbone functional meaning, but is unproblematic if the scenario matrix is practised as foundation.

In Figure 4.8, however, the scenario matrix is not referred to at all. The four scenarios are disconnected from the scenario matrix: they are presented as four possibilities (or 'destinations'). The scenario matrix can be removed: the futures

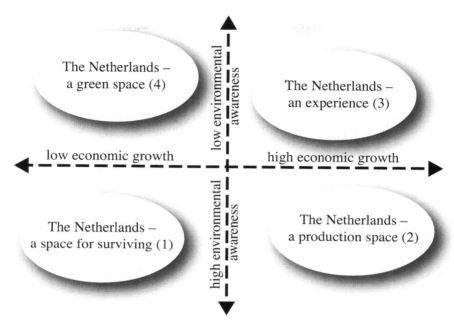

Figure 4.7 *Scenario matrix as two-dimensional possibility space*

Source: adapted from van 't Klooster and van Asselt (2006); van 't Klooster (2007)

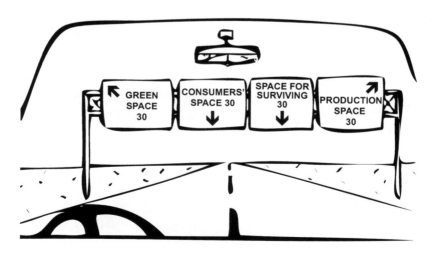

Figure 4.8 *Scenario matrix used as scaffold*

Source: adapted from van 't Klooster (2007)

told have a life of their own. This is a departure from the backbone meaning as this representation suggests that the scenario matrix serves no purpose in the descriptions of the future. However, as we will detail below, Figure 4.8 also departs from the foundation functional meaning and hints at a third mode of ordering.

Multiplicity continues to reign: The scaffold functional meaning

In the course of the foresight endeavour, some futurists increasingly questioned the backbone functional meaning. They felt constrained by the scenario matrix and, in the words of one futurist, thought it to be 'too mechanical'. The backbone critics argued that the scenario matrix 'beats down the richness out of the scenarios' and that it fails to give an insight into the complexities and dynamics that underlie the futures described (various field notes). The conclusion was that the scenario matrix should be discharged. In May 2001, a letter was sent to the stakeholders involved in which the scenario matrix was literally referred to as a 'scaffold': a construction device which should be 'broken down after the building is erected'. With *scaffold*, the futurists themselves inscribed a different functional meaning in a metaphor. In this functional meaning, the scenario matrix is not intrinsic to the futures (to be) told, but is a heuristic to stimulate variety between scenarios – useful at the start, but an obstacle in later stages. Dumping the scenario matrix is a precondition in the scaffold logic: its removal is needed to enable futurists to develop complex and relevant scenarios.

The anti-backbone lobby even began to criticize the scenario axes themselves. It was claimed that 'the axes are not plausible and well formulated'. An intriguing statement! If the scenario matrix is 'just' a scaffold, the choice of the axes is of minor concern, if not irrelevant. Nevertheless, the futurists advancing the scaffold logic still reified the backbone vocabulary. This may be a case of what Thompson et al (1990) described as 'stolen rhetoric' – namely, the use of core values, vocabulary and style by opponents adhering to a different perspective in a way that supports their own position, on the one hand, and undermines the opponents' stance on the other. Practising of the backbone logic by scaffold proponents may be a case of stolen rhetoric as a strategy to gain support; but it may also point to the 'stickiness' of the backbone functional meaning (i.e. it is difficult to leave the backbone idea behind and adopt another functional meaning).

The scaffold functional meaning was strongly supported, and it may even have been suggested by the director of the institute responsible for the whole foresight endeavour. One futurist explained that: 'Our director [stated] that he does not want to see the scenario matrix in the final reports' (Field notes, 21 May 2002). Whether through hierarchical pressure[8] or not, the scaffold gained visibility at the expense of the backbone and the foundation functional meanings. In the final report (Dammers et al, 2003), the scaffold even dominated: it was asserted that the scenario matrix was practised as 'a scaffold to position the scenarios and to guarantee that they would diverge sufficiently', and that once the set of scenarios contained sufficient variety, the scaffold was to be abandoned.

However, the end of our story is not the triumph of the scaffold. We would like to argue that the three functional meanings figuring in the SCENE project – namely, backbone, foundation and scaffold – continued to play a part in the foresight endeavour until the very end. The scaffold was not welcomed by all futurists, not even by a majority, notwithstanding its dominance in front stage portrayals.

A number of futurists questioned the idea of discarding the scenario matrix and continued to advance the idea of its use as a foundation. They argued that dismissal of the scenario matrix would result in the futures told collapsing like a house of cards. A backbone defence would present epistemological arguments, such as claiming that profound research has revealed that these driving forces *are* the most important and that without them there are no scenarios. The futurists advancing the foundation functional meaning, however, mobilized social arguments, such as 'We should meet the expectations of the workshop participants who expect that we worked with the scenario matrix' and 'The scenario matrix did function as a structuring device ... we should keep the method transparent' (Field notes, 16 January 2002). Furthermore, past investments and achievements were invoked in their opposition to the scaffold idea. One futurist stated that they 'already spent a lot of time writing about the scenario matrix' and he considered it a waste of time and effort if written texts were discarded (Field notes, 16 January 2002).

Where the proponents of the scaffold appear to cope with, and even establish, radical changes in the foresight process, those adhering to the foundation functional meaning stress continuity in the foresight endeavour. Unique to the foundation logic is that the scenario matrix is needed as an account of the process. Such accounts of the SCENE project can be found in some of the reports of sub-projects, some of which were, however, never completed, remained unpublished or were not widely distributed.

Just as the backbone rhetoric did not disappear after the introduction of the foundation functional meaning, the foundation metaphor continued to be practised in the SCENE project in face of the scaffold functional meaning. The backbone vocabulary was still mobilized, even by scaffold adherents. No closure was ever established on the issue of functional meaning.

We argue that the cover of the final report (see Figure 4.9) is an enactment[9] of the scenario matrix that sits comfortably with multiple functional meanings. The cover of the report can be read as a symbol of the scaffold because of the removal of the scenario matrix. But we can also argue that the scenario matrix is actually *visibly absent*: the two axes and the four quadrants are implied by the positioning of the four scenario symbols. This visible absence can be interpreted as a reference to the foundation logic still in use and/or as an acknowledgement of the textbook backbone functional meaning.

Figure 4.9 *Enactment that sits comfortably with multiple functional meanings*

Source: adapted from Dammers et al (2003)
Note: The report title translates as 'SCENE: a quartet of spatial scenarios for the Netherlands'. Ruimtelijk Planbureau translates as 'The Netherlands Institute for Spatial Research'.

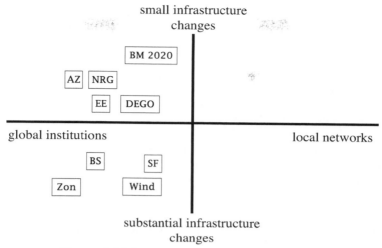

Figure 4.10 *Scenario matrix used as showcase*

Note: The small boxes with characters refer to scenarios developed in the BETER project.
Source: Field notes, 10 December 2003

More functional meanings: The showcase

The three functional meanings practised in the SCENE project (backbone, foundation and scaffold) are not necessarily the only enactments of the scenario matrix feasible in foresight practice. We witnessed in other endeavours that futurists developed scenarios without any use of any scenario matrix. We will not go into the details of how they told their futures, but mention that scenario matrices such as the one in Figure 4.10 appeared in the final phase of the BETER project.

We propose inscribing this functional meaning with the metaphor of a *showcase*, as the scenario matrix was used to position the scenarios as a means of exploring or communicating differences and similarities. In the backbone functional meaning, the scenario matrix is by definition a 2 × 2 matrix. The foundation logic accepts a 2 × 2 matrix or a two-dimensional space. In the showcase functional meaning, the scenario matrix is, by definition, a two-dimensional space in which images of the future are presented. The axes do not necessarily represent driving forces: the horizontal axis in Figure 4.10, for example, refers to two different configurations of energy supply infrastructure. We noticed that the use of scenario matrices as a showcase has consequences for the time and effort invested in the construction of the scenario matrix. In contrast to the SCENE project, ample time and effort, usually an hour or an afternoon, was invested in constructing axes in the showcase use of the scenario matrix. In addition, multiple scenario matrices were applied simultaneously. Neither serious construction of, nor closure on, a particular set of axes is needed in the showcase functional meaning, while closure on two axes is required in the foundation and scaffold functional meaning.

The scenario matrix as a showcase is neither a legitimization of the futures told (as in the backbone functional meaning) nor an account of the process of foresight (as in the foundation functional meaning). By contrast, the scaffold is used as an ordering device in the early phase, to be discarded later on. In the showcase functional meaning, however, the scenario matrix appears later in the foresight endeavour. It is used merely to present or evaluate scenarios.

Conclusions

In this chapter we have described the functional meanings associated with a tool referred to as standard in the futurists' community. We detailed how futurists practise various functional meanings yielding different uses of the scenario matrix, which we inscribed as backbone, foundation, scaffold and showcase. Informed by our observations, we concluded that the state of affairs is adequately described as a situation of multiplicity, as defined by Mol (2002): no closure with regard to functional meaning was established as none of the functional meanings were fully dismissed when alternative functional meanings were introduced. We conclude that it is too easily taken for granted that the scenario matrix is a standard device. What does standard mean when there are very different ways to practise it?

An important difference can be observed between the backbone, on the one hand, and the foundation, scaffold and showcase, on the other hand. The backbone functional meaning inhibits a positivistic stance with regard to knowledge production, while the other functional meanings qualify as constructivist. The latter qualification means that it is acknowledged that foresight is not, and cannot be, a matter of unravelling facts, as there are no future facts, but only images of the future composed by individuals or groups. In Chapter 1, we argued that almost all futurists whom we have encountered would agree assessing the future is obviously, if not by definition, a constructivist endeavour. At the same time, we have shown that vocabulary associated with the positivistic backbone functional meaning advanced in textbooks is reified in practice, notwithstanding the fact that the functional meanings which are actually practised (foundation, scaffold and showcase) have in common that they seriously depart from the backbone idea. The constructivist nature of the latter functional meanings would be consistent with the epistemological perspective of most futurists and with the kind of work involved in foresight in action. Nevertheless, many futurists still stick to the backbone functional meaning as their front-stage methodological account and continue to invoke backbone rhetoric. As a result, we observe a friction in foresight practice between reification, or at least stickiness, of the rhetoric associated with the positivistic backbone functional meaning, on the one hand, and the constructivist nature of foresight in action, on the other hand.

What does the scenario matrix story tell us about how experts assess the future? Although the scenario matrix is often presented as standard, we have observed that in foresight in action it is used in different ways that also differ

Table 4.1 *Functional meanings of the scenario matrix*

| To be dropped | Constructivist functional meanings | | |
Backbone myth	Foundation	Scaffold	Showcase
Positivistic	Scenario matrix is the result of an intensive social construction process*	Ample time invested in constructing scenario matrices	
Two driving forces constitute the scenario matrix	Requires closure on two axes		No closure on axes is required: multiple scenario matrices can be used
Found in textbooks and front stage portrayals	Scenario matrix is used in developing scenarios		Used in late(r) stage of foresight
Scenario matrix determines the scenarios	Procedural device: ensuring common ground while preventing overlap	Ordering device: useful at the start, but obstacle in later stages	Scenario matrices are used in presenting or evaluating scenarios
Scenario matrix is, by definition, 2 × 2 matrix	Matrix could be 2 × 2 matrix or two-dimensional possibility space		A scenario matrix is, by definition, a two-dimensional possibility space
Scenario matrix legitimizes the futures told	Scenario matrix is account of the process	Scenario matrix is to be abandoned in the course of foresight endeavour	

Note: * In our observations the scenario matrix used as scaffold was also the result of an intensive and lengthy social construction process. However, if the idea of a heuristic in order to initiate the process is taken seriously, the question can be raised whether the social construction process needs to be so intensive and lengthy. It seems probable that in the scaffold functional meaning, constructing a scenario matrix might be a quick endeavour.

from how the tool is presented in textbooks. This story demonstrates that some futurists use the scenario matrix as foundation, scaffold or showcase in constructing scenarios or in evaluating constructed scenarios. In textbooks, the scenario matrix is nevertheless still presented in terms of the backbone. Informed by our observations, we conclude that textbooks need to be updated. It should be recognized that the scenario matrix is used in different ways. The idea of backbone should be dropped in textbooks. The backbone functional meaning obscures the constructivist nature of the actual work. Explicitly discarding it in textbooks is likely to counteract further reification of the backbone myth.

We also observed a multiplicity of functional meanings. Closure, for example, was not established. Although the futurists managed to proceed, the question is whether multiplicity is a desired state of affairs. We have inscribed how the scenario matrix is actually practised (foundation, scaffold, showcase). This overview of multiple functional meanings (summarized in Table 4.1) might help practitioners to organize closure. Furthermore, the differences between the various functional meanings can facilitate a more informed weighing of pros and cons. Such a better informed discussion on how the scenario matrix could be used might also stimulate the search for, and reflections on, alternative approaches to scenario construction in which the scenario matrix is not employed at all.

Notes

1   We would also like to thank our former colleague Maud Radstake, who in a faculty workshop where we presented our observations also suggested that, in the analysis, it could be worthwhile to 'follow a tool'.

2   The use of the notion 'enactment' as analytic vocabulary was not Mol's invention. It has been used earlier by organization theorist Karl Weick (1979, 1999). We owe this concept history to Geoffrey Bowker.

3   The 'oil crisis success story' retold among futurists (Dobbinga, 2001; van Notten, 2005) also 'reifies' the image of Shell's leadership in futuristic methodology. This story, told in various versions, has it that due to scenario analysis, Shell was able to anticipate the oil crisis and arguably acted accordingly and better than its competitors. The notion of 'reify', or 'reification', which has Marxist roots, was reintroduced by Latour and Woolgar (1986) as a reference to stabilization and solidification of statements and stories that are handed down over time and travel in many ways so that they become a taken-for-granted part of practices in ways that further increase complacency. Both Wack and Van der Heijden worked for Shell. Adding this detail lends credibility to the association of the scenario matrix with Shell, and it is the kind of association shared and emphasized among futurists (otherwise, how would we know?).

4   These kinds of 2 x 2 diagrams enjoy widespread popularity both in scholarly and professional contexts. We consider it beyond the scope of this chapter to treat the scenario matrix in such broader contexts of use. Here, we confine ourselves to its use in the context of foresight.

5   The Canadian sociologist Erving Goffman (1959) proposed a theoretical framework to analyse social interactions as theatrical performances. He argued that, similar to an actor playing a character, in everyday life, people use setting, clothing and their verbal and non-verbal actions to foster a particular, preferably favourable, impression. In this context, Goffman uses the term 'front stage' to refer to all actions that are part of the performance and visible to the audience, while the term 'backstage' denotes the behaviours in which people engage when no audience is present. Goffman contends that the distinction between front stage and backstage performances and mechanisms of impression management with the aim of convincing audiences are observable in social life. More recently, STS scholars have translated and adapted this dramaturgical view to the sociology of science and expertise (e.g. Hilgartner, 2003; Bijker et al, 2009). The distinction between 'front stage' and 'backstage' performances is central to these scholars' explanations of how experts produce scientific credibility, legitimacy and objectivity in science advice. Dobbinga (2001) used the same concepts in her analyses of a scenario endeavour at a Dutch ministry. The way in which we use the notions of backstage and front stage is in line with how it is used in Hilgartner (2003) and Bijker et al (2009).

6   So how original is our metaphor? It can be argued that we just had to pick it up and add analytic value.

7   For a detailed account, see van 't Klooster and van Asselt (2006) and van 't Klooster (2007).

8   It is beyond the scope of our expertise to tell stories about the role and impact of power and hierarchy on foresight endeavours.

9   As mentioned before, Mol used the verb 'enact' in medical practice to inscribe the coexistence of many answers to the question of what a particular disease *is*: in each answer a version of the disease is enacted. Likewise, multiplicity in the context of foresight implies that various functional meanings of the scenario matrix are enacted in foresight practice, while limits exist to what futurists will accept as enactment of the scenario matrix.

Reflections

5

Dealing with Prospective Uncertainty

Prospective uncertainty

In the previous chapter, we addressed foresight in action through an analysis of observations about the scenario matrix. By analysing a multiplicity of functional meanings, we aimed to contribute to the understanding of how policy-oriented foresight is actually carried out. In this chapter, we describe and analyse observations about the approaches that futurists use in the face of uncertainty. It is generally agreed among futurists that foresight involves dealing with 'prospective uncertainty', which we define as instances in which futurists have doubts about the future, partly or fully, because (scientific) knowledge is perceived as limited (compare van Asselt, 2005, and van Asselt et al, 2007a). Fontela's complaint reveals that prospective uncertainty is inherent to foresight (Fontela, 2000, pp10–14):

> *We know little about the past and present in a multidisciplinary way. We know that sociological and political factors influence economic factors and vice versa. We know that technological developments lead to innovation that modify productive structures; we know, indeed, that the facts that determine change are many and that our scientific knowledge of the processes of change is clearly insufficient ... to explore [the future].*

The acknowledgement of prospective uncertainty is common in the foresight community. Foresight is frequently presented as the art of understanding or even managing uncertainty (see, for example, Cinquegrani, 2002; Burt and van der Heijden, 2003; Tonn, 2003; Cariola and Rolfo, 2004). Foresight scholars routinely refer to uncertainty as intrinsic to the future (e.g. Cinquegrani, 2002; Puglisi and Marvin, 2002; Aligica, 2003; Burt and van der Heijden, 2003;

Tonn, 2003; Wilkinson and Eidinow, 2003; Wilkinson et al, 2003; Dortmans and Eiffe, 2004; and Hayward, 2004). In the previous chapter, we noted that 'uncertainty' is one of the criteria used to qualify driving forces when selecting the axes of the scenario matrix. Therefore, even in the positivistic perspective (backbone functional meaning), prospective uncertainty is genuinely acknowledged.

In Dutch foresight, it is also routinely acknowledged that foresight involves dealing with prospective uncertainty. For example, the Dutch Scientific Council for Government Policy (WRR), a governmental agency and pioneer in the field of foresight, stated in a retrospective study that 'future studies are primarily about uncertainties' (WRR, 2000). In the fifth environmental outlook (RIVM, 2000), it is explicitly argued that 'the future is uncertain' and that 'The processes described ... in this ... outlook are interlarded with uncertainties.' Dobbinga (2001) noted that prospective uncertainty was an explicit point of departure in a scenario project at the Dutch Ministry of Transport.

Uncertainty is crucial in many portrayals of current day foresight practice. But at the same time, it is also argued that dealing with uncertainty in foresight is an 'at present taken-for-granted and disattended [sic] social process' (Brown et al, 2000, pxii). Furthermore, we observed that futurists' self-accounts, if available, usually do not address how uncertainty is attended to in practice. The intriguing question is, thus, how do futurists sort out uncertainty in actual foresight endeavours.[1] Schön (1983) and Nowotny et al (2001) suggest that clues may be discovered from studying uncertainty manners in use. The concept of 'uncertainty manner' is shorthand for a frequently observed behavioural pattern pertaining to prospective uncertainty. Brown et al (2000) explicitly recommended that empirical social scientific research should play an important role in making transparent how prospective uncertainty is actually managed in foresight. In this chapter we aim to disclose such uncertainty manners. To this end, we first examine uncertainty awareness in foresight practice.

Uncertainty awareness

References to prospective uncertainty were made in many of the work sessions that we attended. We heard, for example, futurists talking about 'many uncertainties' and 'the uncertainties the future offers us', qualifying particular statements about the future as 'highly uncertain', as well as arguing that 'the further [we extend] into the future, the more uncertain it gets' and 'it is very uncertain, but we have to say something' (various Field notes and interviews). In addition, in sessions in which uncertainty was not explicitly mentioned, obvious references to prospective uncertainties abound. In such sessions (e.g. Field notes, 28 August 2003), futurists asserted that they do not know or that they know 'too little'.

Also in foresight practice, prospective uncertainty is presented as the core of foresight. In a meeting report in an early phase of a foresight endeavour, it was argued:

It is expected that in the years to come, society will change fast...
Because of that, innovative, scientifically based foresight is
needed... It is especially important to identify uncertainties.
(Field notes, 16 January 2002)

And in another meeting, this foresight endeavour was presented as aiming at 'anticipating uncertainty' (14 December 2001).

In some utterances, particular sources of uncertainty are specified, such as insufficient reliable data and long time series, as well as a limited understanding of what is and what is not included in particular data sources (Field notes, 15 March 2004). We also attended a meeting in which a number of futurists presented the computer models used in their foresight endeavour (3 December 2002). Most modellers devoted a large amount of their presentation time to discussing uncertainties, such as uncertainty related to datasets and questionable assumptions, uncertainty pertaining to causal relationships, uncertainty related to the question of whether phenomena are modelled on the appropriate geographical scale, uncertainty pertaining to the dynamics of change, and uncertainty with regard to distributional issues (geographically and socially). It was even argued that 'The model involves uncertainties; actually each [model] step is uncertain.' The futurists concluded that this meeting helped them to understand uncertainty.

However, we witnessed that in many cases in which prospective uncertainty is explicitly acknowledged, this uncertainty is, generally speaking, not further elaborated upon or examined. Even in the above session (3 December 2002), we heard one modeller arguing 'it is terribly uncertain. The ranges are gigantically large', without further specification or examination of the involved uncertainties. Formed by such and similar experiences, we have the impression that uncertainty often serves as a black box that can remain closed. Uncertainty is acknowledged, but not seriously examined or elaborated upon.

Notwithstanding the fact that prospective uncertainty is acknowledged on the futurists' shop floor, we also observed that in some obvious instances of uncertainty, prospective uncertainty is not acknowledged, but concealed as an 'assumption' and 'research question'. In one of the sessions we attended (Field notes, 19 March 2002), the futurists discussed the uncertain relationship between investments in research and development (R&D), innovation and economic growth in relation to a particular scenario. It was not explicitly stated that this is an instance of prospective uncertainty. Instead, the futurists discussed the issue in terms of 'assumptions' and talked about the importance of being explicit. In comparable situations where prospective uncertainty was not explicitly on the table, seemingly strong claims about the future were softened as 'assumptions' and statements presented as assumptions were qualified as 'super-speculative' or as 'subjective' (various field notes). From the attitude towards the notion of 'assumptions', we conclude that in the context of foresight, an assumption should be read as a particular statement with regard to an issue that the futurists consider to be a matter of prospective uncertainty. It is a hypothesis about the uncertain future. It needs serious reflection in order to realize that assumptions actually refer to uncertainty.

Prospective uncertainty could also be inferred from references to themes as 'research questions'. In one of the sessions we attended, the futurists discussed demographic futures – in particular, the number of children per family (Field notes, 21 May 2002). Confronted with uncertainty, the group could not reach consensus and the issue was parked as a 'research question'. The same tendency was observed later in the same meeting, as well as in other meetings (e.g. Field notes, 14 December 2001). It is interesting that, notwithstanding the general awareness of uncertainty, futurists prefer to portray prospective uncertainty as 'research questions', instead of acknowledging that it is actually an instance in which they have doubts about the future, partly or fully because (scientific) knowledge is limited. Noordegraaf (2000), Mesman (2002), Uggla (2004), van Asselt (2005) and van Asselt et al (2007a, 2007b) observe that more generally scientific uncertainties are partly managed with reference to future research. It is usually emphasized that further investigation is pending or needed, which serves as a reassuring suggestion of complete knowledge in the future. In other words, by referring to uncertainty in terms of research questions and issues for further research, the future is depicted as a world of scientific certainty (Collins, 1987). It is surprising that this approach to uncertainty is also practised in a knowledge practice that presents itself as engaging with an uncertain future.

Prospective uncertainty is not only routinely acknowledged in scholarly writings and futurists' reports, but it is also a common feature in foresight practice. In assessing the future, futurists encounter issues which they characterize as uncertain. Practitioners consider dealing with prospective uncertainty a difficult challenge. For example, a futurist reflecting on one of the observed foresight endeavours claimed that one of the issues addressed turned out to be the most problematical because of the high level of uncertainty (Field notes, 12 August 2002). We also heard a practitioner say that it is demanding to hold onto uncertainty because 'you want to have the feeling that your work makes sense' (Field notes, 12 May 2003). And we heard futurists stating that they find dealing with prospective uncertainty very difficult (Field notes, 23 January 2003).

We witnessed a high level of uncertainty awareness in futurists' writings. However, the picture is mixed with regard to foresight practice. Acknowledgement of prospective uncertainty is commonplace; but at the same time uncertainties are black-boxed and concealed as assumptions and research questions. Furthermore, practitioners in foresight practice expressed that they consider dealing with uncertainty a difficult challenge.

Uncertainty manners

We observed that futurists are aware of prospective uncertainty, while at the same time the above observations suggest that acting in line with this awareness is not straightforward. We therefore decided to attend in closer detail to the kind of behaviours on the shop floor in instances of prospective uncertainty. How do uncertainty-aware futurists deal with prospective uncertainty? The familiar and broadly reified[2] picture among professional futurists is that 'You put most of the uncertainties in the scenarios, in principle' (interview quote, van Asselt, 2000).[3] In other words, professional futurists simply list prospective uncertainties and then provide various interpretations of these uncertainties, referred to as 'scenarios'. Also on the shop floor, the use of scenarios is motivated by referring to uncertainty 'because the future is not fixed' and 'the further you extend in to the future, the more uncertain it becomes' (Field notes, 15 March 2004). We also heard a futurist arguing that 'when the uncertainties are much larger', the assessments of the future should be presented as 'scenarios' and not as 'prognoses' (Field notes, 7 November 2002). It is further argued that 'in order to be able to deal with the uncertainties the future is offering us', the scenarios need to differ (Field notes, 18 September 2003). Or as another futurist phrased it: 'If you don't know what will happen with energy demand', it is important to realize that there is 'not just one possibility' (Field notes, 28 August 2003). Van 't Klooster (2007) refers to this foresight aspiration in light of uncertainty as the 'variation ambition'. This concept refers to the idea that, in the face of prospective uncertainty, various (sometimes even conflicting) views of the future are, in principle, legitimate. In practice, this ambition entails creating sufficiently varying scenarios in order to provide users with as much information as possible on the uncertainties of the future.

Our observations suggest that futurists use the notion of scenarios as a self-account of how uncertainty is dealt with. References to variations in ambition also seem to serve as self-accounts. However, we are not convinced that these self-accounts are adequate representations of how futurists deal with uncertainty in practice. In the previous chapter, we revealed the assumptions on which the use of the scenario matrix is based. We demonstrated how much work is needed to construct a scenario matrix and that the 'same' scenario matrix is quite different depending upon the functional meaning ascribed to it. Informed by this experience, we do not accept the familiar idea of scenarios as internally consistent interpretations of various prospective uncertainties as a sufficient explanation of how futurists deal with prospective uncertainty. We expect that more interesting and relevant insights into futurists' ways of understanding and managing prospective uncertainty can be gained through empirical research. We believe that different and more insightful stories can be told about how futurists actually approach uncertain issues.[4]

Informed by our empirical research, we thus aim to address how futurists deal with prospective uncertainty. This is easier said than done. Even in sessions on the shop floor where we expected to hear how futurists deal with prospective uncertainty, we did not find clues, as is evidenced in the following remark in our field notes: 'If it [dealing with uncertainty] doesn't happen here, where does it?!' (Field notes, 21 May 2002). So how did we examine behavioural patterns pertaining to prospective uncertainty? Futurists are not the only professionals who are challenged to deal with prospective uncertainty. For example, medical staff are also confronted with it. Since Fox's seminal *Training for Uncertainty* (1957), the question of how uncertainty is dealt with in medical practice is addressed in medical-sociological studies, such as those by Light Jr. (1979); Atkinson (1984); Katz (1984); Fox (2000); Mesman (2002, 2005, 2008, 2009); and Fosket (2004). We mobilized these insights to develop a categorization of uncertainty manners (see van Asselt, 2005, and van Asselt et al, 2007a). We also compared our preliminary findings with insights informed by empirical research on how actors deal with uncertainty in policy domains, in general (Noordegraaf, 2000), and in environmental and health risk management contexts, in particular (Dunsby, 2004; Schmid, 2004; Uggla, 2004; Wells Bedsworth et al, 2004), as well as by research on how patients deal with uncertainty (Brashers, 2001). This categorization was then used as a heuristic to interpret our observations, which in turn helped to further categorize and elaborate upon the different uncertainty manners. In this iterative way, we clustered our observations on the role of uncertainty in foresight practice into the following categories:

- Construction of solidity: assumptions and probable, possible and preferred futures are treated as a future fact.
- Typical exemplars: experiences in other countries, personal experiences and statements about the future in previous foresight and particular historical developments are used to draw conclusions about the uncertain future.
- Expertise as anchor: expert judgement, expert consultation and consensus-building among experts are used as a filter to sift uncertainties and as a basis for establishing foresight models and outlooks.
- Numeric discourse: numbers, broadly treated as certainties, are used as building blocks in foresight practice, although practitioners are well aware and/or critical of the certainty connotation of numbers.
- Communication habits: vagueness in communication is employed, not just as an act of camouflage, but also as an attempt to communicate uncertainty.
- Delegation: dealing with prospective uncertainty is assigned to other people (particular practitioners and policy-makers) or is postponed.

Below, we detail the various uncertainty manners with observations from foresight practice.

Construction of solidity

Solidity is created through a particular trading of uncertainty. Possibilities and probabilities are transformed into firm assumptions. The conditionality is ignored and the possibilities are treated as a (future) reality.[5] For example, in the fifth *Environmental Outlook* (RIVM, 2000), it is argued that new technologies, thought of as 'solutions' for persistent environmental problems, may create new problems in the next 30 years. The possibility is then transformed into the assumption that it will happen, which is subsequently used as a solid basis for further assessment. The result is an unconditional recommendation on particular strategies to prepare for the future. More generally, we observed that in this *Environmental Outlook* the firm tone overruled the conditional content (van Asselt, 2004). In her retrospective reflection on the famous *Limits to Growth* foresight activities by the Club of Rome in the 1970s, Nowotny (2008) also mentioned this approach to uncertainty: 'By substituting probabilities calculated by the computer model for certainties, guarantees for the future were constructed' (Nowotny, 2008, p110). Another example of such trading of uncertainty is visible in the following exchange between futurists on the issue of demography (Field notes, 28 August 2003):

> M in response to G: *What do you expect in terms of population size? I do not expect much of a change.*
>
> A: *The population will stay constant, about 8 to 9 million households.*
>
> Futurist A presents this expectation as a matter of fact, which remains undisputed.

A similar way of dealing with uncertainty could be observed in other sessions (Field notes, 28 August 2003; 15 March 2004) in which assumptions were solidified by way of qualifications, such as 'best guess', 'expectation' and 'this is an assumption, but of course verified by experts', without further explanation of what the expert verification of assumptions entails. In other sessions, we also witnessed that assumptions were presented and discussed as fact-like statements, which have to be underpinned in a scientific manner (e.g. Field notes, 21 March 2002; 21 May 2002). In such instances, assumptions are stated without discussing alternatives. This pattern also occurred in the content analysis of the series of *Environmental Outlooks* (van Asselt, 2004): alternative assumptions were not presented, let alone discussed. As argued above, the notion of 'assumption' in principle hints at prospective uncertainty; but in practice, uncertainty becomes concealed in inferences based on assumptions, in the undisputed presentation of assumptions as matters of fact and/or in the expert authority attached to it.

Not only probabilities, possibilities and assumptions, but also policy norms, which describe a preferred future, are treated as a future reality. In this way, futurists manage to disarm particular prospective uncertainties. This is nicely illustrated by the following exchange between some futurists (Field notes, van Asselt, 2000):

> Futurist J: *The health effects and the effects on ecosystems: we don't know them very well. The uncertainties there are much larger than earlier in the chain.*

Futurist F: *And that is extraordinarily alarming …*

Futurist K: *In Europe we have said … we call it a norm ….*

Futurist F: *You hide behind the norm.*

Futurist K: *Indeed, but that is practical.*

Futurist F: *Yes, but it doesn't solve the problem.*

Futurist K: *Well, but we have got rid of that very large uncertainty.*

The policy norm – namely, a preferred future – is not treated as one of the many possible futures, but as a future fact. In the above exchange, futurists realized that in so doing, uncertainty was actually removed from the plate. Notwithstanding this awareness, they treated a preferred future as future reality. Similar behaviour is observed by de Vries (2008), who examined uncertainty manners employed in the drafting of four policy reports by two Dutch planning agencies, also including a case of foresight in action. De Vries describes how particular uncertainties were not included in a figure about allowed greenhouse gas emissions, as it was *assumed* that the Kyoto Protocol would be attained (de Vries, 2008, p114). These examples illustrate that prospective uncertainty is rendered invisible by treating a policy goal as a future fact.

In another session (Field notes, 14 December 2001), we observed something comparable. Participants, futurists and stakeholders were invited to develop ideas about the future. It was repeatedly stated that environmental policy should be treated as a 'given' (compare Chapter 2). Also here, a preferred future (environmental policy is implemented and as effectively as desired) is assumed to materialize – this assumption is used as a solid basis for further assessment. Instead of facing uncertainty with regard to environmental policy, solidity is constructed.

We thus observed that one way of dealing with uncertainty in foresight practice involves treating assumptions and probable, possible and preferred futures as future facts. In this way, solidity is constructed to facilitate the assessment of the future as if it is a fact instead of a realm full of prospective uncertainty.

Typical exemplars

Another way to sort out uncertainty is by using past experience as an anchor. To illustrate this we refer to medical practice, where Mesman (2002, 2008, 2009) coined the notion of 'typical exemplars' – namely, patients in situations which are considered comparable in one way or another. Typical exemplars are used to draw conclusions about the future of the patient.

We observed that professional futurists have their own repertoire of typical exemplars. For example, they use such experiences in other parts of the world, such as New York, Silicon Valley, Kiev and Jutland (a partly Danish, partly

German peninsula) in discussing the Dutch future (Field notes, 16 January 2002; 14 December 2001). Typical exemplars also involve personal experiences. We witnessed that in discussing future possibilities in work arrangements, futurists used colleagues and friends as typical exemplars to demonstrate a particular work arrangement (Field notes, 15 May 2004). In addition, their own building was mobilized to think about energy-efficient futures, and previous work experience in a home for the elderly was used to think about the long-term consequences of ageing (Field notes, 15 May 2004). In another foresight endeavour, futurists discussing future means of transport described their own experiences and preferences when addressing prospective uncertainty (Field notes, 3 December 2002).

Furthermore, futurists frequently use historical events and processes as a typical exemplar. Such use of historical developments is visible in the reference to so-called 'trends'. We observed that futurists anchor their assessments of the future in this way. As argued above, scenario exercises are usually explicitly motivated with reference to prospective uncertainty. Taking that into account, the following scene is all the more noteworthy:

> *In a meeting of a scenario project, various teams presented their work in progress. One of the futurists stated: 'We reason from current trends to future developments.' According to this futurist, the key question in the development of the scenarios is: 'What are the trends? And from that, what are the future developments?' A colleague futurist also started his presentation of [his team's] work in progress ... with an overview of 'trends'. In his reasoning into the future, these past and current trends are presented as pointing to an 'inevitable' direction.*[6] *Another colleague stated that for a particular issue addressed in the scenario exercise, 'the emphasis is on extrapolating trends'.* (Field notes, 19 March 2002)

Similar statements were made in other foresight endeavours (Field notes, 3 December 2002): 'We look to the past and that is extrapolated'; 'You examine the trend during the last 25 years, which you extrapolate. Based on that extrapolation, a higher and lower variant are developed'; and 'We look to trends in the past, which we take as medium pathway into the future.' This way of using trends to assess the uncertain future is qualified as 'realistic' and as 'plausible'. One futurist, for example, argued: 'You want to say something reliable, something plausible about the future. Therefore, you look at what happened in the last 25 years.'

We observed that trends were used as typical exemplars. The term describes past patterns that are used to draw conclusions about the future in the same way as past patients are used to draw conclusions about the future prospects of current patients. We also observed a different way of using historical trends as an anchor: trends are presented as a kind of measuring rod 'to evaluate the extremity of the scenarios'. Past patterns are used as a point of departure and the question that futurists asked is 'whether we will ... extrapolate the trend or ... the opposite'. The notion of the trend is thus presented as a kind of 'reference future' and is used here as an anchor in assessing the uncertain future (Field notes, 19 March 2002).

This way of dealing with uncertainty is, however, controversial. In a session where maps of The Netherlands were developed for each of the scenarios, one futurist complained that only extrapolations were presented and that 'surprises and new developments' were omitted (Field notes, 9 April 2002). In another meeting, a futurist warned: 'this sounds very much like forecasting' and 'the scenarios shouldn't become trend extrapolations' (Field notes, 19 March 2002). Similar warnings pertaining to the tension between the idea of scenarios and 'extrapolating the present' were given in other meetings (e.g. 16 January 2002; 25 February 2003). Colleague futurists also questioned the assumed degree of realism of extrapolated futures (e.g. Field notes, 3 December 2002). However, such interventions did not seem to have much effect. They did not lead to discernible changes in the manner in which the maps were developed.

Statements about the future from previous futures studies seem to serve as typical exemplars as well (compare Chapter 2). We observed that scenarios developed by other futurists are considered comparable, which provides a basis for drawing conclusions about the uncertain future. For example, prospective uncertainty with regard to immigration was mentioned in one of the foresight endeavours. Instead of discussing the uncertainty, a futurist referred to the prospective estimates used in another Dutch foresight study – namely, the *Environmental Outlooks* of the Environmental Assessment Agency. These estimates were adopted without further discussion (Field notes, 3 December 2002).

Expertise as an anchor

Expertise can be seen as a synthesis of collective experience and experts as the embodiment of expertise. We witnessed that futurists draw upon expert judgement in instances of prospective uncertainty in the context of foresight. In line with the vocabulary proposed by van der Sluijs and colleagues (van der Sluijs, 1997; van der Sluijs et al, 1998), we refer to this use of uncertainty as expertise as an anchor.

In interviews as well as in the many meetings we attended, there were references to 'expert judgement'. Confronted with uncertainty, futurists consider it important 'to refer back to what others have done' or said (Field notes, 14 December 2001), and 'if you are uncertain about something, you consult each other' (interview quote, van Asselt, 2000).[7] We heard that 'expert judgement is used to assess unknown relationships', 'you may have uncertainty ... we discuss about it and an expert judgement is passed' and 'a large part of the input is expert judgement' (interview quotes, van Asselt, 2000). The following excerpt of a discussion among futurists exemplifies the role of expert judgement in dealing with prospective uncertainty (Field notes, van Asselt, 2000):

Futurist F: *You have to realize that it [dealing with prospective uncertainty] is a trick that we learned over time ...*

Futurist R: *I may be too little concerned about the theory behind it; we are working intuitively.*

Futurist J: *Very intuitively.*

One of three then argues that this also holds for other professional futurists, and that they do not act differently. Later in the discussion one of the participants asks about the evaluation of uncertainty:

Futurist K: *Does that mean that we do it intuitively?*

Futurist R: *Yes.*

In the second part of the discussion, it becomes clear that it is not 'just' a matter of intuition, but also of expert judgement:

Futurist R: *We can consider how [uncertainty] impacts upon the policy recommendations. I am sure that we do that [consider the impact of uncertainty], what is the uncertainty ... what is the mistake you may make?*

One of the practitioners who was not directly involved in the foresight activities asserted:

Futurist J: *I cannot imagine that the experts who put the assessment together have not among themselves thought about issues as 'can we defend this', 'can the conclusion be justified', 'do we believe this'.*

During our participation in foresight practice, we observed many situations of prospective uncertainty in which experts were invited and consulted. For example, in a session on 25 February 2003, an external expert participated who was invited to be consulted by the futurists. References to such consultations were often made to advance closure on a particular idea about the uncertain future. It was claimed that consultation was used as a method to tackle 'unknowns' (interview quote, van Asselt, 2000). Such consultation does not have to be a formal process, but is often informal and *ad hoc*. Choices on particular details of an image of the future were more than once motivated with reference to such informal bilateral exchanges.

We also observed another pattern in drawing on experts to tackle uncertainty. In a discussion on a particular uncertainty, the futurists tended to question assumptions used by others. One of the futurists reframed the uncertainty question as an issue of trust in other experts: 'Do we take the position "those are conscientious people"? The question is: do we want to question the assumption or do we adopt the assumption?' (Field notes, 3 December 2002). Instead of discussing the uncertainty, the choice was presented in terms of whether or not to rely on the assumption used by others. A similar way of dealing with uncertainty was observed later on in the same session when output was used that derived from a model developed and run by another foresight institute. In an exchange about a particular assumption, it became clear that the futurists talked about an assumption ingrained in that external model. One of the futurists involved concluded: 'That is something we have to accept: we cannot exercise any influence.' Another futurist added that they cannot sift out all the assumptions in the model: the other authoritative institute can, but they cannot. So here, too, the issue of uncertainty is reframed as a matter of whether other experts are trustworthy enough to adopt their assumptions. The situation was presented as depending upon those experts and it was suggested that the choice was between accepting the assumptions in the model or being empty-handed. As a consequence, supposedly indispensable expertise was used to solidify certain assumptions.

Consensus formation is a more thorough form of using expertise as an anchor.[8] Professional futurists themselves emphasize that consensus is sought when confronted with prospective uncertainty: 'Creation of support for the numbers was important. To that end, it was attempted to gain consensus for what we were doing … with a large number of external institutes' (interview quote, van Asselt, 2000). A futurist observed that in this process 'the edges of [uncertainty] ranges disappear', while a colleague wondered: 'It is striking that we use … [consultation] for a reduction or removal of uncertainties' (interview quotes, van Asselt, 2000). Although one interviewed futurist argued that consultation could be a way of identifying uncertainties, our observations suggest that consultation is predominantly practised to advance closure around prospective uncertainty. For example, in one of the workshops, we observed that practitioners strived for consensus in their assessment of the future: what they disagreed on was not included in the outlook (Field notes, 14 December 2001). Disagreement is a strong indicator of uncertainty (see van Asselt, 2000); but instead of examining the disagreement, it was used as a filter to put prospective uncertainty aside. Not all participants in this workshop agreed with this way of treating uncertainty. Some qualified the output as 'a without discussion model' and argued that you should include various perspectives: 'Robust policy requires taking various perspectives into consideration' (Field notes, 14 December 2001). However, notwithstanding these objections, disagreement among experts was used to disarm prospective uncertainty.

We thus conclude that experience is used as an anchor when confronted with uncertainty. We observed that, generally speaking, expert judgement and consultation and consensus-building among experts are used as a filter to remove uncertainties and to solidify foresight models and outlooks.

Numeric discourse

Because of its factual precision and comparability, a numeric description seems to be more reliable, objective and fact like. For this reason, numbers are often treated as certainties (compare Porter, 1995; Stone, 1997; and Fosket, 2004). We propose referring to this social phenomenon as the 'certainty connotation' of numbers, which may be used to discuss the future even when the foresight is presented as a qualitative endeavour – see, for example, *The Netherlands 2030* (VROM, 1997) and *SCENE: A Quartet Spatial Scenarios for the Netherlands* (Dammers et al, 2003).

One of the observed foresight endeavours (the BETER project) emerged from a numeric debate, or even conflict, about certain numbers, also referred to as 'data'. The aim of the foresight endeavour was to resolve the disagreement and to create a 'comprehensive dataset' (various project documents, various field notes 2002–2003). Due to this framing, we initially thought that the futurists were talking about (past and present) facts, whereas they were, in fact, referring to numbers *about the future*. In this case, the term 'data', *de facto* a reference to future possibilities expressed in numbers, concealed a disagreement about prospective uncertainty.

The importance of numbers as a way to proceed in a situation of prospective uncertainty could also be observed in other encounters with prospective uncertainty. In a meeting with a number of futurists (Field notes, 23 January 2003), it was obvious to those involved that there was significant uncertainty pertaining to the future of 'the water system'. At a certain point, the futurist conducting the assessment revealed that he would not be able to carry out all the work envisioned. This created discomfort among his colleagues. He was interrogated as to whether he would deliver 'the numbers', and his colleagues expressed relief when he said he would. In another meeting (Field notes, 12 November 2002), a futurist reported about 'old and new numbers' with regard to a particular data set used as input for one of the models used in the foresight endeavour. The old and new numbers would be compared arguably in order to identify 'uncertainties'. However, instead of examining the uncertainties, the question which dominated the further discussion was whether an 'update' was needed in which the new numbers were used. In both instances, numbers enabled the futurists to proceed without examining the prospective uncertainty.

A special case in this context is the use of mathematical models in futurists' practice.[9] We observed that Dutch futurists in the public sector use models as number generators, as well as in cases where the idea of trend extrapolation and forecasting is explicitly rejected. At least in Dutch practice, computer models are often used in efforts where the aim is to explore the future by means of different scenarios.[10] Futurists involved in these exercises shared with us that 'People tend to believe their own model. I'm struggling with the question of how to stimulate them to distance themselves and qualify the numbers' (Field notes, 2 October 2002). This particular futurist wanted to know whether the quantitative ranges derived from various model runs were 'hard' or 'soft' in order to get some better idea of the uncertainties. Nevertheless, she found it difficult to gain that kind of insight.

Our observations also indicate that the certainty connotation takes place through active 'black-boxing'[11] of the models, either by the futurists, their clients or as a result of the interplay between clients and futurists. As an informant phrased it: 'It is not considered appropriate to question the models' (interview quotes, van Asselt, 2000). The resistance towards questioning models was also visible in some of the scenes associated with using expertise as an anchor. These black-boxed models then serve as solid ground. Therefore, in the case of foresight, the numeric discourse as a way of dealing with prospective uncertainty is not confined to numbers, but includes mathematical models as well.

In interviews and discussions, Dutch futurists are critical about the numeric discourse as a way of approaching prospective uncertainty. One futurist argued that 'In this way, the result is a rather quantitative story that creates quasi-certainty.' Another informant told us: 'There is a tendency to quantification. In that way, you create a certain quasi-certainty about the future' (interview quotes, van Asselt, 2000). Futurists also argued that attention given to uncertainty may stimulate 'the escape into statistics' and the creation of a 'statistical quasi-reality' (interview quotes, van Asselt, 2000). In other words, due to the association of uncertainty with statistics, the numeric discourse might also arise out of references to prospective uncertainty. A qualification of the numbers in an appendix of a foresight report revealed a similar awareness of the certainty connotation of numbers and could be read as an effort to 'soften' this aura of certainty:

> For easy reference the numbers are rounded off to one decimal place with a maximum of three significant digits. This way of rounding off does not represent the number of 'certain' digits in the calculated emission levels. (RIVM, 2000)

At the same time, futurists aim to use numbers to express uncertainty (compare van der Sluijs et al, 1998). Wardekker et al (2008) suggest that quantifying uncertainty is even the preferred approach in communicating about uncertainty. In doing so, different types of ranges are provided instead of providing a single number with a higher connotation of certainty (examples are taken from RIVM, 2000):[12]

- percentages, such as in 'the global emission of CO_2 will increase by at least 70 per cent with a maximum of 190 per cent';
- absolute intervals as 250 to 285 million kilogram CO_2 equivalents;
- orders of magnitude, such as 'four times to six times' and 'twofold to three-fold'.

One could argue that in doing so the futurists (aim to) deconstruct the apparent certainty of numbers as they provide uncertainty information through these ranges. After all, they convey an acknowledgement of prospective uncertainty and provide some indication of the degree of uncertainty. However, at the same time, prospective uncertainty appears to be bounded and precisely known, and is thus controlled.

The certainty connotation of numbers and models is broadly agreed upon, both in scholarly literature and in foresight practice (compare Wardekker et al, 2008, and de Vries, 2008). Because of this certainty connotation, the numeric discourse serves as a particular way of constructing solidity amidst prospective uncertainty. Although we encountered futurists who were critical of the numeric discourse, many foresights use numbers, including qualitative and narrative assessments of the future. Alternative non-numerical representations are rarely advanced. In some endeavours we witnessed that futurists tried to soften the numbers or even attempted to use them to communicate uncertainty – for example, by means of qualifications or by employing different kinds of ranges. The numeric discourse is mobilized in foresight practice in situations of prospective uncertainty, but in more diverse ways than merely as building blocks in the construction of solidity.

Communication habits

In medical-sociological research, it is argued that vague references and promises enable professionals to deal with uncertainty (e.g. Bosk, 1980; Mesman, 2002). The habit of vagueness in communication as way of managing prospective uncertainty is explicitly acknowledged by some futurists. One informant, for example, said that they 'always tried to get around this', with formulations such as 'it is probable that', or 'this is supposed to be the minimum' or 'it goes in that direction', etc. (interview quotes, van Asselt, 2000). Another futurist observed that 'Often it is written down in a rather hidden way that it is based on estimates or that it involves major [uncertainty]'. Another referred to the use of 'prudent formulations' (interview quotes, van Asselt, 2000). Close reading of the series of *Environmental Outlooks* (RIVM, 1988, 1991/1992, 1993, 1997, 2000) revealed that futurists routinely use expressions such as forms of 'estimate', 'expect' and 'assume'; adverbs such as 'almost', 'approximately', 'around', 'probably', 'circa' and 'roughly'; and phrases such as 'it is difficult to describe/predict', 'it is unclear whether' and 'it seems possible' (van Asselt, 2000, 2004).[13] Petersen (2006) and de Vries (2008), who studied uncertainty manners in foresight practice from a slightly different angle, also witnessed that statements about uncertainty are often kept vague.

Vagueness can act as camouflage, as is suggested in medical-sociological literature. However, our observations in foresight practice suggest that the strategy of vagueness can be read as an attempt to be open about uncertainty. Deliberate and conscious use of prudent formulations and styles can also be a way of disclosing uncertainty, as the following assertions of professional futurists suggest: 'you try to report ranges in formulation, you round off numbers through words such as "about" and "roughly"' (interview quotes, van Asselt, 2000). On the shop floor we also heard a futurist arguing: 'The housing need is very uncertain up to 2030... We therefore have to keep it general [in our communication], then we don't pretend it is the truth' (Field notes, 25 February 2003). Futurists in policy-oriented foresight practice argued that prospective uncertainties have to be, and are, communicated in case 'the experts really don't know' and 'we think a policy-maker can use it'. De Vries (2008) also observed that whether and how uncertainty is communicated depends upon futurists' assumptions with regard to the usefulness of uncertainty information to policy-makers. One futurist asserted that: 'In that case [fine dust], we say that there are large health effects. We are not sure about the cause. You have to communicate to the policy-maker that there is uncertainty, like with climate change.' Futurists deem prospective uncertainties relevant for policy in case 'they have policy consequences', if 'they substantially influence the conclusions' or when 'policy-makers can base their policy on it' (interview quotes, van Asselt, 2000). Communication of prospective uncertainty allows others, the users of the foresight, to consider uncertainty and to take a responsible decision while knowing the odds.

However, it is questionable whether communication of uncertainty through vagueness is an explicit strategy. Content analysis of how uncertainty has been communicated in the series of *Environmental Outlooks* suggested that uncertainty communication in foresight practice is often an *ad hoc* affair (van Asselt, 2004). Informed by the analysis of foresight reports, we argue that it is necessary to differentiate between two types of uncertainty communication:

1   communication expressing uncertainty awareness to stimulate a sense of uncertainty (communicating uncertainty); and
2   uncertainty information – namely, communication about the source and the nature of specific uncertainties and/or the consequences of these uncertainties for statements about the future and for policy-making (communicating about uncertainty).

Only the second form of uncertainty communication enables policy actors to further consider uncertainty. However, our analysis of foresight reports suggests that most uncertainty communication is of the first type.

We thus observed that vagueness as a communication habit is used in dealing with prospective uncertainty. However, as opposed to what is suggested in medical-sociological literature, it is not merely used as an act of camouflage, but also as an ambivalent attempt to communicate uncertainty to policy audiences.

Delegation of uncertainty

Dealing with prospective uncertainty can be delegated to other individuals. In some foresight contexts, particular practitioners were charged with a distinct responsibility with regard to dealing with uncertainty in the foresight endeavour. Usually these people were portrayed as uncertainty experts in one way or another. These experts attempted to help their colleagues in dealing with uncertainty; but more often than not they felt that the issue of uncertainty was fully delegated to them, which they did not intend or like. The experts then complained that they did not have enough time, that they did not have the necessary abilities or that they lacked a thorough overview of relevant uncertainties to be able to satisfy the job.

As implied in the previous section, communicating uncertainty could also mean delegating the issue of uncertainty to policy-makers. This is not necessarily a bad thing: policy-oriented foresight might help policy-makers to identify prospective uncertainty and to take responsible decisions while knowing the odds. On the other hand, it is questionable whether it is acceptable to present foresight as the art of understanding or even managing uncertainty, as is often done in futurists' writings. In this case, uncertainty should be seriously examined in order to be understood; this understanding should then be transferred in one way or another to policy audiences. To facilitate policy-makers in taking on the delegated uncertainty, it is not sufficient to merely communicate prospective uncertainty. It is also necessary to provide uncertainty information (communication about uncertainty). We already suggested that the latter form of uncertainty communication is not systematically practised in Dutch foresight. Friedman et al (1999) observe that, in general, the communication of uncertainty is usually limited to reporting that there 'is' uncertainty. In such a context, delegating uncertainty could easily come down to pushing uncertainty onto policy-makers without helping them to understand, let alone to manage, prospective uncertainty.

Another method is the use of procrastination: understanding or managing uncertainty is postponed. This may pertain to decision-making under uncertainty or to an uncertain issue. Usually this entails collecting more information through research. From our ethnographic research in Dutch foresight practice, it became clear that if a topic is too uncertain, it is not included in the foresight. Uncertainty is used as a filter, as can be seen from the following quotes:

> On the basis of indications of uncertainty in the outcomes, the project team can decide to downplay it in the overall picture. (interview quote, van Asselt, 2000)

> This is an uncertainty: we should examine it, but not in this project. (Field notes, 23 June 2003)

See also the following excerpt of a discussion among some futurists (Field notes, van Asselt, 2000):

Futurist K: *If something becomes very uncertain ... a researcher could reason that it is of no use to report a range ...*

Futurist J: *... then the issue is dropped. It is a kind of filter.*

Futurist F: *It is so uncertain, we wash our hands of it.*

These observations reveal that futurists deal with prospective uncertainty by postponing its resolution. The explicit suggestion or ambition is that through time and research more knowledge can be gained so that the issue may be certain enough to consider in the next foresight endeavour. In the beginning of this chapter, we argued that in the context of foresight in action, 'research questions' can be considered implicit references to uncertainty. This suggests that it is not just an implicit reference, but that portraying prospective uncertainty as a research question also enables futurists to deal with it in a particular way. Research questions can be postponed and deferred to the future. Hence, instead of dealing with prospective uncertainty, uncertainty is delegated to the future.

A comparable delegation was observed in foresight endeavours in which models were used to assess the future. It was suggested in various meetings that particular assumptions ingrained in the model foreclosed the examination of uncertainty or that the models did not allow the assessment of alternative futures. We witnessed how such situations were 'resolved'. Futurists agreed that they had to use these models, deemed inadequate in light of uncertainty, and that they had to develop an agenda for new, better models (Field notes, 3 December 2002). So, instead of finding ways of dealing with uncertainty in another way, dealing with uncertainty is deferred to the future, when, hopefully, models will become available that allow for more flexibility with regard to assumptions and alternative runs.

Delegation of uncertainty is an intriguing manner of dealing with uncertainty as it stands in stark contrast to the frequent claim that foresight is the art of managing uncertainty. It can, of course, be argued that the Dutch foresight practice is peculiar or amateurish. However, this objection cannot be substantiated as empirical research on dealing with uncertainty in other foresight practices is lacking. One of the rare papers dealing with prospective uncertainty elsewhere suggests that delegation of prospective uncertainty in foresight practice is more common. Uggla (2004) examined how Scandinavian risk assessors dealt with prospective uncertainty in the context of waste disposal. In a peer-reviewed paper published in *Futures*, Uggla observed how prospective uncertainty was delegated: 'nature is expected to supplement possible shortcomings, from weaknesses in safety analysis to errors in encapsulation of the waste' (Uggla, 2004, p559). Through serving as a 'barrier and buffer', nature is expected to cover up for any unknowns. In addition, prospective uncertainty is not understood, dealt with or managed by the risk assessors/futurists, but is delegated to the future.

Our observations in foresight practice reveal that dealing with uncertainty is delegated to other people (particular futurists or policy-makers) or is postponed. With Uggla (2004), we fear that this way of dealing with uncertainty is a matter of 'delegating the problem'.

The danger of 'certainification'

We have argued in this chapter that in dealing with prospective uncertainty, Dutch futurists, consciously or unconsciously, apply different ways of constructing solidity, and we have discussed the role of typical exemplars and expertise as an anchor. We have addressed the use of the numeric discourse in the context of dealing with uncertainty. Besides that, we described the multi-purpose use of vagueness as a communication habit as well as a behaviour that could be characterized in terms of delegation. We would like to emphasize that although these approaches can be distinguished on an analytical level, in practice they are harder to separate. We also emphasize that we do not claim comprehensiveness. Uncertainty manners practised in foresight may exist that we have not yet noticed. However, we have addressed all instances where the futurists referred to uncertainty. Observations which we coded as pertaining to uncertainty have been scrutinized. Therefore, although we do not claim completeness, we also do not claim that these manners are representative of all foresight in action. What we suggest is that the approaches to uncertainty described in this chapter are the most dominant in the observed foresight endeavours.

The described uncertainty manners – namely, the ways in which prospective uncertainty is coped with – are *ex-post* descriptions informed by our analysis of the observations in foresight practice. They are not a description of strategies that futurists have considered or designed and put in practice. Our analysis demonstrates various uncertainty manners (see Table 5.1 for a summary); but no systematic methodical strategy for dealing with prospective uncertainty in foresight in action has been identified. The uncertainty manners are more adequately qualified as coping mechanisms, and wrestling with uncertainty seems to be a more proper portrayal of foresight practice than notions of managing and understanding uncertainty.

Furthermore, we fear that 'certainification' may be the practical outcome of the dominant uncertainty manners. With certainification we refer to a paradoxical course in which initial uncertainty awareness is compromised by increasing uncertainty intolerance and all kinds of solidifying efforts, which in the end lead to outlooks presented as definite and solid accounts about an uncertain future. We have reported that we came across many references to prospective uncertainty on the foresight shop floor. At the same time, we witnessed that in many cases in which prospective uncertainties are explicitly acknowledged, they are not further elaborated upon or examined. In addition, we observed that prospective uncertainties were black-boxed and concealed within assumptions and research questions. Our informants also stated that they considered dealing with uncertainty a tough challenge. In examining actual behaviour when confronted with prospective uncertainty, we demonstrated that futurists treat

Table 5.1 *Uncertainty manners observed in foresight practice*

Uncertainty manners					
Construction of solidity	Typical exemplars	Expertise as anchor	Numeric discourse	Communication habits	Delegation
Assumptions and probable, possible and preferred futures are treated as future facts.	Historical 'trends', experiences in other countries, personal experiences and statements about the future in other foresights are used to draw conclusions about the uncertain future.	Expert judgement, expert consultation and consensus-building among experts are used to tackle uncertainty.	Certainty connotation of numbers is used.	Vagueness is employed, both as a camouflage and as an ambivalent attempt to raise awareness about uncertainty.	Dealing with prospective uncertainty is assigned to other people or is postponed.

assumptions and possible, probable and preferred futures as a future fact (construction of solidity). We also reported that past patterns are often used to draw conclusions about the uncertain future (typical exemplars) and that expert judgement, expert consultation and consensus-building among experts are used as a filter to sift out uncertainties (expertise as an anchor). Furthermore, numbers, generally interpreted as certainties, are used as building blocks in foresight practice, although practitioners are well aware and/or critical of the certainty connotation of numbers (numeric discourse). Vagueness is employed (communication habits), not merely as an act of camouflage, but also as an ambivalent attempt to communicate uncertainty. However, the question is whether just a sense of uncertainty is communicated, or whether uncertainty information is provided. Informed by our observations, we are afraid that the latter is often lacking. Finally, we observed that dealing with uncertainty is delegated either to other people or in time (delegation). In sum, as witnesses to foresight in action, we observed that, in practice, notwithstanding initial openness to and awareness of uncertainty, actual behaviour with regard to prospective uncertainty involved concealing, black-boxing, understudying and camouflaging uncertainty; treating assumptions, potential futures and historical trends as future facts; using numbers notwithstanding the certainty connotation; and delegating uncertainty in careless ways. This myriad of behaviours can be qualified as uncertainty intolerant.

Also on the shop floor, we encountered futurists critical of coping manners; however, as far as we observed, they did not manage to forestall or marginalize uncertainty intolerant behaviour. We do not claim that all foresight endeavours observed fell into the certainification trap. However, we did witness certainification tendencies on the shop floor that contradict self-accounts in which foresight is presented as the art of understanding and managing uncertainty.

Our empirical research in foresight practice suggests that it is very difficult to live up to that expectation. We are not alone in questioning the routinely uttered claims with regard to prospective uncertainty and actual foresight practice. Dobbinga (2001) observed that in the case of foresight at a Dutch ministry, uncertainty was acknowledged in the early stages, but it was brushed aside over the course of time. Schooneboom (2003) observed that many of the scenarios he encountered lack a questioning attitude. According to Schooneboom, they look like competing certainties. Wilkinson and Eidinow (2008) and Bizikova et al (forthcoming) also suggest that in foresight practice there is a tendency to focus on 'known unknowns' (or 'certain uncertainties'; van Asselt, 2000), and that the more fundamental uncertainties are ignored. They furthermore suggest that uncertainty is 'resolved' by consensus-building; that notwithstanding initial uncertainty awareness, the focus in foresight practice often moves to the reduction of uncertainty; that uncertainty is not addressed in meaningful ways; and that uncertainty is not communicated in ways that are understandable and approachable. These observations of foresight practitioners provide some further support for the idea of certainification as a pattern observable in foresight in action. Experiences from Burt and van der Heijden (2003) suggest that in foresight in the private sector, prospective uncertainty causes discomfort or even fear among managers (namely, the foresights' clients) and that they have a preference for 'forecast' and a 'single future'. According to Burt and van der Heijden (2003), managers are aware of prospective uncertainty; but they nevertheless resort to forecasting and to what we call 'certainified' outlooks. Also in this context, the (initial) uncertainty awareness seems to go hand in glove with uncertainty intolerance. This might suggest that certainification is a potential pitfall beyond policy-oriented foresight.

It is interesting that futurists on the shop floor recognize that certainification is actually taking place, although they seem to assume that this is primarily the case in foresight endeavours by others. For example, informants qualified the scenarios produced by another institute as 'uncertainty denying' outlooks (e.g. Field notes, 12 May 2003). Our observations provide clues about drivers of certainification. One of our informants argued that certainification is related to the kind of questions that policy-makers ask. He told us that his experience was that 'civil servants search for certainty', that ministries demand prognoses and numbers, and that they ask 'What will happen in 2030?' (Field notes, 12 May 2003). He recognized the dilemma: 'because [prospective] uncertainty is not fundamentally accepted, I'm pushed in a weird position' (Field notes, 12 May 2003). Years later the same informant, now working as a chief scientist at one of the ministries, shared his experiences pertaining to the use of foresight in public policy. He told us that he was amazed by the extent to which a particular foresight was used as a prediction, and he feared that policy-makers employed it as if it provided prospective certainty (pers comm, 13 July 2009). On the shop floor, we encountered many futurists expressing their impression that policy-makers prefer what we refer to as certainified outlooks. We observed that particular ways of dealing with prospective uncertainty, such as construction of solidity, were defended with reference to 'the client' (Field notes, 14 December 2001). Furthermore, futurists demonstrated that they found it difficult to communicate uncertainty – for example, by means of radically different scenarios – as they feared irrelevance. They were afraid that a study with extreme scenarios would not be taken seriously in the policy arena. In one of the foresight endeavours, a session was organized with policy-makers to introduce and discuss the draft scenarios (Field notes, 31 May 2005). In this session, policy-makers expressed relief that the scenarios and, especially, the numbers did not differ much from the previous set of scenarios.

We did not research policy-makers' attitudes towards uncertainty, so we cannot draw any empirically informed conclusions on whether they search for prospective certainty, an attitude that would arguably invite certainification in foresight practice. The reason we share these observations is that we want to illustrate the kind of experiences that futurists seem to have with policy-makers. These experiences influence futurists' views on policy-makers' attitudes towards prospective uncertainty. In such a context, futurists may feel encouraged or are even seduced to certainify, although they are aware of prospective uncertainty. Frewer et al (2003) have revealed that experts who fear that audiences cannot handle uncertainty preferred not to communicate uncertainty. De Vries (2008, p211) also identified this tendency: 'authors dealt with uncertainties according to presupposed user perceptions'.

Certainification enables practitioners to proceed in the short term. But the question is whether this is a sustainable strategy in the long run. In the context of foresight, it is easy to question and/or deconstruct the certainty of certainified claims. Certainification may sooner or later jeopardize basic foresight ambitions of relevance. Those audiences aware of prospective uncertainty may become annoyed by certainified claims (see, for example, Schooneboom, 2003). Second, those decision-makers who had turned to futurists to solve their problems are likely to lose faith when they discover the uncertain character of the certainified claims. One response may be to disregard the long-term assessment altogether. As Jasanoff (1991) suggests, it is also feasible that as a response, policy-makers require even higher levels of certainty, which futurists cannot provide. This is likely to result in a problematic and troublesome relationship, and in the long run may bring about a deep aversion towards policy-oriented foresight. Therefore, although certainification appears to be stimulated by the ambition to serve the client, it is a short-sighted strategy that in the long run may ruin any interest in policy-oriented foresight.

Conclusions

Foresight is routinely presented as the art of understanding and managing prospective uncertainty. At the same time, self-accounts do not provide insight into how uncertainty is understood and dealt with, whereas practical dealing with uncertainty is understudied. Informed by our empirical research in foresight practice, we conclude that dealing with prospective uncertainty is a tough challenge. It requires finding alternatives to comfortable uncertainty manners and fighting tendencies towards certainification. Just being aware of prospective uncertainty is not enough. In Dutch foresight practice, the awareness of uncertainty and the ambition to deal with it in an adequate manner are high (see also de Vries, 2008; Wardekker et al, 2008). Uncertainty awareness is a necessary, but insufficient, condition to prevent the use of uncertainty manners that tend to bring about certainification.

In the previous chapter, we called for a revision of current textbooks. The reality of how the scenario matrix is presented in the literature does not do justice to the much more sophisticated ways in which the scenario matrix is actually practised. Taking into account uncertainty manners and tendencies towards certainification, the portrayal of foresight as the art of understanding and managing prospective uncertainty is also inadequate. However, in this case, we would like to argue in favour of the textbooks' ambitions. The implications of current practice are that foresight is insufficient in providing policy actors with quasi-certainty about the uncertain future. If they take such quasi-certainty for absolute certainty, they are most likely less prepared for the future than without foresight. So, what would be left of the whole idea of foresight in cases where uncertainty is not the focus of attention? The importance of uncertainty is too easily taken for granted. Acknowledging uncertainty is just a first step. Our analysis indicates that it is a tough challenge to assess the future consistently in an uncertainty-tolerant mode.

What guidance do we, informed by our observations in foresight practice, have to offer? Uncertainty is often black-boxed. Our analysis suggests that it is important to examine and elaborate upon instances of uncertainty. It is not enough to conclude that there 'is' uncertainty; but it should be *put* centre stage and seriously scrutinized (compare WRR, 2009). Reflection in action would entail being aware of the comfortable uncertainty manners. Futurists need to recognize that they construct solidity, that they too easily employ typical exemplars, that expertise is too literally used as an anchor, that the numeric discourse is an inadequate resort, that vagueness is a dubious way to communicate uncertainty, and that careless delegation of uncertainty is problematic. The first step towards uncertainty-tolerant foresight would be for futurists to recognize and question the use of these uncertainty manners in actual foresight endeavours. They should agree among themselves that practising uncertainty-intolerant manners is bad practice. They should no longer accept certainification.

For scholars studying foresight, our observations suggest that this should not be the last attempt to describe how uncertainty is attended to in foresight practice. Follow-up empirical research is needed to identify more appropriate ways of dealing with prospective uncertainty in policy-oriented foresight. It might be difficult to find good practices; but taking into account the importance of dealing with prospective uncertainty, it is worth trying.

Notes

1   Uncertainty is not just an important issue for the foresight field. Uncertainty is perceived as a hallmark of our era (Nowotny et al, 2001). As Funtowicz and Ravetz (1990) and Morgan and Henrion (1990) emphasized, dealing with uncertainty in science for policy is not a straightforward endeavour, as it challenges the classical positivist paradigm (see also Wynne, 1992; Ravetz, 1971; van der Sluijs et al, 1998; van Asselt, 2000; Krayer von Kraus et al, 2005). Insight into how futurists deal with prospective uncertainty is thus of general importance.

2   See, for example, Schwartz (1991), Schoemaker (1991) and van der Heijden (1996) for classical textbook versions and the Ministry of International Affairs and Kingdom Relations (Ministerie van Binnenlandse Zaken en Koninkrijksrelaties, 2003) for a reification of this image in Dutch practice.

3   If we use interview quote, van Asselt (2000) or field notes, van Asselt (2000), as a source, we refer to interviews conducted in the context of that PhD project. However, many of the quotes used here are not cited in van Asselt (2000).

4   We did not investigate whether and how issues were characterized as uncertain, nor did we assume that it is possible to objectively list all uncertainties. In the analysis reported in this chapter, we selected instances that the futurists themselves, whether proactively, reactively or prompted, referred to in terms of uncertainty (or closely related notions).

5   Van der Sluijs et al (1998) investigated how prospective uncertainty was dealt with in climate risk assessment, and observed another variant of construction of solidity. They demonstrated how the temperature range of 1.5°C to 4.5°C, usually referred to as climate sensitivity, was kept constant over decades, notwithstanding significant prospective uncertainty. In this case, the hypothetical character of what was originally a best guess was ignored. Instead, the hypothesized range was treated as a matter of fact and served as an 'anchoring device'. This construction of solidity had another perverse effect: upholding the 1.5°C to 4.5°C range required narrowing down all kinds of uncertainty that could affect that range.

6   In other meetings, we also observed that particular historical trends were treated in this way (for example, field notes, 16 January 2002).

7   Compare the findings of Noordegraaf (2000), who studied how civil servants deal with uncertainty. He also observed 'involving relevant others' as a way of proceeding in situations of uncertainty.

8   Van der Sluijs et al (1998) described and analysed an extreme variant of consensus formation in their case study of the climate sensitivity concept.

9   See, for example, Ministerie van Binnenlandse Zaken en Koninkrijksrelaties (2003), van der Sluijs et al (1998), Petersen (2006) and van Asselt and Rotmans (2002) for social-scientific treatments of this topic in the context of futures studies in the fields of energy, climate change and sustainable development.

10   Similar arguments about Dutch foresight practice are advanced in van den Berg et al (1993), Halffman and Hoppe (2005) and Huitema (2005).

11   The notion of black-boxing is used here in a similar sense as it was used by Latour and Woolgar (1986). They described how the production of 'facts' is black-boxed – namely, the history is actively forgotten in order to gain the status of truth and/or proof. Only the output is brought to the fore, not the process of production. In practice, black-boxing complicates or even pre-empts questioning and inquiring (Latour, 1987)

12 Not all ranges provided in a foresight communication can be read as a form of uncertainty communication. It should be derived from the context whether the range refers to uncertainty.

13 Not all words listed here are always expressions of uncertainty, so qualifying such words and linguistic constructions as expressions of uncertainty is only possible through contextual and close reading (van Asselt, 2004). Furthermore, it is interesting to observe that notwithstanding obvious differences in the general technical jargon between foresight and medical practice, in light of uncertainty, quite similar vocabulary is used. Stocking (1999) studied how journalists are dealing with uncertainty and found rather similar wordings and phrasings. These similarities suggest that uncertainty vocabulary is not part of the disciplinary jargon, so professionals seem to rely on common language.

Reflections

6

The Past, the Present and the Future

Introduction

Foresight involves the study of time, particularly the time ahead of us. The future refers to what has not yet happened (van der Steen, 2009). Futurists formulate knowledge claims about what might happen.[1] The meaning of time is basic to futures studies. Inayatullah (1993), a well-respected Pakistani-born futurist living in Australia, emphasised that '[any] adequate theory of the future must be able to problematize time and negotiate the meanings of time' (cited in Bell, 2000, p251). Bell (2000), a prominent US futurist, stated that 'a conception of time is itself among the most basic assumptions of futurist thought' (Bell, 2000, p116). Or as van der Steen (2009, p31) phrased it: 'perception and conceptualization of time are critical for conceptions of the future. Assessment of the future is assessment of "time"' (our translation). However, the meaning of time in foresight is usually not explicitly reflected upon.[2]

In the previous chapters, we investigated the ways in which futurists assess the long term through the lens of a particular tool (the scenario matrix) (see Chapter 3) and according to prospective uncertainty (see Chapter 4). Foresight is routinely presented as the art of understanding and managing uncertainty. However, our analysis indicated that futurists consciously or unconsciously employ uncertainty manners that tend to contribute to what we refer to as certainification: a paradoxical course in which initial uncertainty awareness is compromised by increasing uncertainty intolerance and all kinds of solidifying efforts which, in the end, lead to outlooks presented as definite and solid accounts about an uncertain future. This picture of foresight in action fundamentally contradicts the constitutive idea of foresight. Since dealing with time is even more fundamental to the idea of foresight than dealing with prospective uncertainty, we expect that empirically informed analysis of how futurists relate to time sheds some more light on the troublesome practical relationship with prospective uncertainty.

Meantime

How do futurists understand time? Brier (2005), who analysed a number of foresight studies and conducted a survey among futurists, observed that when futurists write about the future, it is often unclear 'whether the author means tomorrow, next week, next decade, or next century' (Brier, 2005, p833). Brier (2005) refers to a particular understanding of the future, usually referred to as 'time horizon'. In scholarly writings, time horizon is defined as 'the chosen cut-off time of the scenario stories' (van der Heijden, 1996, p227) and 'how far into the future one's thinking goes' (Brier, 2005, p833). Both definitions reveal that in the context of foresight, the future is not eternity, but a 'meantime' – namely, a period in between now and somewhere in the future. So futurists delimit the future and decide how far their outlooks extend beyond the present.

Our observations in policy-oriented foresight practice suggest that the years 2020, 2030, 2040 and 2050 are popular cut-off times, yielding time horizons varying from a little more than a decade to 50 years at most. Dutch futurists told us that they consider outlooks which extend to 100, hundreds or even 1000 years as pure speculation (various Field notes). Brier noticed that futurists are afraid that 'increasing their time horizon could create the perception that their work would be characterized as science fiction' (Brier, 2005, p844). Our observations in Dutch practice are in line with this finding. Delimiting the future to decades might be considered an attempt to create a respectable reputation (compare Chapter 1).

On the other hand, delimiting the future might also be cast as another attempt to reduce prospective uncertainty. Both in scholarly writings and on the shop floor, it is argued that prospective uncertainty increases the further into the future the outlook extends. As reported in Chapter 5, futurists told us that 'the further into the future, the more uncertain it gets' and 'We cannot know the future and the further into the future we want to look, the less we know.' So the long term is associated with excessive prospective uncertainty. As a consequence, treating the future as relatively close to the present is perceived as significantly curtailing prospective uncertainty.

We aim to address the question of how futurists understand time. The above shows that the future is conceptualized as an in between period of some decades, at most. This curtailing of the future is motivated with regard to 'relevance' and prospective uncertainty. Put differently, delimiting the time horizon reduces prospective uncertainty to manageable proportions.

Temporal repertoires

Dealing with time in terms of a fixed meantime indicates a static understanding. Instead of following time horizons in a similar way as we scrutinized the scenario matrix (see Chapter 3), we decided to look at the issue from another angle. Time can also be understood as a dynamic process of relating past, present and future. In science and technology studies (STS) literature and literature employed in STS (see, for example, Koselleck, 1985; Adam, 1994; Nowotny, 1994; and Mesman, 2002), the notion of 'repertoire' is used to refer to stabilized patterns of reasoning and ways of doing things (Wenger, 1998; Bijker et al, 2009). A repertoire 'includes the discourse by which members [of a community of practice] create meaningful statements about the world' (Wenger, 1998, pp82–83). In order to emphasize that we refer to futurists as a community of practice and their meanings of time, we use the notion 'temporal repertoire' (van 't Klooster, 2007) to refer to the ways of reasoning about how past, present and future are related and the associated ways of creating statements about the future. In the context of foresight, a temporal repertoire includes the set of principles that futurists employ with regard to their use of (scientific) knowledge about the past and the present in assessing the future. Understanding the temporal repertoire(s) in use helps to better comprehend how futurists understand time in a dynamic sense.

Before we returned to our observations of foresight practice, we had another look at textbooks and scholarly foresight writings. We analysed how the relationships between past, present and future were conceptualized. Bell (2000) stated that futurists assume that 'Some things that now exist or are developing can be expected to continue in the future and to have implications for shaping the future' (Bell, 2000, p178). Although Bell did not claim that the future is predictable in the strict sense, he stated that if historical situations are sufficiently similar to future situations envisioned, 'reasonable deduction from past knowledge[3] to future possibilities' is permitted (Bell, 2000, p177). Michael (2000) argued that futurists project onto the future what they, informed by past-based knowledge, consider 'fundamental or foundational'. In so doing, 'They are thus making claims about the longevity of certain fundamental aspects of the present' (Michael, 2000; p29). In this temporal repertoire, past, present and future are conceived as inextricably bound up with each other. This temporal continuity provides a strong basis for conceptualizing and assessing the future as a 'world' determined by the past and present. We therefore refer to it as 'historic determinism'.

In scholarly writings on foresight, we discerned another temporal repertoire. In this perspective on time, the relationship between past and present, on the one hand, and the future, on the other, is postulated as rather loose. It is stressed that the future will be different from the past. For example, Herman Kahn (Kahn and Wiener, 1967, p264), broadly considered one of the founders of policy-oriented foresight, wrote:

> *History is likely to write scenarios that most observers would find implausible not only prospectively but sometimes, even in retrospect. Many sequences of events seem plausible now only because they have actually occurred; a man who knew no history*

might not believe any. Future events may not be drawn from the restricted list of those we have learned are possible; we should expect to go on being surprised.

Brooks (1986, p31) argued that in order to be able to prepare for the 'not-impossible eventualities', foresight has to embrace 'shocks, non-linear responses and discontinuous behaviour'. More recently, Lempert et al (2003, p30) explicitly supposed that 'the future is ... not determined by the past and the present'. And even Bell (2000, pp147–148) argued: 'Sometimes, though, we must forget the past and transcend the present, if we want to create a new, different, more desirable future. In such cases, knowledge of the past may be more of an obstacle than a help, acting like blinders and narrowing our vision.' A survey among members of the Dutch futurist network Netwerk Toekomstverkenning (January 2003) revealed that Dutch futurists agreed that discontinuity is important in foresight (van Notten, 2005). Other authors also argued that scenarios should be used to identify discontinuity (such as Davis et al, 1998; Berkhout and Hertin, 2002, and futurists of the Global Business Network, www.gbn.org, accessed 15 October 2003). Such futurists argued that historical knowledge is a poor resource, contradicting the historic deterministic repertoire. Exploration of possible futures is regarded as an activity that requires a great deal of imagination (see, for example, Dammers, 2000). Instead of temporal continuity and causality, discontinuity, non-linearity and change are emphasized in this second temporal repertoire, which we refer to as 'futuristic difference'.

In light of our interest in the question of how experts assess the long term, the follow-up question is whether and how these temporal repertoires are practised in foresight in action.

A case in time[4]

In one of the observed foresight endeavours, known as *Welvaart en Leefomgeving* (WLO) (which would literally translate as 'welfare and environment', but the futurists themselves used the following translation: 'the future of the built and natural environment'), we attended in detail to the temporal repertoires in use. Below, we first discuss the point of departure and then analyse the actual assessment behaviours through the lens of temporal repertoires.

Point of departure

As a first step, we tried to identify the temporal repertoire that served as point of departure for their assessment of the future. In the first phase of the assessment, the futurists implicitly questioned the historic determinism temporal repertoire in the document outlining their planned approach:

What can we really say about the circumstances 40 years ahead? Forty years ago, there was no PC nor internet and rarely television. We had a compartmentalised society,[5] which revolved around the wage earner family,[6] with very few immigrants. Goods were predominantly transported by railway and boats and we were just converting from coal to gas. What would we at the time have predicted for the Netherlands in the year 2000? (WLO internal working document, 2003, p4)

In this excerpt, the futurists communicated their view on how much the future will differ from the past and present. With examples, they emphasized major non-linear and discontinuous changes. Through this retrospective consideration of what might happen in 40 years time, the futurists expressed a line of reasoning consistent with the futuristic difference repertoire. Furthermore, they explicitly proposed envisioning and examining a number of discontinuous phenomena, such as 'extreme sea-level rise', 'an early demographic turn'[7], 'long-lasting energy shortage', 'new energy sources' and 'new modes of transport' (WLO internal working document, 2003). The futurists even unequivocally stated that in order to assess the future one must depart from 'current cultures and structures' (WLO internal working document, 2003). They hinted that the past and the present cannot be considered determinants of the future. In meetings, we heard: 'After 2020, many unfamiliar things will happen. The dynamic of change might be quite different' (Field notes, 17 August 2004), and 'past mechanisms ... might play out quite differently than how they did in the past' (Field notes, 23 August 2004). The futurists proposed '*ontwerpend denken*' (best translated as 'creative, constructive thinking') as their foresight approach. They stated that they wanted to depart from the certainties of the past and that they aimed to closely examine new non-existent cultures, structures and developments (various project documents). The discourse and the proposed approach were consistent with what we refer to as futuristic difference. Furthermore, the futurists obviously distanced themselves from the historic determinism repertoire.

The next question is what this approach entailed in practice. How did these futurists, who subscribed to futuristic difference, actually assess the future?

Slicing time

The WLO futurists viewed time in terms of a time horizon and used 2040 as their cut-off date. It is often implicitly assumed that in foresight the future starts in, or directly after, the present. However, in the WLO practice, the future partly occurred in the past. The starting point was the current state of affairs. However, the data available is never perfectly up to date. So in this foresight, which started in 2003, the future actually began around the year 2000 or thereabouts.

Notwithstanding futuristic difference as the point of departure, we observed that the futurists also agreed that prospective uncertainty increases the further into the future the outlook extends – or, in other words, the possibility of futuristic difference increases over time. Building upon this belief, the futurists decided to divide the 40-year time horizon into two periods: 2000 to 2020 and 2020 to 2040. They proposed treating the two future periods differently. This might appear to be a sensible practical decision. However, further analysis revealed that this seemingly minor act facilitated a barely noticeable change in the temporal repertoire, as we explain below.

The 2000 to 2020 time period was characterized as 'the short term' and the futurists assumed that for this period they could tell the 'probable future', as knowledge of 'mechanisms of the last 20 years is largely usable to identify and assess probable trends' (discussion document, 2003). They stated they could use past-based datasets or 'time series' to extrapolate variables. And we saw that the futurists employed data and time series in this particular way. The futurists explicitly characterized this approach as '(trend) extrapolation' (various project documents, various field notes). They assumed that the closer to the present, the more predictable the future is on the basis of past-based knowledge. In their thinking about the 2000 to 2020 period in terms of 'probability', the futurists presumed a strong temporal continuity. In other words, the futurists' understanding of time and their assessment approach of the 2000 to 2020 time period was more appropriately characterized as consistent with the historic determinism temporal repertoire, notwithstanding adherence to futuristic difference as a point of departure.

In the early phase of the foresight endeavour, the way in which the futurists talked about the second period, 2020 to 2040, was consistent with the futuristic difference repertoire. This foresight period was characterized as 'the long term' and 'the distant future'. The futurists alleged that in the long term, structures and mechanisms will transform and give way to new ones. With regard to this time period, the futurists stated that they 'doubted their ability to identify probable developments' (discussion document, 2003). It became their aim to assess 'uncertainties' and to envision different possible futures. The futurists presented their endeavour as follows: 'We assess in broad outlines playfully as what-if exercises, what might happen' and discard 'the usual level of detail' (discussion document, 2003). The futurists explicitly stated that for this long term, they considered it 'acceptable' that the assessment would only be informed by past-based knowledge to a limited extent (Field notes, 19 October 2004). While for the 2000 to 2020 period the assessment approach was framed as describing the probable future grounded in past-based knowledge, the futurists aimed at envisioning different possible futures for the 2020 to 2040 period. The assessment approach was described in terms of creative 'what if' thought experiments.

Notwithstanding the futuristic difference temporal repertoire as the point of departure, we observed that by dividing (slicing) time into two periods, the discarded historic determinism repertoire was reintroduced for the 'short term' of 2000 to 2020. Futuristic difference was only maintained for the 2020 to 2040 period.

Co-existence

The futurists continued to refer to the 2020 to 2040 period in ways consistent with the futuristic difference repertoire. How did they assess this period? We observed how early in the assessment process, some futurists began to evaluate work in progress on the 2020 to 2040 period in terms consistent with the historic determinist temporal repertoire. Notwithstanding the alleged adherence to the futuristic difference repertoire, we heard a futurist arguing about proposed scenarios for the 2020 to 2040 period:

> *This deviates tremendously from historical trends. We should be able to explain why the trend changes... The larger the deviation from the average trend, the less realistic [the scenarios] become.*
> (Field notes, 23 August 2004)

> *I have difficulty writing consistent and coherent stories [about these outlooks]. In my view, there is friction [with the past].*
> (Field notes, 23 August 2004)

Over time, we observed a growing tendency to disqualify statements about the 2020 to 2040 period which could not be directly traced back to past observations or backed up by historical knowledge. In the actual assessment process, proposed possible futures were disqualified in ways and with arguments consistent with the historic deterministic repertoire. This occurred despite futurists' intentions that were consistent with futuristic difference as well as their publicly distancing themselves from historic determinism. We witnessed that the historic determinist repertoire, which was reintroduced for the 2000 to 2020 period, started to spill over to the 2020 to 2040 time frame.

The majority of futurists defended futuristic difference for the 2020 to 2040 period. We heard them argue:

> *Your belief in assumptions is strongly grounded in the conviction that you have to look back over the past 30 to 40 years.* (Field notes, 23 August 2004)

> *A deviation from historic trends doesn't mean that the statements are not realistic. Why would new circumstances always closely fit with current trends? You should not forget that we develop scenarios: what-if stories. You cannot calculate scenarios from A to Z. It is very difficult to determine causality through a [mathematical] equation informed by a statistical analysis. We need to take qualitative decisions consistent with the scenario. We need to realize that we are talking about a period of nothing less than 40 years. A lot can happen.* (Field notes, 23 August 2004)

These futurists argued that it was not realistic to extrapolate past trends into the future because 'the fact that it happened this way in the past doesn't mean that it will happen the same way in the future' (Field notes, 23 March 2004). We heard another futurist say:

> *Extrapolation can be a pitfall. If you look 20 to 30 years back in time and you discover an unequivocal relationship between two variables that was constant in the past, it doesn't mean that the two variables are causally related in the future. You should not assume that you can extrapolate those trends into the next 30 years in which things will change.* (Field notes, 24 August 2004)

> *... we can discuss the degree and the pace [of change]; but there will be scenarios that counter historic trends.* (Field notes, 23 August 2004)

In a different meeting, another futurist was very explicit on this issue:

> *How important is it to underpin everything empirically [i.e. with past-based knowledge]? We are developing scenarios! So there is a degree of creativity. Creativity combined with intellect, but we don't have to substantiate each claim with past records.* (Field notes, 23 March 2004)

A similar contribution was made in another work session:

> *We are concerned with the next 40 years. My goodness: has not a huge amount happened over the last 40 years? We could not have imagined that in the 1960s. So we have to use the scenarios to play with the degrees of freedom associated with the uncertain future and with past mechanisms which may severely change in the future.* (Field notes, 19 October 2004)

As a result, the foresight approach associated with the historic deterministic repertoire was explicitly and heavily questioned for the second 'long-term' future period. In the previous futurists' quotes, it was argued that the past and the present should not be considered determinants of the future. Futurists referred to prospective uncertainty to defend the futurist difference temporal repertoire, as is visible in the previous quote as well as in the next:

> *It is the question whether you should fully base scenarios on empirical facts about the past. The future is by definition uncertain, so we could better direct our efforts on assessing ... [possibilities] and question ourselves whether we have fully thought things through.* (Field notes, 23 March 2004)

Prospective uncertainty was mobilized as an argument to assess the long-term future (2020 to 2040) in terms of possible futures (futuristic difference), instead of assessing the future considered most probable in terms of being consistent with the past (historic determinism).

Our impression was that the futurist difference repertoire was dominant in the early phase of the assessment of the 2020 to 2040 period. Historic determinism was explicitly disregarded. But the historic deterministic repertoire reappeared, not just with regard to the assessment of the 2000 to 2020 time frame, but also in exchanges pertaining to the assessment of the 2020 to 2040 period. It was, however, not recognized that the two different temporal repertoires coexisted. At face value, the futurists looked united, as was demonstrated with the use of similar vocabulary ('scenarios', 'variation', 'change' and 'consistency'). However, more detailed analysis of the vocabulary used (see Table 6.1.) indicates that the notions have different meanings depending upon the temporal repertoire that is mobilized. Futurists whose line of argumentation was consistent with the historic deterministic repertoire stated that:

> [Variation is possible] within realistic limits. Within realistic ranges there is room for ... different scenarios and for changes compared to the past. (Field notes, 23 August 2004)

> In this view, future scenarios are limited by the degree of variation observed in the past. Change is accepted as long as the degree of change is in line with past records. In foresight literature, this view is referred to as 'unchanged change' (Bell, 2000), or, as one of the futurist phrased it: 'If the trend changes, I want to have a historic period that is in line with that change'. (Field notes, 11 May 2005)

In the futurist difference repertoire, however, the idea of change pertains to new possibilities, as well as to options that did not happen in the past. According to futuristic difference, scenarios should be radically different and should significantly deviate from the past. The future need not be an extension of the past. In Table 6.1, we summarize the main differences that we observed between the two temporal repertoires, but which were not recognized or addressed on the shop floor.

Although the futuristic difference repertoire served as a point of departure, the historic deterministic and the futuristic difference temporal repertoires actually coexisted in the foresight process. The historic deterministic repertoire was reintroduced for the short-term future (2000 to 2020) and we observed that some futurists started to employ the historic determinism repertoire with regard to the assessment of the long-term future (2020 to 2040), notwithstanding the obvious futuristic difference preference for the assessment of the latter time period.

Table 6.1 *Empirically informed description of temporal repertoires employed in foresight*

	Historic deterministic temporal repertoire	Futurist difference temporal repertoire
Key principle	Temporal continuity	Prospective uncertainty
Key values	Reliability, plausibility	Variety, change
Assessment approach	Grounded in past-based knowledge	Creativity and intellect
Type of future assessed	Probable future	Possible futures
Vocabulary		
Change	Extrapolation of degree and intensity of observed change (unchanged change)	Assessment of new patterns, structures, mechanisms, possibilities, etc.
Scenarios	Variants within the range of observed change in the past	Radically different stories about possible futures
Range/variation	Limited by past records	Limited by degree of uncertainty
Consistency	In line with historical trends and developments	Internally consistent stories

In the course of the foresight endeavour, the coexistence of the two temporal repertoires increasingly surfaced, although we had the impression that the futurists did not recognize it or did not consider it important. The two repertoires were apparent in the long drawn-out discussion on the degree of difference among the scenarios. It was often presented as a closed debate, but it was not. The futurists committed to the futuristic difference repertoire kept complaining about the lack of variety in the scenarios, while those who felt at ease with the historic deterministic repertoire continued to resist radically different stories about the future.

The rise of historic determinism

It is possible that different repertoires coexist. However, when such frames of reference are contradictory, conflicts will occur, either openly or beneath the surface (compare van Lente, 1993, 2000; Bijker, 1995; van Eeten, 1999; and Mesman, 2002). The historic determinist and the futurist difference temporal repertoires are contradictory: the set of principles that futurists hold with regard to the use of scientific knowledge about the past and the present in assessing the future is incommensurable. In historic determinism, future outlooks have to be grounded in historical knowledge. As a result, the future is constrained by the past. In the futuristic difference repertoire, on the other hand, historical knowledge is just one of the many resources in an envisioning endeavour. The past and present provide a starting point for the assessment, but not in a determinist, constrained manner. The essence of the futuristic difference repertoire is creative thinking that is informed by scientific knowledge, while extrapolation informed by historical knowledge is the dominant assessment approach consistent with the historic determinist repertoire. It is not to be expected that the two temporal repertoires would continue to coexist. So what did happen?

The long drawn-out debate among the futurists about the degree of variety in the set of scenarios could be seen as a clash between the two temporal repertoires, as is demonstrated in the following exchange:

> *One of the futurists stated that he feared that in the end the scenarios will not differ enough from one another. He explained his concerns. Another futurist responded that in this particular case it would be acceptable to divert from the model outcomes. However, another futurist intervened and questioned the degree to which it is acceptable to divert because choices which are not supported by historical knowledge are 'arbitrary'. Another futurist disagreed. He considered the notion 'arbitrary' as inappropriate: 'the choices have to fit in the storyline. If you develop scenarios, they are always arbitrary. The future is uncertain. Nobody knows the future, so in the end any choice is arbitrary.' The futurist who coined the notion 'arbitrary' reacted that the choices have to be 'based on something'.* (Field notes, 14 December 2004)

In this scene, both historic determinism and futuristic difference are visible, as is the tension rooted in the coexistence of these two competing repertoires.

We witnessed that over the course of the foresight endeavour, the historic deterministic repertoire grew stronger. We saw that futurists advocating a style of foresight in line with the futuristic difference repertoire began to use lines of reasoning that sounded like historic deterministic arguments defending against criticism. The following scene illustrates this process:

> *Of the eight futurists in the room, E was the only true proponent of historic determinism. He literally stated that 'the historical trends should be a yardstick' in the foresight endeavour. He disqualified proposed scenarios that violated historic trends as 'unrealistic', 'not defendable', 'not plausible' and as 'a completely new reality'. The other futurists opposed his point of view and disqualified his attitude as 'trend prognosis', and argued: 'We know that is not what we want.' However, at the same time, historic determinism arguments were part of their own frame of reference. When S asked P whether he thought a particular idea was realistic, P responded: 'Historically, it isn't.' And M claimed that 'the further you go away from the average trend ... the less realistic it gets.' In a discussion about a particular choice in one of the scenarios, B argued in favour of that choice: 'That is very pragmatic, but we should have it, because that is the trend.' And S openly admitted: 'I don't get it clear ... to what extent should the past set the scenarios?'* (Field notes, 14 December 2004)

This scene shows that futurists opposing the historic deterministic repertoire also employed historic determinism vocabulary and/or arguments. Other examples of futuristic difference proponents using historic deterministic vocabulary and reasoning abounded. In a project document authored by one of these futurists, it was argued that the difference between the scenarios was too small. At the same time, developments observed over the last 30 years were used to demonstrate the plausibility of a larger variety in the outlooks: while taking differences in the past into account, 'it is not very plausible that this [pattern] would happen in all scenarios' (project document, 22 November 2004). In a meeting in December 2004, it was also argued:

> 'This [the set of scenarios] looks strange ... there is little differentiation... We don't consider that plausible, taking into account what happened over the last 30 years. (Field notes, 14 December 2004)

The futuristic difference stance was defended with historic deterministic arguments. Although used from a futuristic difference perspective, this use of historic determinism reasoning lent credence to the vocabulary. We witnessed that key values associated with the historic deterministic repertoire, such as plausibility, were used in strong defences of assessment in line with the futuristic difference repertoire (see also the following excerpt):

> ... we have said, from the beginning, the models are just tools. It is about the scenarios, about the stories. We try to use models as much as possible because of the plausibility, but there are limits to what you can do with models. (Field notes, 14 December 2004)

In this way, the historic deterministic temporal repertoire and associated framings and values, such as plausibility, obtained a stronger position in the futurists' discourse.

We observed that over the course of the assessment endeavour, the discarded historic deterministic temporal repertoire was not only reintroduced, but became stronger. Ironically, the rise of historic determinism was actually supported by futurists who used vocabulary and lines of reasoning consistent with historic determinism to defend the futuristic difference approach. The countervailing consequence was that historic deterministic arguments increasingly featured in the assessment discourse, which contributed to normalization of the historic deterministic temporal repertoire. At a certain stage, historic determinism was no longer tied to the short-term future or to the attitude of a minority, but crept into the lines of reasoning at the group level. We witnessed that in the next stage, historic determinism began to shape the actual assessment behaviour.

The fall of futuristic difference

Over the course of the foresight endeavour, the degree to which the futurists considered proposed possibilities for the future 'plausible' became increasingly referred to in terms of the degree to which the statement could be anchored in historical knowledge. We witnessed that the efforts to disqualify those statements about the future that could neither be unequivocally linked with observations in the past and present, nor backed up by past-based knowledge, were increasingly effective. As a result, the ideas for futures that departed from historic trends were dismissed. Models were increasingly portrayed as embodiments of 'expert judgement' and departures from model outcomes were disqualified. For example: 'To say in an *ad hoc manner* ... [it] will be so and so ... I do not consider that an appropriate basis [for our assessment of the future]' (Field notes, 19 October 2004).

Efforts to assess possible futures that radically differed from the past were thwarted time and again by historic deterministic counterarguments. Furthermore, statements about the future that were consistent with the futuristic difference repertoire were ever more criticized. Over time the idea of 'knowing' the future informed by historical knowledge appeared to be more appealing. We have some indication that this was facilitated by two mutually reinforcing mechanisms. On the one hand, it appeared as if the futurists became uncertain about assessing the uncertain future as a realm of different futures. To be able to deal with their uncertainty about handling prospective uncertainty, they therefore preferred to resort to ways of reasoning and doing things that were familiar. On the other hand, the futurists wanted to be authoritative (compare Chapter 1) and therefore leaned towards arguments and ways of doing things that were arguably considered (more) academic. This is also illustrated by the stance defended in the SCENE foresight project (discussed in Chapter 3). SCENE futurists contended that they needed to employ academic knowledge 'to prevent that scenarios end up being mere science fiction' (cited in a project document of the SCENE project).

We witnessed in the course of the WLO endeavour that the 'academic' argument was increasingly played as a trump card. In one of the exchanges, a proponent of the historic determinism read the pleas for more diversity between the scenarios as criticism of the model outcomes he delivered. He defended his work with the following arguments:

> *This is thorough, rigorous analysis, well founded, sound and presented to various scientists several times. So that cannot be the cause of concern.* (Field notes, 14 December 2004)

Notwithstanding opposition to the historic deterministic temporal repertoire, this kind of reasoning also resonated among futurists who adhered to the futuristic difference temporal repertoire, as is demonstrated by the following statement: 'I don't agree with 'intuition' [as qualification of our assessment approach]. We work academically' (Field notes, 19 October 2004).

The 'academic' argument favoured strong reliance on past-based academic knowledge. In our view, the aspiration of 'academic' foresight facilitated the gradual shift to the historic determinism temporal repertoire as the dominant understanding of time, which in turn shaped the assessment behaviour. This shift was also facilitated by the use of past-based computer models with their connotation of 'certainty' (see also Chapter 4), which aided the historic deterministic style of practising foresight.

We observed that in the course of the project, it turned out to be difficult to uphold statements about the future that were not grounded in historical knowledge. Ideas about possible futures that violated historic trends were dismissed. It was not that the futurists explicitly decided to discard the idea of assessing possible futures (consistent with the futuristic difference repertoire), but the possible futures proposed were rejected in light of historic deterministic criticism. As a consequence, only the ideas on the future that qualified as probable in the context of historical knowledge survived. The postulated difference between the short-term future (2000 to 2020) and the long-term future (2020 to 2040) blurred over time. In the final report (see Box 6.1 for quotes that we consider representative), the future was no longer 'sliced' into two time periods that need to be treated in a different manner. Generally, the future claims were about 'the next decades', without differentiating between a short-term and a long-term future. This way of treating the future in the final report supports our conclusion that the postulated difference blurred over the course of the assessment. Furthermore, the tone of the final report was as overtly historic deterministic. Past, present and future were presented as a continuum, as a coherent whole. No discontinuities were included. Probability, instead of possibility, dominated in the lines of reasoning in the final report. Most future claims were anchored in historical knowledge: the futurists defended their future claims with reference to what had happened in the past. In the report, the futurists presented their approach to the assessment of the future in the following terms:

> *Consistency and plausibility are the key words in this analytic approach. Consistency means ... considering established causalities. There is no general theory that integrates all issues [covered in this foresight]. Nevertheless, in the assessment we use ... the available knowledge about relevant causal mechanisms. In this way, the scenarios are as much as possible elaborated quantitatively.* (Janssen et al, 2006, p37)

In this self-account of their approach, futuristic difference as the initial point of the departure even fully disappeared. The futurists still referred to prospective uncertainty in their self-account to defend the scenario approach, but in one and the same breath, they talked about 'rational assumptions' (Janssen et al, 2006, p37) (see our analysis of framing prospective uncertainty in terms of 'assumptions' in Chapter 5). The historic deterministic character of the final

Box 6.1 Quotes from the *Welvaart en Leefomgeving* (WLO) final report

The following quotes illustrate how the WLO futurists presented their assessment of the future in the final report:

- *With regard to migration that is currently dominant in quantitative terms bringing about population growth, the authors say that 'It is expected that this trend will continue in all scenarios' (p59).*[8]
- *With regard to migration within The Netherlands, it is stated that 'it is assumed that [the pattern] observed in the past will continue' (p61).*
- *Future claims with regard to types of houses and quarters are defended as extensions of the realizations in the past and extrapolations of historical trends (p75).*
- *'[During] the last decades, air quality improved substantially. This improvement will continue in the next decades' (p94).*
- *Claims with regard to transport safety in the future are presented in the following terms: 'Consistent with the trend in the next decades' (p98).*
- *With regard to the clash between economical demands and societal demands of agriculture, the authors state that 'In the coming decades, this will not be different than in previous years' (p104).*
- *With regard to their quantitative future claims regarding waste, the futurists argued that they are 'based on trend developments' (p122).*
- *'[During] the last decades, the use of artificial and natural manure decreased and it is expected that it will continue to decrease' (p123).*
- *About future claims with regard to nature, the futurists stated that 'In none of the scenarios, we expect any improvement, because agriculture will remain dominant ... and will further intensify [as it did in the past]' (p140; see also p144).*
- *With regard to agriculture, nature and landscape, the futurists claimed that 'the current trend will intensify' (p192).*

report supports our conclusion about the rise of historic determinism and the fall of futuristic difference over the course of the foresight.

In sum, notwithstanding the stated preference for the futuristic difference repertoire, the historic deterministic repertoire was reintroduced in the 'slicing' of time and it became important in reasoning and doing things. Considering the incommensurability between the two temporal repertoires, it was to be expected that one repertoire would 'lose'. However, in view of the ambitions associated with foresight, it is surprising that the futuristic difference repertoire was discarded. In the course of the foresight endeavour, futurists adopted the very temporal repertoire that they initially openly distanced themselves from.

Discontinuity in foresight[9]

In this chapter, we have described how time was addressed in a particular foresight endeavour, where temporal continuity became the key value in evaluating proposed futures. Despite the futurists' original ambitions, they had

BOX 6.2 RELEVANT OBSERVATIONS IN OTHER ENDEAVOURS

In our analysis of the meaning of time in foresight practice, we focussed on the *Welvaart en Leefomgeving* (WLO) endeavour. However, we observed that critical points similar to the ones in the WLO story also occurred in the other foresight projects. It is impossible to share all those observations in a meaningful way, so we limit ourselves to some highlights:

- In one of the workshops, a participant warned of 'the danger of linear thinking' (Field notes, 14 December 2001), which could be read as criticizing ways of reasoning and/or assessment behaviour consistent with the historic determinism temporal repertoire. This short excerpt suggests that the two temporal repertoires also coexisted in this particular foresight endeavour.
- We observed the following exchange among futurists about particular assumptions. Futurist H argued that a particular city in relation to a particular indicator 'did badly in the past, so it will in the future. These kind of assumptions [are built into the model].' Futurist O added: 'The past is dominant for the future.' Futurist S objected: 'Is that realistic?' And Futurist F concluded: 'The model doesn't consider that the future might be fundamentally different.' Regarding another foresight model, Futurist H told his colleagues: 'It requires quite some thinking to include new phenomena' (Field notes, 3 December 2002). The two temporal repertoires are also visible in this exchange.
- In a bilateral exchange, a high-level senior futurist referred to a foresight for 2000 produced in 1950 and argued that 'Everything that happens now, is not described. Only trends were extrapolated… No thoughts about possible trend breaks. That [namely, discontinuity] is good theme for us; however, it is also a scary theme.' In his view, futurists with a natural scientific background 'have little interest in discontinuity'. He said that he is in favour of what he referred to as 'searching for discontinuity'. He compared discontinuity with cryptograms: 'They seem fully illogical, but if you see the solution, you think, "of course!". That is fascinating… I hate scenarios that pretend "this is how it will be".' His view of foresight is that it helps to imagine the future and what that might mean. He also told us that in his view many of the searches for discontinuity in the ongoing assessment failed – for example, 'they [other futurists in this foresight endeavour] did not investigate whether ageing might result in completely different ways of living. Neither did they seriously consider the question [of] what it would mean if people have a second home, not just as a countryside cottage.' At the same time, he also stressed that it is important not 'to propose airy fairy fantasies' to avoid becoming 'immune to criticism'. He explained: 'You have to be able to question each other. You should be able to refer back to what others have done' and to what can be found in the academic literature. 'We do value [scientific] truth' (Field notes, 14 May 2003). These expressions reveal a similar ambivalence with regard to discontinuity and comparable assessment challenges as we witnessed in the WLO endeavour.
- With regard to the interplay with policy, a high-level senior futurist told us that this is relevant in case ministries ask 'what are the prognoses and numbers for 2030?' (compare Chapter 5). In other words, ministries request what the probable future is in relation to a historic deterministic perspective. According to the senior futurist, planning agencies will agree, notwithstanding their own view. In the same exchange, he also told us that 'the outside world will not understand that various futures are possible' (Field notes, 14 May 2003). This suggests another way in which historic determinism may be (re)introduced in foresight practice – namely, via policy clients.

trouble dealing with discontinuity. We decided to examine whether this is a typical Dutch problem or whether tackling discontinuity is a challenge for foresight practice generally. Therefore, we took a closer look at discontinuity as described in foresight literature and the manners in which it is addressed in foresight practices elsewhere.

Next to systematic searches for discontinuity in the foresight literature, references to the academic literature were also collected through discussions with European scholars and practitioners in the field of foresight. In so doing, we established an overview of how discontinuity is talked about in the foresight literature. We then analysed a diverse set of 25 foresight studies in order to assess whether and how temporal discontinuity was addressed. In this way, we aimed to shed further light on the meaning of time in terms of temporal repertoires in foresight practice.

Discontinuity in foresight literature

In *The Age of Discontinuity* (Drucker, 1968, pxxvii), Drucker[10] described discontinuities as 'the unsuspected and apparently insignificant [that] derail the massive and seemingly invincible trends of today'. Drucker stated that discontinuities are not the prominent trends of today, but the 'shapers of tomorrow's society' and that they are different from 'what most of us still perceive as "today"' (Drucker, 1968, pxxix). He discussed a number of discontinuities that he felt worth considering at the time of writing in 1968. From the examples he discussed, it can be concluded that Drucker focused on discontinuity as a social phenomenon. The inconspicuous and apparently insignificant, and the notion of breaks in time as well as in the character of trends, are central features of Drucker's understanding of discontinuity. Van Notten (2005) argued that Drucker's description was complemented by Ayres (2000), whose article was published in the futurists' journal *Technological Forecasting and Social Change*. Ayres provided some criteria for discontinuity – namely, a high rate of change, the magnitude of change and the consequences and (partial) irreversibility.[11] Ayres pointed out that whether a development can be considered a discontinuity is often a question of perspective. For example, what seems discontinuous in the short term might appear continuous when regarded from a long-term perspective, and vice versa.

We found a number of interpretations of discontinuity in the foresight literature (Brooks, 1986; Svedin and Aniansson, 1987; Clark, 1988; Kates and Clark, 1996; Glantz et al, 1998; Schneider et al, 1998; Ayres, 2000), several of which referred to Brooks's classification of discontinuity (Brooks, 1986):

- unexpected discrete events;
- discontinuities in long-term trends;
- sudden emergence into political consciousness of new information.

We encountered a number of discontinuity-related terms in the foresight literature, such as surprises (Svedin and Aniansson, 1987; Clark, 1988; Achebe et al, 1990; Moyer, 1996; Glantz et al, 1998; Ringland, 1998; Rotmans et al, 2000; Kieken, 2002; UNEP, 2002); wild cards (Global Business Network, 1996b; McCorduck and Ramsey, 1996; Ringland, 1998; Petersen, 1999; Western Australian Planning Commission, 2000; Scott, 2002; Mendonça et al, 2004); contingent events (Dammers, 2000); sideswipe (Gallopín et al, 1997); extreme events (Clark, 1988); *faites porteurs d'avenir*[12] (Dansereau, 1988); dislocations (Polak, 1971); trend breaches (Banister et al, 2000); shocks (Ringland et al, 1999); bifurcation (Rotmans et al, 2000); and paradigm busters (Ringland et al, 1999). Of the discontinuity-related concepts, surprise and wild card (sometimes used as synonyms – for example, in Mendonça et al, 2004) are the most common. The definitions of surprise (e.g. Holling, 1986; Schneider et al, 1998; Glantz et al, 1998, several of which provided overviews of definitions of surprises) share the idea of the unexpected. However, change is surprising only in relation to a particular set of convictions (e.g. Thomson et al, 1990). In terms of temporal repertoires, it could be argued that discontinuity is primarily a surprise for the proponents of the historic deterministic repertoire.

Wild cards are described as 'low-probability, high-impact events that happen quickly' (Petersen, 1999) and as 'sudden and unique incidents that can constitute turning points in the evolution of a certain trend or system' (Mendonça et al, 2004, p201). In the wild card literature (usually practitioners' writings as opposed to academic publications), we came across the following typology of wild cards (Global Business Network, 1996b):

- a wholly discontinuous event that interrupts our lives;
- catalytic developments so different in degree or scale that they are different in kind; one can distinguish between developments that involve progress and those that set it back;
- discontinuities that might be anticipated but have significant unintended consequences.

While the definitions of surprises share a high degree of unexpectedness, definitions of wild cards emphasize the high impact.

Indications of future discontinuity are referred to as weak signals (Mendonça et al, 2004), early warnings (Petersen, 1999), seeds of change (Masini, 1999) and seeds of time (Ansoff, 1982), the latter with reference to Shakespeare's *Macbeth* where Banquo challenges the three witches by saying: 'If you can look into the seeds of time and say which grain will grow and which will not, then speak to me' (cited by van Steenbergen, 1996, p680).

Masini (1999, p1163) describes seeds of change as:

> *Those aspects of society that are in the process of developing and that require new modes of understanding that go beyond the rational and work at levels of intuition and emotion.*

Molitor (1998) even claims that 'of every change traces can be found, often in a very early stage'. We treat weak signals, early warnings and seeds of time as almost synonymous for signals of change – namely, warnings, events or developments, which are too incomplete to permit an accurate estimation, but which might be first symptoms and indications of impending change (compare Ansoff, 1982; Petersen, 1999; and Mendonça et al, 2004).

Examples found in the foresight literature involved environmental, political, social and economic discontinuities. Examples of environmental discontinuities included climatic discontinuities, extreme natural disasters, shifts in environmental conditions and environmental collapses. Political discontinuities brought forward in the foresight literature ranged from violent conflict to energy crisis, from nuclear war to non-violent political changes. Examples of social discontinuities are shifts in worldviews and beliefs, demographic changes, epidemics and pandemics, massive (im)migration, profound changes in consumption and production patterns, and techno-scientific (r)evolutions. Finally, economic discontinuities, in the form of various kinds of socio-economic acceleration and stagnation, were discussed. These examples involve disrupting events, temporary or permanent trend breaks, breaks with the status quo and/or changes in dominant societal conditions. Most reference is made to disruptive events as opposed to gradual processes. We refer to such events as 'abrupt discontinuity' (van Notten, 2005). But it is clear from our literature review that discontinuity also involves gradual processes of change and system changes. We refer to the latter type of discontinuity as 'gradual discontinuity'(van Notten, 2005). The main difference between these types of discontinuity is the speed of change. Although events dominate in abrupt discontinuity as long-term dynamics of change do in gradual discontinuity, both types of discontinuity are the upshot of interactions between events and dynamics of change. Abrupt discontinuity gives society a jolt, even if only temporarily. It manifests itself instantaneously. Gradual discontinuity, on the other hand, refers to steady transformation over a longer or even long period of time. In many cases, it might be difficult to distinguish between the two types of discontinuity. Nevertheless, we use the distinction as a way of making sense of nuances as presented in the foresight literature.

The development of scenarios is presented as a way of considering future discontinuity in the literature. Or to put it even stronger, the basic idea of scenarios as portrayed in textbooks and scholarly writings is that they present different futures that break away from the past and the present. So, in a sense, discontinuity is assumed in the idea of scenarios. Berkhout et al (2001, p8) argue that 'scenarios provide a response to the problems of discontinuity'. Professional futurists argue that scenarios 'embrace the potential for sharp discontinuities' (www.gbn.org; accessed 15 October 2003) and help to prepare for 'surprising' change (Davis, 1998). Similar arguments with regard to the potential of foresight in terms of understanding new circumstances and challenging assumptions can be found in Jungermann and Thuring (1987), Schwartz (1991), Bood and Postma (1995) and van der Heijden (1996). Adam and Groves (2007, p32) described the ambitions of future-telling by means of scenarios in terms of recognizing the problem of uncertainty, avoiding illusions about a knowable future and understanding 'emerging situations while they are still in flux'. They stated that in foresight 'deterministic assumptions are inappropriate' (Adam and Groves, 2007, p32). Imagination is considered more important in assessing discontinuity than the analysis of past and present trends (Petersen, 1999; Dammers, 2000; Mendonça et al, 2004). Following these authors, futuristic difference is the temporal repertoire to be practised in foresight. But in writings on discontinuity, we also found pleas for academic credibility, arguably in order to ensure consistency and avoid arbitrariness (Harremoës et al, 2001). Such pleas for academic credibility, probably unconsciously, open a window of opportunity for strong reliance on historical knowledge. As we observed in the Dutch case, this may place the foresight endeavour on a slippery slope from futuristic difference to the historic determinism.

Discontinuity is a theme in foresight literature, although the number of reflections is somewhat limited. Our synthesis of how discontinuity is treated in the literature enables us to reformulate the challenge associated with assessing the long term in a way that is consistent with the futuristic difference temporal repertoire. When the relationship between past and present, on the one hand, and the future, on the other, is postulated as rather loose, the challenge is to use imagination and knowledge of the past and present to 'spot' and give meaning to signals of change. Scenarios are then considered as stories about future change and embrace discontinuity.

Discontinuity in foresight practice

As a next step, we assessed whether and how discontinuity was actually assessed in a sample set of 25 foresight studies[13] from around the globe.[14] We first discuss the findings related to those studies that omitted discontinuity. Then we discuss the foresight studies that included discontinuity.

Foresights that omitted discontinuity

Half of the set did not consider discontinuity. In seven studies, *Foresight Futures 2020* (Department of Trade and Industry, 2002); Questa (Ministerie van Verkeer en Waterstaat, 1998; WRR, 2000; Vleugel, 2000; Dobbinga, 2001), *The European Environment at the Turn of the Century* (EEA, 1999; European Environment Agency and DHV, 2000), *Scenarios Europe 2010* (Bertrand et al, 1999; Bertrand and Michalski, 2001; European Environment Agency and Alcamo, 2001), *Possum* (Banister et al, 2000), and *Tunis* (Barbanente et al, 2002), we did not find any noteworthy traces of discontinuities or any reasoning why discontinuity was ignored. Some even presented the scenarios as 'surprise free' (*Questa*), 'neutral', 'baseline' or 'business as usual' (*The European Environment at the Turn of the Century*) through which exclusion of discontinuity is explicitly flagged. All of these studies were presented as scenario studies; but the actual outlooks were, in fact, consistent with the historic deterministic temporal repertoire. Berkhout and Hertin (2002) reviewed one of these studies – namely, the UK *Foresight Futures 2020* (Department of Trade and Industry, 2002). They concluded:

> *The ... approach used in these scenarios suggests that change occurs gradually along a single trajectory. Future states are seen as being the outcome of an accumulation of changes over time... But not all change is like this. The direction of change may itself vary over time, with one set of conditions being replaced by a new set. This change in direction may take place slowly ... or it may happen suddenly as a result of major, surprise external events.* (Berkhout and Hertin, 2002, p93)

This conclusion of Berkhout and Hertin (2002) supports our reading of the study. Furthermore, they explicitly criticized the fact that discontinuity was omitted in this study.

In some cases, it was explained why discontinuity was omitted. In one foresight endeavour, British Airways (Moyer, 1996), it was openly assumed that the future would not significantly vary from the past. This reasoning – consistent with historic determinism – was used to endorse a 'discontinuity-free' assessment approach. We found similar assumptions about stability and continuity in other foresight studies – namely, *Port of Rotterdam* (Global Business Network, 1996a) and *Schooling for Tomorrow* (OECD, 2001; Miller, 2003). In light of assumed temporal continuity, consideration of discontinuous change was deemed a redundant exercise. As in the above described WLO study, we also found the argument that the *near* future will not be radically different from the past. So the time horizon of the study was mobilized to defend the assumption of continuity and the omission of discontinuity:

> *... we do not develop extreme scenarios, which sometimes appear in studies that have a very long time frame. The emphasis in our study is on the period up to 2020.* (de Mooij and Tang, 2003, p176)

In other cases, discontinuity was considered possible; but these cases were considered irrelevant, for example, in the Intergovernmental Panel on Climate Change (IPCC) emissions scenarios (IPCC, 2000; European Environment Agency and Alcamo, 2001):

> *Many of ... [these] scenarios suggest that catastrophic develop-ments may draw the world into a state of chaos within one or two decades. In such scenarios GHG [greenhouse gas] emissions might be low because of low or negative economic growth, but it seems unlikely that they would receive much attention in the light of more immediate problems.* (IPCC, 2000, Box 4.2)

We also observed that potential factors of change were referred to, but considered too weak to cause any significant deviation of current trends. This is another way of claiming that discontinuity is irrelevant.

In another study, Ringland (1998) argued that discontinuities were relevant, but that the best way to consider them was not to incorporate them in the scenarios. So although future discontinuity was considered relevant, its assessment was nevertheless circumvented. A similar approach was taken in *Shell 2001 Global Scenarios* (Shell International, 2002). The two scenarios, presented as snapshots, which only implicitly addressed the events, developments and processes that shape the scenarios, did not contain discontinuities. The possible impact of the then recent 11 September 2001 attacks was only considered in a separate caption. In doing so, the relevance of discontinuity in foresight is addressed. Yet, instead of assessing discontinuities in the future, only the impact of a past discontinuity upon the future was investigated. This assessment behaviour implicitly conveyed the message that discontinuity was only worth looking into once it actually occurred.

Interestingly, in one study, Possum (Banister et al, 2000), we read that an advantage of scenario development over other approaches to the future is the larger emphasis on trend breaks. However, no such discontinuities were found in the scenarios.

In a foresight endeavour on security in Europe (Hyde-Price, 1991), the explicit decision to exclude discontinuity was defended by quoting Buchan (1969) in approval: foresight 'cannot successfully take account of the element of chance in human affairs, the incidence of wars, economic or social catastrophe, or the emergence of powerful idiosyncratic leaders' (Hyde-Price, 1991, p84). Moreover, it was argued that no study written during the 1970s could have predicted the impact of Gorbachev's *glasnost* and *perestroika* on the international scene. In this case, neither the relevance of discontinuity nor the relevance of assessing it was questioned, but the human ability to assess discontinuity was doubted to such an extent that it was considered impossible to assess discontinuity.

We interviewed some futurists who were involved in studies that omitted discontinuity, such as *Port of Rotterdam* (Global Business Network, 1996a; interviews in van Notten, 2005). One of the futurists interviewed (10 June 2002) told us that the client of the foresight study did not want to consider uncertainty and potential disruption. A comparable situation was hinted at by another interviewed futurist (26 July 2002), who stated that in so-called desirable scenarios, which they were asked to develop, no room was left for the consideration of radical change. In order words, both futurists' comments implied that the foresight study was supposed to reassure its audience rather than upset it. This approach implied a focus on discontinuity-free scenarios and discontinuity was ignored to avoid discomfort. Myers (1995) refers to this phenomenon as 'ignore-ance', which can be read as the *arrogance* to *ignore*.

Dobbinga (2001) studied the development process of one of the foresights (*Questa*) where we found no traces of discontinuity. In her view, the scenario process was hampered by the organizational culture. Despite publicly encouraging the scenario team to think the unthinkable, according to Dobbinga, management held tight reins on the foresight endeavour and futurists were not allowed to stray beyond the established thinking. Consequently, they opted, partly unconsciously, for the security of the dominant mode of thought and behaviour. This probably impaired the exploration of discontinuity.

The futuristic difference repertoire prescribed that potential discontinuity needs to be considered in one way or another. We have witnessed how in Dutch foresight in action, practitioners had difficulty in finding ways of accepting discontinuity. We had a closer look at a set of 25 international scenario studies in order to better understand the challenge of dealing with discontinuity. We observed that half of the set of relatively randomly selected scenario studies did not consider discontinuity. Further analysis indicated that in most studies discontinuity was omitted without any reflection. In the other studies, the following arguments were advanced or postulated to motivate a discontinuity-free assessment of the future: discontinuity would not occur, discontinuity is improbable or irrelevant, people are not able to assess discontinuity, and discontinuity creates discomfort. In other words, implicitly or explicitly, the historic deterministic temporal repertoire was advanced in discarding discontinuity in assessing the long term.

Foresights that included discontinuity

We now present an analysis of the ways in which discontinuity was addressed in those studies that did include discontinuity Table 6.2 summarizes the approaches used and the examples of discontinuities addressed in the various foresights.

We observed three manners in which discontinuity was presented in the scenario studies. First, discontinuities were addressed in a separate caption or box alongside the scenarios. We also observed two ways in which discontinuity was integrated within the scenarios themselves. Several scenarios reasoned from a, usually abrupt, discontinuity at the beginning of the scenario story that set off a chain of other discontinuous events or gradual changes. Another approach observed was to have the scenario revolve around the description of the causes, the occurrence and the consequences of a discontinuity that occurred somewhere in the middle of the scenario.

We observed reasoning in line with the futuristic difference temporal repertoire in statements such as 'the landscape changes too rapidly, and the cascading developments ... in closely related fields ... make predictions obsolete almost at the moment they are uttered' (World Business Council for Sustainable Development, 2000, p5), and in the remark that scenarios help people to look for 'signs of ... unexpected futures' (Bobbitt, 2002, p718). Bobbitt (2002), in particular, demonstrated a high awareness of the possibility of 'radical ... discontinuities' (p717), 'high-impact and low-probability contingencies' (p718) and 'unexpected futures' (p718).

Table 6.2 *Summary of foresights that included discontinuity*

Foresight	Examples of abrupt discontinuity	Examples of gradual discontinuity	Approach used to assess discontinuity[15]
Surprising Futures (Svedin and Aniansson, 1987)	• Epidemics • Collapse of UN in aftermath of hostage crisis • Riots and bloodshed over tax inequalities	• India's rise to world power • Reversal of urbanization • Downfall of science and end of knowledge accumulation in Europe	• Kates and Clark's (Clark and Munn, 1986; Kates and Clark, 1996) approach to exploring surprise: development of so-called 'conventional wisdom' scenario from which the others break away
Beyond Hunger (Achebe et al, 1990)	• Technological breakthroughs • Collapse of tourism • Failed experiment with biological weapons → massive death	• Transition from dictatorship to democracy • Sustained economic recovery	• Kates and Clark's (Clark and Munn, 1986; Kates and Clark, 1996) approach to exploring surprise: development of so-called 'conventional wisdom' scenario from which the others break away
The Futures of Women (McCorduck and Ramsey, 1996)	• Suspension of environmental protection measures	• Employment and wide-ranging currency fluctuations	• Unexplained
WBCSD Biotech (World Business Council for Sustainable Development, 2000)	• Deaths of patients with gene therapy → media attention → collapse of biotech business	• Societal transformation movement away from biotech • Biotech develops into integral part of human life	• Interviews, workshops, explicit attention for unintended consequences
Norway 2030 (Øverland et al, 2000)	• Cascading series of events triggered by technological breakthroughs culminating in a global socio-political crisis		• Wild-card scenario, approach proposed by Schwartz and Ogilvy (Schwartz and Ogilvy, 1998)
Finnish Aquaculture (Bruun et al, 2002)	• Dramatic fluctuations in VAT • New poisonous algae species in Baltic Sea	• Transformation of communities • Erosion of aquaculture due to oil tanker traffic	• Not elaborated
The Shield of Achilles (Bobbitt, 2002)	• War on the Korean peninsula • Nuclear conflict in South Asia • Unprecedented immigration as result of revolution in Mexico • Sharp drops in population growth • Weather epidemics[16]	• Emergence of new international institutions • Improved quality of life and longevity due to technological advances • Genetic screening at birth	• No indications that a specific discontinuity-oriented approach was used

Mont Fleur (Ringland, 1998; Le Roux et al, 1992; Kahane, 1998)	• A populist government's unstable economic policies collapse → recession	• Responsible governance towards prosperity	• No indications that a specific discontinuity-oriented approach was used
Destino Colombia (Global Business Network, 1998)	• Spiral of decline halted by dialogue • Spiral of decline halted by strong government		• No indications that a specific discontinuity-oriented approach was used
Which World? (Hammond, 1998)	• Mentality changes • Fundamental change through visionary green plans, drastic cuts in US greenhouse gas emissions, a revolution in industrial efficiency and urban renaissance • Multiple complex environmental disasters: collapse of fishery → loss of food, deaths from smog, violent conflicts over water resources → criminal organizations in charge • Collapse of Africa → refugees and millions of fatalities per year due to violence, hunger and disease		• No indications that a specific discontinuity-oriented approach was used
GEO-3 (UNEP, 2002)	• Economic crashes and recessions • Environmental disasters • Armed conflicts • Widespread water contamination in Asia • Major food scare in Europe	• Transition to sustainable society supported by change in social values and institutions	• No specific discontinuity-oriented methodology was used; built upon scenarios developed in *Which World?* and *Visions*

In principle, the studies that included discontinuity displayed assessment behaviour in line with the futuristic difference repertoire. However, we observed ambivalence with regard to discontinuity similar to that witnessed in Dutch foresight practice. For example, in the set of studies that included discontinuity to a greater or lesser extent, we read that the aim was to develop scenarios that were 'not so surprising that they were entirely "science fiction"... Thus we were not so much looking for extreme surprises, as "great, but still interesting" ones' (Svedin and Aniansson, 1987, p1). In the discontinuity approach advocated by Kates and Clark (Clark and Munn, 1986; Kates and Clark, 1996), which was adopted in two of the foresights analysed, the idea is first to develop a purely historic determinist scenario as a basis from which the others break away. In doing so, the historic deterministic approach to the future is reintroduced, and by presenting this historic determinism scenario as 'conventional wisdom' scenario, instead of, for example, the discontinuity free scenario, it is even probably unconsciously, suggested that this is a clever approach.

In another study, the *Norway 2030* foresight (Øverland et al, 2000), the futurists wrote that they chose not to include discontinuity in their scenarios. The cited reasons for this position were that the discontinuities considered did not conform to the images portrayed in the scenarios, that they seemed too violent or too immediately improbable, and that they might have too provocative or negative an effect. Similar reasons were employed in studies that fully omitted discontinuity. In spite of these considerations, the futurists involved (Øverland et al, 2000) wanted to present their ideas about potential discontinuity. To this end, they merely developed a 'wild card' scenario in which several discontinuities were merged. In doing so, discontinuity was addressed separately: set aside from the actual assessment of the future.

In one of the other scenario studies that included discontinuity (McCorduck and Ramsey, 1996), the futurists used the notion of wild cards, which they illustrated using examples such as atomic and biological terrorism, climate change and dramatic new fertility and contraceptive technologies. However, despite acknowledging the relevance of discontinuity, the futurists indicated that wild cards were only briefly considered in their study without further motivation. Even futurists who demonstrated lines of reasoning and assessment behaviour consistent with the futuristic difference temporal repertoire (Bobbitt, 2002) continued to advance historic deterministic notions such as 'probability', which is at odds with futuristic difference. In other words, although the two temporal repertoires conflict, even in foresights that include discontinuity, historic determinism lurked around the corner.

Although half of the analysed foresight studies included discontinuity to some degree (consistent with futuristic difference), the idea of discontinuity was approached in an ambivalent manner. We found numerous statements and decisions that were more consistent with historic determinism.

Dutch practice in perspective

We reviewed the foresight literature and a diverse set of scenario studies from around the globe in order to be able to put the observations with regard to temporal repertoires in Dutch foresight practice into perspective. In half of the set of scenario studies, discontinuity was omitted. The cited reasons for this position were in line with the historic deterministic temporal repertoire. In the studies that through inclusion of discontinuity expressed assessment behaviour that conformed to futuristic difference, the idea of discontinuity was approached in an ambivalent manner. Also in these foresights, we found reasoning and decisions in line with historic determinism. We only analysed the foresight output in the review of the 25 international studies, while we observed foresight in action in the study of Dutch foresight practice. Although our findings of the two different approaches are difficult to compare, they suggest that struggling with the two temporal repertoires is not only a typical Dutch foresight affair.

Further support for this view on foresight in action is found in other reflections on foresight practice. Dammers (2000) contended that few scenarios take contingent events into account. Marien (2002) argued that scenarios 'often ignore the "wild cards"'. Kieken (2002) concluded that in most model-based assessments of the long term, the assumption of incremental progress dominates. Bruun et al (2002) maintained that the overwhelming majority of scenarios can be characterized as conventional and trend based. In an earlier study, van Asselt and co-authors (Greeuw et al, 2000) analysed scenarios pertaining to sustainability issues. Informed by that set of scenario studies, we concluded that many of the scenarios considered had a 'business-as-usual' character, assuming that current conditions will continue to exist for decades. Even if the scenario studies did not simply extrapolate trends, the changes that the scenarios described were merely incremental, to which Bell (2003) referred as 'unchanged change'. Zeisler and Dyer (2000) argued that scenarios often portray the future most likely from a historical perspective, or that they are mere variations on a current theme.

In the rare theoretical reflections on discontinuity in foresight (Brooks, 1986; Morgan, 2002; Adam and Groves, 2007), we found concepts that are similar to what we subsume under historic determinism. Brooks (1986, p326), for example, coined the notion 'evolutionary paradigm'. He lamented that:

> *Most visions of the future are based on an evolutionary paradigm that involves the gradual incremental unfolding of the world system through time and ... space.*

Morgan (2002, p891), in his turn, talked about 'the progressive image of the future', which he described as:

The progressive image of the future contains the idea of continuous and perpetual social change that supposedly 'progresses' due to developments in science, technology and social organization... It does not make a break with the past or the present. It is continuous and more of the same; it does not incorporate the notion of discontinuous change or fundamental reconstruction.

Adam and Groves (2007, p24) qualified the dominant approach to the future as the 'past-based scientific perspective', which they describe as:

... a contemporary mode of [future-telling] ... that is rooted in linear causality and positivism – that is, a commitment to past-based empirically verifiable explanations.

Our analysis of the foresight literature and a set of foresights suggest that what might have been perceived as a contingent Dutch problem is rather a severe challenge for futurists around the globe. It is a challenge that was first observed as many as 20 to 25 years ago and that is not yet resolved.

On the other hand, the analysis of the Dutch WLO foresight endeavour also enables us to put the analysis of foresight reports and associated conclusions on the state of the art into perspective. If the WLO report had been analysed in the same way as we analysed the other foresight output, it would have been qualified as a foresight that omitted discontinuity. In such an analysis, it could have easily ended up as an exponent of the historic deterministic temporal repertoire. However, our analysis of foresight in action indicates that it is even more problematic. WLO is a story of ambitions in line with the futuristic difference, the reintroduction and rise of historic determinism, and, finally, the fall of futuristic difference. We do not consider the WLO foresight an example of a foresight in which discontinuity was not included. The futurists aimed to conduct a foresight in the spirit of futuristic difference. In their proposal, they highlighted discontinuities; but in the actual assessment process they did not resist historic determinism attacks and attractions.

Our analysis of foresight in action suggests that it is too easy to conclude that in studies that result in reports with scenarios which do not include discontinuities, historic determinism was the point of departure. The futurists may have wrestled with discontinuity. They may not have managed to carry out a foresight in line with futuristic difference. The final scenarios and the tone of the report might be overtly historic determinist, but the original ambitions may have been different. The analysis of the WLO endeavour suggests that we should be careful in drawing conclusions from the analysis of foresight reports. Although in many cases discontinuities are not included in the final scenarios, it might well be that the futurists had different ambitions, but that they, like the WLO futurists, did not find a way to live up to these ambitions. Although foresight in a way prescribes futuristic difference as the temporal repertoire, our analysis of foresight in action and foresight output suggests that this is easier said than done, and that the challenge of futuristic difference is not just profound, but also subtle.

Conclusions

The aim of this chapter was to investigate how futurists in foresight practice understand time. We observed that futurists curtailed and sliced time. The future was commonly approached as being a few decades away from the present. The next question that we tried to answer was: how do futurists assess this 'meantime'? We identified two temporal repertoires – namely, historic determinism and futuristic difference. In the historic deterministic temporal repertoire, the future is conceptualized and assessed as a 'world' determined by the past and the present, whereas in the futuristic difference temporal repertoire, the relationship between past and present, on the one hand, and the future, on the other, is postulated as rather loose. Instead of temporal continuity and causality, discontinuity, non-linearity and change are emphasized. These repertoires thus inhibit different views on how (academic) knowledge about past and present is used in assessing the future.

We witnessed that in a foresight endeavour that started from the futuristic difference temporal repertoire, historic determinism, although initially discarded, was reintroduced. Indeed, it grew stronger and, ultimately and implicitly, defined the assessment approach. An analysis of a set of 25 scenario studies also revealed that in many other foresight endeavours, historic determinism is advanced. Even studies that found ways to consider discontinuity did so ambivalently. It is also clear from other reflections on foresight in action that historic determinism is a persistent mode of telling the future that might become dominant even in endeavours that initiated from ambitions in line with futuristic difference. We therefore conclude that the question of how to deal with the past and the present in assessing the future is both a severe and a subtle challenge.

This story on the past, present and the future puts our observations on dealing with prospective uncertainty (see Chapter 5) into another perspective. Our analysis indicated that uncertainty manners employed tend to contribute to a pattern that we inscribed as certainification – namely, a pattern in which initial uncertainty awareness is compromised by increasing uncertainty intolerance and all kinds of solidifying efforts which, in the end, leads to outlooks presented as definite and solid accounts about an uncertain future. We witnessed how the use of (historical) trends as typical exemplars, among other uncertainty-intolerant manners of coping with prospective uncertainty, endorsed certainification. In the current chapter, we portrayed another pattern in which the futuristic difference ambition was undermined, curtailed and, in the end, defeated. This resulted in assessment behaviours and outlooks that are consistent with historic determinism. We also observed that the two paradoxical patterns intertwine or even mutually reinforce each other. The long-term future is associated with increasing prospective uncertainty. Curtailing the future 'reduces' uncertainty to terms considered manageable, while at the same time reducing the 'meantime' – in other words, the future time span considered in the assessment. A shorter time frame is not only associated with less prospective uncertainty, but also nourishes the idea that it is possible to assess the future in terms of probability. Curtailing the future thus provides an opportunity for the (re)introduction of the historic deterministic temporal repertoire. Futurists committed to the futuristic difference repertoire employ prospective uncertainty in criticizing historic determinism. However, the stronger the historic determinism repertoire gets, the more the emphasis shifts from uncertainty and possible futures to temporal continuity and the future defined as most probable, congruent with the past and present. With this shift in values, defences of the futuristic difference repertoire with reference to prospective uncertainty are increasingly ineffective.

In view of the intertwining paradoxical patterns of certainification and dominance of historic determinism, it seems relevant to reflect on the relationship between uncertainty and discontinuity. Prospective uncertainty means that what might happen is unknown, so that there are various possibilities. Discontinuity refers to the possibility of change, either in an abrupt or in a gradual manner. Prospective uncertainty and discontinuity are different concepts, but in the context of foresight they are related. Both ideas are associated with futuristic difference. On the other hand, uncertainty intolerance supports a preference for the historic deterministic temporal repertoire, while ambivalence with regard to discontinuity encourages uncertainty intolerance. Both tendencies seem to be nourished by the ambition of serious futurists to be respected as 'academic' experts, which makes it harder to deviate from what is seen as academic knowledge and conventional academic practice.

Foresight textbooks are ambivalent to temporal repertoires. Both historic determinism and futuristic difference could be traced. However, in view of foresight as the art of understanding and managing uncertainty, the historic deterministic temporal repertoire is very problematic: it supports uncertainty intolerance and assessment behaviour that contradicts the idea of exploration of possible futures. This should be recognized in foresight textbooks. It should be made crystal clear that futuristic difference is the temporal repertoire to be adopted in practising foresight. As we have shown in this chapter, historic determinism undermines and contradicts the key ambitions of foresight. Futurists should be aware that, especially in contexts where futurists aim to be respected as academic experts, the historic deterministic temporal repertoire is attractive or even very seductive. What we have learned from this analysis is that good foresight adheres to futuristic difference. Good practitioners are aware that retreat to historic determinism is a major pitfall. Our observations indicate personal ambitions, group dynamics and institutional, or even cultural, incentives that endorse retreat to historic determinism. Such reflection on action can help futurists to better reflect in action. In this way, they should be able to recognize and to oppose historic deterministic tendencies in a foresight endeavour.

Notes

1   One would expect that futurists formulate their knowledge claims in the future tense. We observed that, in practice, they often use the present tense. We did not investigate why they do so.
2   Adam and Groves (2007) also observe this lack of reflection on the meaning of time in the context of various modes of future-telling. Their book is a thorough theoretical reflection on the meaning of future time. Another exception is the PhD thesis by Martijn van der Steen, a political scientist, who wrote a solid chapter (in Dutch): 'Time and future in theory: What is future and who makes future' (van der Steen, 2009, pp31–105).
3   Bell (2000) uses the term 'past knowledge', which we consider a loose term, because it might refer to knowledge in the past or to knowledge on what happened in the past, or to both. We have the impression that he refers to the latter type of knowledge, for which reason we follow Adam and Groves (2007) in using the notion 'past-based knowledge'. However, for the sake of readability, we also sometimes use the term 'historical' as a synonym.
4   See also Chapter 5 in van 't Klooster (2007).
5   Dutch society used to be compartmentalized along religious and socio-political lines: Catholic, Protestant and Social Democrat.
6   A working husband, a mothering housewife and children.
7   Dutch demography is generally expected to change due to ageing and a declining number of births. The notion of 'early demographic turn' refers to a future in which this discontinuity will happen much earlier than is usually expected.
8   The problematic idea of 'robust trends' is addressed in endnote 1 of Chapter 3.
9   See also Chapter 3 and 4 in van Notten (2005) and van Notten et al (2005).
10 The famous scenario analyst Peter Schwartz qualified Drucker as an 'authority on business management and the future' (Schwartz, 1991, p76). Schwartz used Drucker's description in his own reflection on discontinuity in the context of scenario analyses (p151).
11 Ayres himself talked about irreversibility. However, his examples also refer to cases where partial irreversibility is a more accurate description.
12 In the opinion of the authors, '*faites porteurs d'avenir*' translates (poorly) as 'heavy trends and seed events'.
13 See van Notten (2005) and van Notten et al (2005) for a more detailed account of this analysis. In this assessment, we did not limit ourselves to policy-oriented foresight, but included some foresight projects developed in a business context – namely, British Airways, ICL and Shell. This explains why we refer to 25 studies in this chapter, instead of 22, as in Chapter 2.
14 We surveyed the literature and the internet for scenario studies. Because of language barriers, we only selected studies available in English and Dutch. The main selection criterion was whether some material was available about the development process in order to be able to examine the study in methodological terms (see van Notten, 2005).
15 For a detailed discussion of the approaches used, see van Notten (2005).
16 Namely, the health consequences of rapidly changing weather patterns/climate change.

Reflections

7

Reflection on Action

Summary of findings

Many professionals assess the long term for policy audiences. They produce statements about prospective conditions, actions and events that have not yet happened, processes in flux, states not yet in existence, and policies not yet in force. We refer to this set of practices as policy-oriented foresight. We studied foresight in action with the aim of addressing the question: how do experts assess the future? Our analysis of foresight in action described in the previous chapters makes clear that there is no simple answer to that question. We did not come across a standard approach. Instead, we described futurists' struggles with policy, with would-be standard tools, with prospective uncertainty, and with temporal repertoires and discontinuity.

In Chapter 2, we reported our first impressions of foresight practice. A first reading of scholarly literature and analysis of publicly available scenario studies served as preparation for our participant observation of foresight in action. We indicated that in futurists' literature, foresight is usually distinguished from forecasting and foresight is generally associated with the development of scenarios. Informed by our first impressions, we argued that experts assess the future by constructing scenarios in which multiple stories are told about possible futures. Scenarios are also referred to as 'what if' thought experiments. First impressions suggested that we could expect that in foresight practice we would meet futurists busy with constructing scenarios, who accept uncertainty and who aim to include even rather radical outlooks.

In Chapter 3, we explored whether it is necessary to distinguish policy-oriented foresight from foresight in business. To that end, we examined how futurists in policy-oriented foresight dealt with policy and concluded that it was a struggle for them. The *policy-free principle*, implicitly or explicitly endorsed in various foresight textbooks, turned out to be of little help in assessing the future in policy contexts. In practice, the futurists diverted from the policy-free principle and aimed to include policy in their scenarios in one way or the other. Despite this, many futurists made clear that they still perceived the policy-free principle as the supreme approach to assessing the future. We observed that as a consequence of this ambivalence, futurists searched for a middle ground. We characterized the resulting stance as the *no (significant) policy change principle*. However, we also witnessed severe problems with putting this principle into practice. As a consequence, the futurists dealt with policy on the tactical level in very pragmatic ways that were at odds with the idea of no (significant) policy change. Coping with policy is therefore a more appropriate description of the state of affairs. This struggling with policy seems particular to foresight in the context of public policy. We concluded that the problematic distinctive issue of dealing with policy warrants that policy-oriented foresight is treated as a special field.

In Chapter 4, we attended in detail to how the scenario matrix, which both practitioners and scholars regard as a standard tool, was used. We inscribed different *functional meanings*, a notion we used to refer to the logics and assumptions associated with the scenario matrix. We observed four functional meanings – namely, backbone, foundation, scaffold and showcase. But more importantly, we saw how various functional meanings coexisted and that no closure with regard to functional meaning was established. Moreover, we observed a friction in foresight practice between the reification of the positivistic backbone functional meaning (backbone), on the one hand, and the constructivist nature of the functional meanings actually practised (foundation, scaffold and showcase), on the other. Although the scenario matrix is often presented as a standard, we observed that in foresight in action it is used in different ways that also differ from how the tool is presented in textbooks. Informed by our analysis of the actual uses of the scenario matrix, the answer to the question 'how do experts assess the future' is: some futurists use the scenario matrix as a foundation, a scaffold or a showcase in constructing scenarios or evaluating constructed scenarios. At the same time, futurists in foresight practice continue to refer to the scenario matrix in terms consistent with the positivistic backbone functional meaning.

In Chapter 5, we described and analysed observations pertaining to manners that futurists employ in the face of prospective uncertainty. Foresight is frequently presented as the art of understanding uncertainty. Dealing with prospective uncertainty is thus staged as the core of practising foresight. In view of this, futurists aim to create scenarios that vary sufficiently. We witnessed that in foresight practice acknowledgement of prospective uncertainty is commonplace; but at the same time uncertainties are black-boxed and concealed as 'assumptions' and 'research questions'. We furthermore observed various uncertainty manners – that is, ways in which prospective uncertainty is coped with: construction of solidity, typical exemplars, expertise as anchor, numeric discourse, communication habits and delegation of uncertainty. No systematic strategy for dealing with prospective uncertainty in foresight in action was identified. Our observations suggest that it is, rather, dealt with at an unreflective level. The manners identified are actually coping mechanisms.

Wrestling with uncertainty seems to be a better portrayal of foresight practice than notions such as understanding and managing uncertainty. We also question the idea (see Chapter 2) that futurists accept or even embrace uncertainty. We actually fear that *certainification* may be the practical outcome of the observed uncertainty manners. Certainification signifies a process in which initial uncertainty awareness is compromised by increasing uncertainty intolerance and various solidifying efforts, which leads to future outlooks presented as definite accounts. In foresight practice, we witnessed such certainification tendencies. Our empirical research suggests that dealing with prospective uncertainty is a tough challenge, which requires both finding alternatives to comfortable uncertainty manners as well as recognizing and fighting tendencies towards certainification.

Foresight can be presented as the study of time. In Chapter 6, we analysed how futurists in foresight endeavours understood time. We observed that time is curtailed and 'sliced'. So, instead of assessing the full future, a so-called meantime is assessed in foresight practice. How do experts assess this future meantime? We used the notion of *temporal repertoire* to refer to ways of reasoning about the relationship between past, present and future and the associated ways of creating statements about the future. We identified two temporal repertoires – namely, *historic determinism* and *futuristic difference*. In historic determinism, the future is conceptualized and assessed as a world determined by the past and the present. Temporal continuity and stability are key principles. In futuristic difference, the relationship between past and present, on the one hand, and future, on the other, is postulated as being rather loose. Discontinuity and change are emphasized. These repertoires thus inhibit different views on how (academic) knowledge about past and present is used in assessing the future. Following the distinction between forecasting and foresight (Chapter 2), it could be argued that historic determinism is the preferred stance in forecasting, while foresight would lean towards futuristic difference. However, our observations indicated that this dichotomy does not hold in practice. In Chapter 6, we detailed a foresight endeavour that started from futuristic difference. Nevertheless, historic determinism, although explicitly discarded, was reintroduced and ultimately shaped the foresight. Further analysis indicated that in many other foresights, historic determinism also dominates. Even studies that find ways of dealing with discontinuity do so ambivalently in terms of the temporal repertoires. Assessing the future in ways that are consistent with futuristic difference is a tough challenge.

In this book, we have told various stories on foresight practice. The aim of researching foresight in action was to inscribe mechanisms and patterns and to provide insight into problems and solutions. Through such an analysis we wanted to answer the question: how do experts assess the future? We do not think that we have a definite and complete answer. We even might have more questions than answers. Nevertheless, it is clear that our provisional and partial answer to the question is at odds with the ways in which foresight is presented in textbooks. In foresight practice, most futurists do, indeed, construct scenarios. However, in policy-oriented foresight, scenarios are not policy free, notwithstanding the policy-free principle advanced in futurists' accounts. In cases where the scenario matrix is used in constructing scenarios, it is applied in ways that differ from the assumed standard approach described in textbooks. Although foresight is presented as the art of understanding uncertainty, we witnessed certainification tendencies. Even though futuristic difference is consistent with the idea of developing multiple scenarios that describe different futures that substantially vary, in foresight practice futurists retreat to historic determinism. As a consequence, scenarios are quite often cast in terms of plausibility rather than possibility.

Informed by our empirical research, we portray foresight as a social endeavour in which futurists in their effort to construct scenarios are confronted with the following problems:

- Futurists perceive the policy-free principle as the supreme approach to assessing the future, while at the same time they consider it unattainable or even undesirable.
- The stance resulting from the previous ambivalence (the *no (significant) policy change principle*) and the pragmatic ways of dealing with policy at the tactical level are at odds with each other.
- In textbooks as well as in foresight practice, the positivistic backbone functional meaning of the scenario matrix is reified, notwithstanding the constructivist nature of the functional meanings (foundation, scaffold and showcase) that are actually used.
- Foresight is presented as the art of accepting, managing and understanding uncertainty. However, certainification is a probable practical outcome of the observed uncertainty manners.
- Although futuristic difference is the temporal repertoire that fits with the idea of foresight, in foresight practice the futurists retreat to the incommensurable historic deterministic temporal repertoire.

Discussion

Is it possible to explain all of these tensions? Are they related in one way or another? In our view, the frictions, ambivalences and conflicts are, indeed, connected. In order to substantiate this proposition, we return to what we referred to as the constructivist thesis and the positivistic ideal:

- The constructivist thesis holds that academic knowledge is socially constructed. Hence, facts and statements are seen as the result of deliberation among experts – that is, as the outcome of an inherently social process.
- The positivistic ideal states that scientific facts about nature and society can be 'revealed' or 'discovered' by means of empirical observation and rational explanation.

In Chapter 1, we argued that the constructivist thesis is the standard epistemology in foresight practice. Science and technology studies (STS) scholars have convincingly demonstrated the validity of the (social) constructivist hypothesis with regard to the production of academic knowledge, but the idea is still controversial and not generally subscribed to in many academic fields. However, we departed from the assumption that in the field of foresight with its conceptual subject of study, the constructivist nature of the activity was widely recognized. Futurists are well aware that foresight is about processes, events and actions that have not (yet) taken place. They realize that foresight is a conceptual practice and that their assessments of the future are social constructions. However, at the same time, as has been an undercurrent in many of our stories on foresight in action, the futurists we met aim to achieve 'academic' foresight. They want to construct or sustain a status as legitimate and recognized academics. Although they seem to be aware that foresight differs from what is usually referred to as 'science', at the same time they hope that their own foresight endeavour is qualified as applied science or at least as scholarly product. Informed by our observations in foresight practice, we hypothesize[1] that with this academic ambition the traditional positivistic paradigm (re-)enters the scene. In foresight practice, positivistic ideals are active as a result of the academic ambition. Both Hilgartner (2000) and Bijker et al (2009) have convincingly demonstrated that expert authority in public policy contexts is treated in positivistic terms. These analyses provide some support for the rationale behind our first hypothesis.

The second hypothesis that we would like to advance is that the positivistic ideals, invoked by academic ambition, create, nourish and sustain the tensions we observed in foresight in action. The hypothesis enables us to recast the above tensions. Positivism portrays academic knowledge production as a value-free activity. Experts should not immerse themselves in normative or political issues. They should distance themselves from politics. Experts are objective and independent. In this view, any act of expertise is policy free. So the preference for policy-free scenarios sits comfortably with positivistic ideals. We already qualified the backbone functional meaning as a way of portraying the scenario matrix in line with positivistic ideals. If it is, indeed, the case that positivistic ideals creep into foresight practice in the slipstream of academic ambitions, then it is of no surprise that the positivistic functional meaning is reified. Leading scholars on the issue of (scientific) uncertainty (Ravetz, 1971, 2006; Wynne, 1980, 1992; Funtowicz and Ravetz, 1990, 1993, 1994; Nowotny et al, 2001; Nowotny, 2008) have argued that the whole idea of (scientific) uncertainty is hostile to the positivistic paradigm. Positivism venerates scientific certainty, which is difficult to combine with the acceptance of uncertainty as the state of affairs. Intolerance towards uncertainty and the preference for solid and definite outlooks are consistent with positivistic ideals. In this perspective, the certainification tendencies that we witnessed are not surprising. The dominance of historic determinism can also be explained in these terms. Historic determinism suggests that there is a past-based empirically verifiable basis for assessing the future. Positivism is strongly associated with the idea of empirical verification (or, more precisely, falsification). So we agree with Adam and Groves (2007) (see also Chapter 6), who refer to historic determinism as the 'past-based scientific perspective', which they explicitly qualify as a mode of future-telling rooted in positivism. By contrast, futuristic difference puts the idea of a strong empirical basis for assessing the future into perspective. In contrast to historic determinism, the futuristic difference temporal repertoire is consistent with the constructivist thesis.

As a result, the problematic tensions that featured in our stories about foresight practice can be understood as manifestations of the conflict between the constructive nature of the activity (futurists construct scenarios in a social endeavour) and the positivistic ideals which are invoked with the ambition of academic foresight. Futurists have to accept that foresight is a constructivist endeavour if they want to practise it in ways that enable the inclusion of policy in assessing the future and in ways consistent with constructivist uses of tools, accepting uncertainty and discontinuity and the futuristic difference as the temporal repertoire. Futurists need to discard the traditional academic standard. In the context of policy-oriented knowledge production, positivistic ideals are activated (Hilgartner, 2000; Bijker et al, 2009). We hypothesize that these ideals create severe tensions, which compromise the ability to address the demanding challenges associated with foresight. Our analysis suggests that positivistic approaches curtail the capacity to engage with the future (see also Adam and Groves, 2007). Familiar research methods are insufficient or are even counterproductive in policy-oriented foresight. The first and most fundamental challenge for futurists is to find ways of being constructivists, both backstage and front stage (see Wilkinson and Eidinow, 2008, for a comparable claim). Even without the problematic tensions described in this book, it will be difficult enough to find rigorous[2] ways of including policy in scenarios, of fostering closure around functional meanings of tools, of finding alternatives to comfortable but problematic uncertainty manners, and of practising futuristic difference in a consistent way.

From reflection on action to reflection in action

We observed that current foresight practice is at odds with the portrayals of foresight in textbooks and scholarly writings. Foresight textbooks have to be rewritten if our advice to accept the constructivist perspective is taken seriously. Furthermore, the idea of policy-free scenarios should be abandoned in the context of policy-oriented foresight. The no (significant) policy change principle that is advanced on the shop floor should also be rejected. Futurists need to find ways of approaching the government as an actor in the dynamics of the future. We realize that, as a consequence, the strategy of using scenarios for wind tunnelling or robustness testing is at least curtailed. Similarly, the potential modes of use have to be rethought and reinvented. In any case, our analysis suggests that it is time to drop the idea of the scenario matrix as a backbone in assessing the future. It might be necessary to discard the scenario matrix altogether, and the constructivist functional meanings must be adopted in any case.

Current practice does not live up to portrayals in futurists' writings of foresight as the art of understanding uncertainty and discontinuity. Although not explicitly stated in those terms, futuristic difference, the temporal repertoire in which discontinuity and change are emphasized, is consistent with the foresight ambitions portrayed in textbooks (compare our first impressions in Chapter 2). There are two possibilities for progress. First, should the futurists' community be unwilling to sacrifice their academic ambitions, it would be advisable to accept the kind of assessment behaviour described in this book as the best (possible) practice. This means that historic determinism is adopted as the assessment paradigm. The assumed distinction between forecasting and foresight will then collapse. According to this perspective, the construction of scenarios as merely variants on historic trends is just one of the possible ways to practise forecasting and there is no need to rewrite the foresight textbooks. Instead, they can be thrown away and replaced by forecasting textbooks, such as Armstrong's (2001), in which scenario analysis is already advanced as a forecasting method.

The second option is the one that we outlined above. Both scholarly and professional futurists accept the constructivist perspective, not just as lip service, but in actual assessment behaviours. This requires being rigorous about dealing with policy, uncertainty and discontinuity. Textbooks should be more explicit in discarding historic determinism and providing guidance on how to employ and adhere to futuristic difference during a foresight endeavour. We consider it important that in textbooks serious attention is paid to uncertainty manners, assessment behaviours, ambitions, group dynamics and incentives that support certainification and retreat to historic determinism. On the shop floor, futurists should agree that certainification and retreat to historic determinism are bad practice. Our reflection on action provides them with insights and vocabulary to practice reflection in action. In this way, they should be able to better recognize and oppose positivistic, certainification and historic deterministic tendencies.

Our analysis of foresight in action enabled us to reflect on what the textbooks say and what practice does. With regard to the scenario matrix and dealing with policy, we argued that the textbooks need to be rewritten. The backbone functional meaning and the policy-free principle are not just inadequate, but inappropriate guidance. Futurists employ more sophisticated functional meanings and policy-oriented foresight requires including policy in one way or another. With regard to dealing with uncertainty and time, we identified bad practice. Both the uncertainty manners in use and the retreat to historic determinism compromise the key ambitions of foresight. More empirical research on foresight in action is needed to identify good practices. Our examination of foresight in action suggests that the key question to be addressed, both by practitioners and by scholars reflecting on foresight, is how to assess the future in uncertainty-tolerant ways consistent with the futuristic difference temporal repertoire. Textbooks could support such reflection in action by describing pitfalls in terms of comfortable uncertainty manners and ways in which the historic deterministic temporal repertoire is endorsed.

Lessons for policy audiences

The aim of policy-oriented foresight is to help policy audiences to address the long term responsibly. What major lessons can be learned from our analysis of foresight in action? Bad foresight – that is, foresight which falls into positivistic, certainification and historic deterministic pitfalls – will likely support uncertainty intolerance and a narrow perspective on the future among policy audiences. In this way, foresight does not help policy audiences to anticipate the uncertain future. The biases of bad foresight are exported to the policy arena. Our analysis, and the vocabulary provided, is supposed to help policy audiences to identify good foresights – namely, those which are uncertainty tolerant and adhere to futuristic difference. On the other hand, our stories also suggest that policy audiences provide incentives that endorse uncertainty intolerance and a preference for positivism and the historic deterministic temporal repertoire. So they are also part of the problem. In a way, policy audiences will get what they, implicitly or explicitly, ask for. The challenge for them, therefore, is to be open to foresight that does not provide quasi-certainties and past-based views on the future.

On the other hand, policy audiences need more guidance in how they can benefit from good foresight. As far as our knowledge extends, the issue of how to use different possible scenarios in policy is not seriously reflected upon by futurists. We indicated in Chapter 3 that the traditional answer (wind-tunnelling/robustness testing) to that question is too simple or even unsuitable. In order to encourage policy audiences to ask for good foresight, they need more and better clues. Futurists should more seriously rethink and think through what good use of good foresight entails. However, developing ideas on how to use uncertainty-tolerant foresight consistent with futuristic difference is not just a responsibility for futurists. Policy audiences need to engage with futurists in order to develop such ideas. As they practise policy, they can evaluate what would be valuable to them. In addition, the issue of how to deal with policy in policy-oriented foresight in meaningful ways demands the expertise, experience and ideas of policy audiences. So policy audiences should not be afraid of, or resistant to, engaging with futurists about questions on how to assess the future. At the same time, futurists should welcome such exchange. Instead of pretending that as experts of the future they know how to do good foresight, they should be willing to admit that, notwithstanding their expertise, experiences and competences, important and tough challenges remain and that bad practice occurs. In order to be able to do good policy-oriented foresight, futurists need the support and input of policy audiences on much more fundamental levels than is usually acknowledged. But this also requires that policy audiences are willing to reflect on their own uncertainty intolerance and positivistic and historic deterministic preferences. Otherwise, it is quite likely that dialogues among futurists and policy actors only contribute to maintaining and sustaining unproductive or even flawed mechanisms and patterns. Good policy-oriented foresight requires foresight-oriented policy audiences.

Notes

1   The notion of hypothesis is quite controversial in social science contexts. 'Hypothesis' is associated with the idea of hypothesis testing common in natural sciences. In the Popperian sense, hypothesis testing involves falsification of the proposition. Popperian philosophy of science is positivistic. Therefore, the notion hypothesis invokes positivistic connotations. Furthermore, in some social science studies, research referred to as hypothesis testing in fact involves searching for evidence that supports the hypothesis (verification), which violates the Popperian idea. So by using the notion of hypothesis, particular connotations and problematic practices are invoked. Nevertheless, we consider the use of 'hypothesis' more appropriate than any synonym we could think of: we use it to denote that, informed by our observations, we speculate about an underlying mechanism.
2   We use the notion of 'rigorous' in line with Andersson (2009, p6), who stated that 'Futures studies have always been criticized for not being scientific enough since we [futurists] cannot apply principles of objectivity and fact (that are the basis for mainstream science) to the future, but this does not mean that we [futurists] cannot be rigorous. We can be rigorous about the principles.'

Reflections

References

Achebe, C., Hyden, G., Magadza, C. and Okeyo, A.P. (1990) *Beyond Hunger in Africa: Conventional Wisdom and an Alternative Vision*, Heinemann, Portsmouth, NH, US

Adam, B. (1994) *Time and Social Theory*, Polity Press, Cambridge, UK

Adam, B. and Groves, C. (2007) *Future Matters: Action, Knowledge, Ethics*, Brill, Leiden and Boston

Aligica, P. D. (2003) 'Prediction, explanation and the epistemology of future studies', *Futures*, vol 35, no 10, pp1027–1040

Aligica, P. D. (2004) 'The challenge of the future and the institutionalization of interdisciplinarity: Notes on Herman Kahn's legacy', *Futures*, vol 36, no 1, pp67–83

Andersson, J. (2009) 'Futures studies for a new era: Experiences from the Swedish Institute for Futures Studies', *International Conference Towards Knowledge Democracy*, RMNO, Leiden, The Netherlands

Ansoff, I. H. (1982) *Strategic Response in Turbulent Environments*, Unpublished, European Institute for Advanced Studies in Management, Brussels, Belgium

Armstrong, S. J. (ed) (2001) *Principles of Forecasting: A Handbook for Researchers and Practitioners*, Kluwer Academics Publishers, Boston/Dordrecht/London

Atkinson, P. (1984) 'Training for certainty', *Social science and medicine*, vol 19, no 9, pp949–956

Ayres, R. U. (2000) 'On forecasting discontinuities', *Technological Forecasting and Social Change*, vol 65, no 1, pp81–97

Banister, D., Stead, D., Steen, P., Akerman, J., Dreborg, K., Nijkamp, P. and Schleicher-Tapeser, R. (2000) *European Transport Policy and Sustainable Mobility*, E. and F. N. Spon, London and New York

Barbanente, A., Khakee, A. and Puglisi, M. (2002) 'Scenario building for metropolis Tunis', *Futures*, vol 34, pp583–596

Bell, W. (2000) *Foundations of Future Studies: Human Science for a New Era*, vol 1, Transaction Publishers, New Brunswick, UK

Bell, W. (2003) *Foundations of Futures Studies: History, Purposes, and Knowledge: Human Science for a New Era* (edition with a new preface; originally published in 1997 edition), vol 1, Transaction Publishers, New Brunswick, UK

Berkhout, F. and Hertin, J. (2002) 'Foresight futures scenarios: Developing and applying a participative strategic planning tool', *Greener Management International*, spring 2002, no 37, pp37–52

Berkhout, F., Hertin, J. and Jordan, A. (2001) 'Socio-economic futures in climate change impact assessment: using scenarios as "learning machines"', Working paper no 3, www.tyndall.ac.uk/sites/default/files/wp3.pdf

Bertrand, G. and Michalski, A. (2001) 'Governance in a larger and more diverse European Union: Lessons from scenarios Europe 2010', in O. De Schutter, N. Lebessis and J. Paterson (eds) *Governance in the European Union*, Forward Studies Unit/ European Commission, Brussels, Belgium

Bertrand, G., Michalski, A. and Pench, L. R. (1999) *Scenarios Europe 2010*, European Commission Forward Studies Unit, Brussels, Belgium

Bijker, W. E. (1995) *Of Bicycles, Bakelites, and Bulbs: Toward a Theory of Sociotechnical Change*, MIT Press, Cambridge, US

Bijker, W., Hughes, T. and Pinch, T. (1987) *The Social Construction of Technological Systems: New Directions in the Sociology and History of Technology*, MIT Press, Cambridge, US

Bijker, W. E., Bal, R. and Hendriks, R. (2009) *The Paradox of Scientific Authority: The Role of Scientific Advice in Democracies*, MIT Press, Cambridge, MA

Bizikova, L., Burch, S., Robinson, J., Shaw, A. and Sheppard, S. (forthcoming) 'Utilizing participatory scenario-based approaches to design proactive responses to climate change in the face of uncertainties', in G. Gramelsberger and J. Feichter (eds) *Dealing with Uncertainty: Insights into the Calculability of Climate Change and Its Influence on Society*, Springer, Berlin, Germany

Bobbitt, P. (2002) *The Shield of Achilles: War, Peace and the Course of History*, Penguin, London, UK

Bood, R. P. and Postma, T. J. B. M. (1995) 'Leren met scenario's?', *Bedrijfskunde*, no 2, pp45–53

Bosk, C. L. (1980) 'Occupational rituals in patient management', *The New England Journal of Medicine*, vol 303, no 2, pp71–76

Bowker, G. C. and Star, S. L. (2000) *Sorting Things Out: Classification and Its Consequences*, MIT Press, Cambridge, US

Bradfield, R., Wright, G., Burt, G., Cairns, G. and van der Heijden, K. (2005) 'The origins and evolution of scenario techniques in long range business planning', *Futures*, vol 37, no 8, pp795–812

Brashers, D. E. (2001) 'Communication and uncertainty management', *Journal of Communication*, September, pp477–497

Brier, D. J. (2005) 'Marking the future: a review of time horizons', *Futures*, vol 37, no 8, pp833–848

Brooks, H. (1986) 'The typology of surprises in technology, institutions, and development', in W. C. Clark and R. E. Munn (eds) *Sustainable Development of the Biosphere*, Cambridge University Press, Cambridge, UK

Brooks, L. J. (2004) *Working in the Future Tense: Materializing Stories of Emerging Technologies and Cyberculture at the Institute of the Future*, PhD thesis, University of California, San Diego, US

Brown, N., Rappert, B. and Webster, A. (2000) *Contested Futures: A Sociology of Prospective Techno-Science*, Ashgate, Aldershot, UK

Bruggink, J. J. C. (2005) *The Next 50 Years: Four European Energy Futures*, ECN, Petten, The Netherlands

Bruun, H., Hukkinen, J. and Ekland, E. (2002) 'Scenarios for coping with contingency: The case of aquaculture in the Finnish Archipelago Sea', *Technological Forecasting and Social Change*, vol 69, pp107–127

Buchan, A. (1969) *Europe's Futures, Europe's Choices: Models for Western Europe in the 1970s*, Chatto and Windus, London, UK

Burt, G. and van der Heijden, K. (2003) 'First steps: Towards purposeful activities in scenario thinking and future studies', *Futures*, vol 35, no 10, pp1011–1026

Burt, G. and Wright, G. (2006) 'Introduction Special Issue: Organisational foresight', *Futures*, vol 38, no 8, pp887–893

Bury, J. B. (1932) *The Idea of Progress: An Inquiry into Its Origins and Growth*, Dover, New York, US

Cariola, M. and Rolfo, S. (2004) 'Evolution in the rationales of foresight in Europe', *Futures*, vol 36, no 10, pp1063–1075

Cinquegrani, R. (2002) 'Futurist networks: Cases of epistemic community?' *Futures*, vol 34, no 8, pp779–783

Clark, W. C. (1988) 'Visions of the 21st century: Conventional wisdom and other surprises in the global interactions of population, technology and environment', in K. Newton, T. Schweiter and J. P. Voyer (eds) *Perspective 2000*, Economic Council of Canada, Ottowa, Canada

Clark, W. C. and Munn, R. E. (eds) (1986) *Sustainable Development of the Biosphere*, Cambridge University Press, Cambridge, UK

Clute, J., Nicholls, P. and Stableford, B. (eds) (1993) *The Encyclopedia of Science Fiction* (first edition 1979), Orbit Books, London, UK

Collins, H. M. (1987) 'Certainty and the public understanding of science: Science on television', *Social Studies of Science*, vol 17, pp689–713

Constable, N. (2003) *Romance on a Global Stage: Pen Pals, Virtual Ethnography and Mail-Order Marriages*, University of California Press, Berkeley, CA, US

CPB (1992) *Scanning the Future: A Long Term Scenario Study of the World Economy 1990–2015*, Sdu Uitgeverij, The Hague, The Netherlands

Dammers, E. (2000) *Leren van de toekomst. Over de rol van scenario's bij strategische beleidsvorming*, PhD thesis, Eburon, Delft, The Netherlands

Dammers, E., Pálsdóttir, H. L., Stroecken, F., Crommentuijn, L., Driessen, E. and Fillius, F. (2003) *SCENE: Een kwartet ruimtelijke scenario's voor Nederland*, NAi Publishers and The Netherlands Institute for Spatial Research (RPB), Rotterdam and the Hague, The Netherlands

Dansereau, P. (1988) 'The edge of dreams', *Perspective 2000: Proceedings of a Conference Sponsored by the Economic Council of Canada*, eds K. Newton, T. Schweitzer and J. P. Voyer, Canadian Government Publishing Centre, Ottawa, Canada, pp32–37

Das, R. and Das, R. (2004) *Future flashes: Views upon Our Water Planet*, Tirion, Baarn, The Netherlands

Davis, A. J., Jenkinson, L. S., Lawton, J. H., Shorrocks, B. and Wood, S. (1998) 'Making mistakes when predicting shifts in response to global warming', *Nature*, vol 391, no 19/2/1998, pp783–786

Davis, G. (1998) 'Creating scenarios for your company's future', Paper presented to the *1998 Conference on Corporate Environmental, Health, and Safety Excellence: Bringing Sustainable Development Down to Earth*, New York City, US

de Baak Management, Futureconsult BV and Squarewise (2005) *Van schone slaapster tot artisitieke vrijstaat Nederland: Vier scenario's voor de Nederlandse kenniseconomie in 2010*, Futureconsult BV, Amsterdam, The Netherlands

de Jong, W. (1997) 'Scenario's 2030 zijn geen wishful thinking' (in Dutch), *NRC Handelsblad*, 14 July

de Jouvenel, B. (1967) *The Art of Conjecture*, Basic Books, New York, US

De Menezes, L. M. (2004) 'Review of "principles of forecasting", in J. Scott Armstrong (ed) *Journal of Forecasting*, vol 23, no 3, pp233–235

de Mooij, R. and Tang, P. (2003) *Four Futures of Europe*, CPB, The Hague, The Netherlands

de Vries, A. (2008) *Towards Do-ability: Dealing with Uncertainty in the Science–Policy Interface*, PhD thesis, Twente University, Enschede, The Netherlands

de Wilde, R. (2000) *De voorspellers: een kritiek op de toekomstindustrie*, Uitgeverij De Balie, Amsterdam, The Netherlands

Department of Trade and Industry (2002) *Foresight Futures 2020: Revised Scenarios and Guidance*, Department of Trade and Industry, London, UK

Dobbinga, E. (2001) *Weerbarstigheid van organisatiecultuur: een organisatie-antropologische studie naar betekenisgeving aan moderne managementinstrumenten*, PhD thesis, Eburon, Delft, The Netherlands

Dortmans, P. J. and Eiffe, E. (2004) 'An examination of future scenarios using historical analogy', *Futures*, vol 36, no 10, pp1049–1062

Drucker, P. F. (1968) *The Age of Discontinuity*, Harper and Row, New York, US

Dunsby, J. (2004) 'Measuring environmental health risks: The negotiation of a public Right-to-Know Law', *Science, Technology and Human Values*, vol 29, no 3, pp269–290

EEA (1999) *Environment in the European Union at the Turn of the Century*, Report no 2, European Environment Agency, Copenhagen, Denmark

Elmore, R. (1980) 'Backward mapping: Implementation research and policy decisions', *Political Science Quarterly*, no 94, pp601–616

Ester, P., Geurts, J. and Vermeulen, M. (eds) (1997) *De makers van de toekomst: Over nut en noodzaak van toekomstverkenningen voor beleidsonderzoek*, Tilburg University Press, Tilburg, The Netherlands

European Environment Agency and Alcamo, J. (2001) *Scenarios as Tools for International Environmental Assessments*, Environmental issue report no 24, European Environment Agency, Copenhagen, Denmark

European Environment Agency and DHV (2000) *Documentation and Evaluation of the EU98 Scenario Process*, DHV Environment and Infrastructure (unpublished), Copenhagen, Denmark

Evans, E., Ashley, R., Hall, J., Penning-Rowsell, E., Sayers, P., Thorne, C. and Watkinson, A. (2004a) *Foresight: Future Flooding. Scientific Summary: Volume I – Future Risks and their Drivers*, London, UK

Evans, E., Ashley, R., Hall, J., Penning-Rowsell, E., Sayers, P., Thorne, C. and Watkinson, A. (2004b) *Foresight: Future Flooding. Scientific Summary: Volume II – Managing Future Risks*, London, UK

Fahey, L. and Randall, R. (1998) *Learning from the Future: Competitive Foresight Scenarios*, Jon Wiley and Sons, US

Flick, U. (1992) 'Triangulation revisited: Strategy of validation of alternative', *Journal for the Theory of Social Behaviour*, vol 22, no 2, pp175–198

Fontela, E. (2000) 'Bridging the gap between scenarios and models', *Foresight*, vol 2, no 1, pp10–14

Fosket, J. (2004) 'Constructing "high-risk women": The development and standardization of a breast cancer risk assessment tool', *Science, Technology and Human Values*, vol 29, no 3, pp291–313

Fox, R. (1957) 'Training for uncertainty', in R. K. Merton, G. G. Reader and P. L. Kendall (eds) *The Student-Physician: Introductory Studies in the Sociology of*

Medical Education, Harvard University Press, Cambridge, Massachusetts, UK and US

Fox, R. (2000) 'Medical uncertainty revisited', in G. L. Albert, R. Fitzpatrick and S. C. Scrimshaw (eds) *Handbook of Social Studies in Health and Medicine*, SAGE, London, UK

Frewer, L. J., Hunt, S., Brennan, M., Kuznesof, S., Ness, M. and Ritson, C. (2003) 'The views of scientific experts on how the public conceptualize uncertainty', *Journal of Risk Research*, vol 2, no 6, pp75–85

Friedman, S. M., Dunwoody, S. and Rogers, C. L. (eds) (1999) *Communicating Uncertainty: Media Coverage of New and Controversial Science*, Lawrence Erlbaum Associates, Mahwah, New Jersey, US

Fuller, T. (1999) 'Futures studies and foresight', in Z. Sardar (ed) *Rescuing All Our Futures: The Future of Futures Studies*, Praeger, Westport, Connecticut, US

Funtowicz, S. O. and Ravetz, J. R. (1990) *Uncertainty and Quality in Science for Policy*, Kluwer, Dordrecht, The Netherlands

Funtowicz, S. O. and Ravetz, J. R. (1993) 'The emergence of post-normal science', in R. von Schomberg (ed) *Science, Politics and Morality: Scientific Uncertainty and Decision-Making*, Kluwer Academic Publishers, Dordrecht, The Netherlands

Funtowicz, S. O. and Ravetz, J. R. (1994) 'Uncertainty, complexity and post-normal science', *Environmental Toxicology and Chemistry*, vol 13, no 12, pp1881–1885

Futureconsult (2006) *Van seniorwash to sixties revival and van rollator tot rolls roys: Scenarios voor vergrijzend Nederland 2016*, Futureconsult BV, Amsterdam, The Netherlands

Gallopín, G. (2004) *La sostenibilidad ambiental del desarrollo en Argentina: Tres futuros*, United Nations, New York, US

Gallopín, G., Hammond, A., Raskin, P. and Swart, R. (1997) *Branch Points: Global Scenarios and Human Choice: A Resource Paper of the Global Scenario Group*, Report Number Polestar Series no 7, Stockholm Environment Institute, Sweden

Galtung, J. (2003) 'What did people predict for the year 2000 and what happened', *Futures*, vol 35, no 2, pp107–121

Geertz, C. (1973/1999) *The Interpretation of Cultures: Selected Essays*, reprinted edition, Basic Books, New York, US

Geertz, C. (1999) 'Preface 1999', in C. Geertz (ed) *The Interpretation of Cultures: Selected Essays*, Basic Books, New York, US

Gemeente Amsterdam (1999) *Stadsvisie 2010: Amsterdam complete stad*, Gemeente Amsterdam, The Netherlands

Gemeente Leiden (2004) *Leiden – Stad van ontdekkingen: Profiel Leiden 2030*, Gemeente Leiden, The Netherlands

Giddens, A. (1991) *Modernity and Identity: Self and Society in the Late Modern Age*, Stanford University Press, Stanford, California, US

Gieryn, T. F. (1983) 'Boundary-work and the demarcation of science from non-science: Strains and interests in professional ideologies of scientists', *American Sociological Review*, vol 48, no 6, pp781–795

Gieryn, T. F. (1995) 'Boundaries of science', in S. Jasanoff, G. E. Markle, R. E. Petersen and T. Pinch (eds) *Handbook of Science and Technology Studies*, SAGE, London, UK

Gilbert, G. N. and Mulkay, M. (1984) *Opening Pandora's Box: A Sociological Analysis of Scientists' Discourse*, Cambridge University Press, Cambridge, UK

Girod, B., Wiek, A., Mieg, H. and Hulme, M. (2009) 'The evolution of the IPCC's emissions scenarios', *Environmental Science and Policy*, vol 12, no 2, pp103–118

Glantz, M. H., Streets, D. G., Stewart, T. R., Bhatti, N., Moore, C. M. and Rosa, C. H. (1998) *Exploring the Concept of Climate Surprises: A Review of the Literature on the Concept of Surprise and How It Is Related to Climate Change*, Argonne National Laboratory, Argonne, US

Global Business Network (1996a) *Port of Rotterdam Scenario Workshop Report*, Unpublished, Global Business Network, The Hague, The Netherlands

Global Business Network (1996b) *Wild Cards*, Global Business Network, San Francisco, US

Global Business Network (1998) 'Destino Colombia', *Deeper News*, www.gbn.org

Godet, M. (2001) *Creating Futures: Scenario Planning as a Strategic Management Tool* Economica, London, UK

Goffman, E. (1959) *The Presentation of Self in Everyday Life*, Doubleday Anchor, New York, US

Grant, R. M. (2003) 'Strategic planning in a turbulent environment: Evidence from the oil majors', *Strategic Management Journal*, vol 24, no 6, pp491–571

Greeuw, S. C. H., van Asselt, M. B. A., Grosskurth, J., Storms, C. A. M. H., Rijkens-Klomp, N., Rothman, D. S. and Rotmans, J. (2000) *Cloudy Crystal Balls: An Assessment of Recent European and Global Scenario Studies and Models*, European Environmental Agency (EEA) Experts' Corner Report no 4: Prospects and Scenarios, Copenhagen, Denmark

Hacking, I. (1999) *The Social Construction of What?*, Harvard, Cambridge, MA

Halffman, W. (2003) *Boundaries of Regulatory Science: Eco/toxicology and Aquatic Hazards of Chemicals in the US, England, and The Netherlands, 1970–1995*, PhD thesis, Universiteit van Amsterdam (UvA), The Netherlands

Halffman, W. and Hoppe, R. (2005) 'Science/policy boundaries: a changing division of labour in Dutch expert policy advice', in S. Maasse and P. Weingart (eds) *Democratization of Expertise? Exploring Novel Forms of Scientific Advice in Political Decision-Making*, Kluwer, Dordrecht, The Netherlands, pp135–152

Hammersley, M. and Atkinson, P. (1995) *Ethnography: Principles in Practice (second edition)*, Routledge, London and New York, UK and US

Hammond, A. (1998) *Which World? Scenarios for the 21st Century: Global Destinies, Regional Choices*, Earthscan Publications Ltd, London, UK

Harremoës, P., Gee, D., MacGarvin, M., Stirling, A., Keys, J., Wynne, B. and Guedez Vaz, S. (2001) *Late Lessons from Early Warnings: The Precautionary Principle 1896–2000*, European Environment Agency, Copenhagen, Denmark

Hayward, P. (2004) 'Futures studies as a catalyst for change', *Futures*, vol 36, no 5, pp611–616

Heinzen, B. (1994) 'Political experiments of the 1990s: The use of scenarios in the public domain', *The Deeper News*, vol 5, no 3, pp20–46

Hess, D. J. (1999) *Science Studies: An Advanced Introduction*, New York University Press, New York, US

Hilgartner, S. (2000) *Science on Stage: Expert Advice as Public Drama*, Stanford University Press, Stanford, US

Hilgartner, S. (2003) 'Expertise and the production of the unknowable', *4S annual meeting*, Atlanta, US

Hine, C. (2000) *Virtual Ethnography*, Sage, London, UK

Hines, A. (2000) 'Where do your trends come from?' *Foresight*, vol 2, no 5, pp533–534

Holling, C. S. (1986) 'The resilience of terrestrial ecosystems', in W. C. Clark and R. E. Munn (eds) *Sustainable Development of the Biosphere*, Cambridge University Press, Cambridge, UK

Hoppe, R. (1980) 'De driehoeksverhouding tussen politiek, planning en toekomstdenken', *Bestuurswetenschappen*, no 5, pp287–302

Hoppe, R. (2002) *Van flipperkast naar grensverkeer. Veranderende visies op de relatie tussen wetenschap en beleid. Achtergrondstudie nr. 25*, Adviesraad voor Wetenschaps– en Technologiebeleid, The Hague, The Netherlands

Horton, A. M. (1999) 'A simple guide to successful foresight', *Foresight*, vol 1, no 1, pp5–9

Huitema, D. (2005) 'Calculating election manifestoes. Election manifestoes as the meeting point for experts and politicians in The Netherlands: the case of the National Institute of Public Health and Environment (RIVM)', Paper presented to the *Public Proofs: Science, Technology, and Democracy Conference, 4th Annual Conference*, Paris, France

Huitema, D. and Turnhout, E. (2009) 'Working at the science–policy interface: A discursive analysis of boundary work at The Netherlands Environmental Assessment Agency', *Environmental Politics*, vol 18, no 4, pp576–594

Hyde-Price, A.G. V. (1991) *European Security beyond the Cold War: Four Scenarios for the Year 2010*, Sage, London, UK

Inayatullah, S. (1990) 'Deconstructing and reconstructing the future: Predictive, cultural and critical epistemologies', *Futures*, vol 22, no 2, pp115–141

Inayatullah, S. (1993) 'From "who am I?" to "when am I?": Framing the shape and time of the future', *Futures*, vol 25, no 3, pp235–253

IPCC (Intergovernmental Panel on Climate Change) (2000) *IPCC Special Report: Emission Scenarios*, Cambridge University Press, Cambridge, www.grida.no/publications/other/ipcc_sr/?src=/Climate/ipcc/emission/091.htm

IPCC (2007) *Climate Change 2007: Synthesis Report: Contribution of Working Groups I, II and III to the Fourth Assessment Report of the Intergovernmental Panel on Climate Change*, Intergovernmental Panel on Climate Change, Geneva, Switzerland

Janssen, L. H. J. M., Okker, V. R. and Schuur. J. (2006) *Welvaart en Leefomgeving, Een scenariostudie voor Nederland in 2040*, Centraal Planbureau, Milieu – en Natuurplanbureau en Ruimtelijk Planbureau, The Netherlands

Jasanoff, S. (1990) *The Fifth Branch: Science Advisers as Policy Makers*, Harvard University Press, Cambridge, US

Jasanoff, S. (1991) 'Acceptable evidence in a pluralistic society', in D. G. Mayo and R. D. Hollander (eds) *Acceptable Evidence: Science and Values in Risk Management*, Oxford University Press, New York, US

Jasanoff, S. (2005) *Designs on Nature: Science and Democracy in Europe and the United States*, Princeton University Press, Princeton, US

Jasanoff, S. and Wynne, B. (1998) 'Science and decision-making', in S. Rayner and E. L. Malone (eds) *Human Choice and Climate Change, vol 1 – The Societal Framework*, Battelle Press, Washington, DC, US, pp1–87

Jick, J. D. (1979) 'Mixing qualitative and quantitative methods: Triangulation in action', *Administrative Science Quarterly*, vol 24, no 4, pp602–611

Jungermann, H. and Thuring, M. (1987) 'The use of mental models for generating scenarios', in G. Wright (ed) *Judgmental Forecasting*, John Wiley and Sons Ltd, Chichester, UK, pp245–266

Kahane, A. (1998) 'Imagining South Africa's Future: How Scenarios Helped Discover Common Ground', in L. Fahey and R. Randall (eds) *Learning from the Future: Competitive Foresight Scenarios*, John Wiley and Sons, New York, US

Kahn, H. and Wiener, A. (1967) *The Year 2000*, MacMillan, New York, US

Kaplan, S. and Garrick, B.J. (1981) 'On the quantitative definition of risk', *Risk Analysis*, vol 1, no 1, pp11–27

Kasemir, B., Jäger, J., Jaeger, C. and Gardner, M. T. (eds) (2003) *Public Participation in Sustainability Science*, Cambridge University Press, Cambridge, UK

Kates, R. W. and Clark, W. (1996) 'Environmental surprise: Expecting the unexpected', *Environment*, vol 38, no 2, pp6–11

Katz, J. (1984), 'Why doctors don't disclose uncertainty', *The Hasting Centre Report*, February, pp35–44

Kieken, H. (2002) 'Integrating structural changes in future research and modelling on the Seine River Basin in integrated assessment and decision support', *Proceedings of the 1st Biennial Meeting of the International Environmental Modelling and Software Society*, eds A. E. Rizolli and A. J. Jakeman, pp237–242

Kleiner, A. (1996) *The Age of Heretics*, Doubleday, New York, US

Knorr-Cetina, K. (1981) *The Manufacture of Knowledge: An Essay on the Constructivist and Contextual Nature of Science*, Pergamon, Oxford, UK

Knorr-Cetina, K. (1995) 'Laboratory studies: The cultural approach to the study of science', in S. Jasanoff, G. E. Markle, J. C. Petersen and T. Pinch (eds) *Handbook of Science and Technology Studies*, Sage, London, UK

Koselleck, R. (1985) *Futures Past: On the Semantics of Historical Time*, MIT Press, Cambridge, MA, US

Krayer von Kraus, M. P., van Asselt, M. B. A., Henze, M., Ravetz, J. and Beck, M. B. (2005) 'Uncertainty and precaution in environmental management', *Water, Science and Technology*, vol 52, no 6, pp1–9

Kuhn, T. S. (1970) *The Structure of Scientific Revolutions*, University of Chicago Press, Chicago, IL, US

Lahsen, M. (2005) 'Technocracy, democracy and US climate politics: The need for demarcations', *Science, Technology and Human Values*, vol 30, no 1, pp137–169

Latour, B. (1987) *Science in Action: How to Follow Scientists and Engineers through Society*, Harvard University Press, Cambridge, Massachusetts, UK and US

Latour, B. and Woolgar, S. (1979/1986) *Laboratory Life: The Social Construction of Scientific Facts*, Sage, Beverly Hills, US

Latour, B. and Woolgar, S. (1986) *Laboratory Life: The Construction of Scientific Facts*, 2nd edition with new postscript by the authors, Princeton University Press, Oxford, UK

Le Roux, P. et al (1992) 'The Mont Fleur scenarios. What will South Africa be like in the year 2002?' *Deeper News*, July 1992, www.gbn.org

Leemhuis, J. P. (1985) 'Using scenarios to develop strategies', *Long Range Plan*, vol 18, no 2, pp30–37

Lempert, R. J., Popper, S. W. and Bankes, S. C. (2003) *Shaping the Next One Hundred Years: New Methods for Quantitative Long-Term Policy Analysis*, RAND, Santa Monica, US

Light Jr, D. (1979) 'Uncertainty and control in professional training', *Journal of Health and Social Behavior*, vol 20, December, pp310–322

Lindgren, M. and Bandhold, H. (2003) *Scenario Planning: The Link between Future and Strategy*, Palgrave-Macmillan, New York, US

Lovins, A. B. (1976) 'Energy strategy: The road not taken?' *Foreign Affairs* no 1, pp63–96

Lynch, M. (1985) *Art and Artifact in Laboratory Science: A Study of Shop Work and Shop Talk in a Research Laboratory*, Routledge and Kegan Paul, London, UK

Marien, M. (2002) 'Futures studies in the 21st century: A reality-based view', *Futures*, vol 34, no 3/4, pp261–281

Masini, E. B. (1999) 'Rethinking futures studies', in Z. Sardar (ed) *Rescuing all Our Futures: The Future of Futures Studies*, Praeger, Westport, Connecticut, US

McCorduck, P. and Ramsey, N. (1996) *The Futures of Women: Scenarios for the 21st Century*, Warner Books, New York, US

Meadows, D. H., Meadows, D. L., Randers, J. and Behrens, W. W. (1972) *The Limits to Growth*, Universe Books, New York, US

Mendonça, S., Cunha, M. P., Kaivo-oja, J. and Ruff, F. (2004) 'Wild cards, weak signals and organisational improvisation', *Futures*, vol 36, no 2, pp201–218

Mesman, J. (2002) *Experienced Pioneers: Dealing with Doubt in the Intensive Care for Neonates* (in Dutch), PhD thesis, Aksant, Amsterdam, The Netherlands

Mesman, J. (2005) 'Prognostic differences and their origins: A topography of experience and expectation in a neonatal intensive care unit', *Qualitative Sociology*, vol 28, no 1, pp49–66

Mesman, J. (2008) *Uncertainty in Medical Innovation: Experienced Pioneers in Neonatal Care Health*, Palgrave MacMillan, Basingstoke, UK

Mesman, J. (2009) 'Channeling erratic flows of actions: Life in the neonatal intensive care unit', in C. Owen, G. Wackers and J. Gregory (eds) *Risky Work: The Ecologies of Human Work within Complex Technological Systems*, MIT Press, Cambridge, US, pp105–128

Michael, M. (2000) 'Futures of the present: From performativity to prehension', in N. Brown, B. Rappert and A. Webster (eds) *Contested Futures: A Sociology of Prospective Techno-Science*, Ashgate, Aldershot, Burlington, Singapore, Sydney

Middelkoop, H., van Asselt, M. B. A., van 't Klooster, S. A., van Deursen, W. P. A., Kwadijk, J. C. J. and Buiteveld, H. (2004) 'Perspectives on flood management in the Rhine and Meuse rivers', *River Research and Applications*, vol 20, pp327–342

Miles, I. (1993) 'Stranger than fiction: How important is science fiction for futures studies?' *Futures*, vol 25, no 3, pp315–321

Milieu en Natuur Planbureau (2006) *Nationale Milieuverkenning 6: 2006–2040*, Report no 500085001, MNP, Bilthoven, The Netherlands

Miljovevic, I. and Inayatullah, S. (2003) 'Futures dreaming outside and on the margins of the western world', *Futures*, vol 35, no 5, pp493–507

Miller, D. and Slater, D. (2000) *The Internet: An Ethnographic Approach*, Berg, Oxford and New York, UK and US

Miller, R. (2003) *The Future of the Tertiary Education Sector*, OECD–CERI, Paris, France

Ministerie van Binnenlandse Zaken en Koninkrijksrelaties (2003) *Scenario's enzo: een handreiking voor scenarioplanning*, Dutch Ministry of Interior Affairs and Kingdom Relations, The Hague, The Netherlands

Ministerie van Verkeer en Waterstaat (1998) *Verplaatsen in de toekomst: Project Questa*, Ministerie van Verkeer en Waterstaat, The Hague, The Netherlands

Mol, A. (2002) *The Body Multiple: Ontology in Medical Practice*, Duke University Press, Durham and London, UK

Molitor, G. T. T. (1998) 'How to spot, track, and forecast change strategies for the new millennium: A world future society conference', Paper presented to the Strategies for the New Millennium: A World Future Society Conference, Chicago, US

Morgan, D. (2002) 'Images of the future: a historical perspective', *Futures*, vol 34, no 9/10, pp883–893

Morgan, G. M. and Henrion, M. (1990) *Uncertainty – A Guide to Dealing with Uncertainty in Quantitative Risk and Policy Analysis*, Cambridge University Press, New York, US

Moyer, K. (1996) 'Scenario planning at British Airways – a case study', *Long Range Planning*, pp172–181

Myers, N. (1995) 'Environmental unknowns', *Science*, vol 269, no 21, July, pp358–360

Nekkers, J. (2006) *Wijzer in de toekomst: Werken met scenario's*, Business Contact, Amsterdam and Antwerp, The Netherlands and Belgium

Neyland, D. (2006) *Privacy, Surveillance and Public Trust*, Palgrave-Macmillan, London, UK

Noordegraaf, M. (2000) *Attention! Work and Behavior of Public Managers amidst Ambiguity*, PhD thesis, Eburon Publishers, Delft, The Netherlands

Nowotny, H. (1994) *Time: The Modern and the Postmodern Experience*, Polity Press, Cambridge, UK

Nowotny, H. (2008) *Insatiable Curiosity: Innovation in a Fragile Future*, MIT Press, Cambridge, MA, US

Nowotny, H., Scott, P. and Gibbons, M. (2001) *Re-thinking Science: Knowledge and the Public in an Age of Uncertainty*, Polity Press in association with Blackwell Publishers, Cambridge, UK

OECD (Organisation for Economic Co-operation and Development) (2001) *Schooling for Tomorrow: What Schools for the Future?*, Paris, France

Øverland, E. F., Neumann, I. B., Dokk Holm, E. and Høviskeland, T. (2000) *Norway 2030*, Royal Ministry of Labour and Government Administration, Oslo, Norway

Pálsdóttir, H. L., Raspe, O., Tisma, A., Verwest, F. and Tiebosch, T. (2002) *Nederland in Europese Context: Toekomstscenario's tot 2030 SCENE op internationaal niveau*, Ruimtelijk Planbureau, The Hague, The Netherlands

Petersen, A. C. (2006) *Simulating Nature: A Philosophical Study of Computer-Simulation Uncertainties and Their Role in Climate Science and Policy Advice*, PhD thesis, Het Spinhuis, Apeldoorn, The Netherlands

Petersen, J. L. (1999) *Out of the Blue: How to Anticipate Big Future Surprises*, Madison Books, Lanham, UK

Polak, F. (1971) *The Image of the Future*, Elsevier, Amsterdam, The Netherlands

Porter, T. M. (1995) *Trust in Numbers: The Pursuit of Objectivity in Science and Public Life*, Princeton University Press, Princeton, New Jersey, US

Puglisi, M. and Marvin, S. (2002) 'Developing urban and regional foresight: Exploring capacities and identifying needs in the North West', *Futures*, vol 34, no 8, pp761–777

Quist, J. (2007) *Backcasting for a Sustainable Future: The Impact after 10 Years*, PhD thesis, Delft University, The Netherlands

Rademaker, P. (ed) (2001) *Met het oog op 2010: De toekomst van het sociale domein, verbeeld in elf essays*, De Balie, Amsterdam, The Netherlands

Ramírez, R. and van der Heijden, K. (2007) 'Scenarios to develop strategic options: A new interactive role for scenarios in strategy', in W. Sharpe and K. van der Heijden (eds) *Scenarios for Success: Turning Insights into Action*, Oxfords Futures Forum, John Wiley and Sons, Chichester, UK

Raskin, P. D. (2005) 'Global scenarios: Background review for the Millennium Ecosystem Assessment', *Ecosystems*, vol 8, no 2, pp133–142

Ravetz, J. R. (1971) *Scientific Knowledge and Its Social Problems*, Oxford University Press, New York, US

Ravetz, J. R. (2006) *The No-Nonsense Guide to Science*, The New Internationalist, Oxford, UK

Reichenbach, H. (1951) *The Rise of Scientific Philosophy*, University of California Press, Berkeley and Los Angeles, US

Ringland, G. (1998) *Scenario Planning: Managing for the Future*, Wiley and Sons, Chichester, UK

Ringland, G. (2002a) *Scenarios in Business*, John Wiley and Sons Ltd, US

Ringland, G. (ed) (2002b) *Scenarios in Public Policy*, John Wiley and Sons Ltd, US

Ringland, G., Edwards, M., Hammond, L., Heinzen, B., Rendell, A., Sparrow, O. and White, E. (1999) 'Shocks and paradigm busters (why do we get surprised?)', *Long Range Planning*, vol 32, no 4, pp403–413

RIVM (1988) *Zorgen voor morgen*, Samson H.D. Tjeenk Willink, Alphen aan de Rijn, The Netherlands

RIVM (1991/1992) *National Environmental Outlook 2 1990–2010*, RIVM, Bilthoven, The Netherlands

RIVM (1993) *National Environmental Outlook 3 1993–2015*, Samsom H. D. Tjeenk Willink, Alphen aan den Rijn, The Netherlands

RIVM (1997) *Nationale Milieuverkenning 4 1997–2020*, Samsom H. D. Tjeenk Willink, Bilthoven, The Netherlands

RIVM (2000) *Nationale Milieuverkenning 5 2000–2030*, Samson, Alphen aan de Rijn, The Netherlands

Robinson, J.B. (2003) 'Future subjunctive: Backcasting as social learning', *Futures*, vol 35, pp839–856

Robinson, J. B. (1982) 'Energy backcasting. A proposed method of policy analysis', *Energy Policy*, pp337–344

Rogers, M.D. (2001) 'Scientific and technological uncertainty, the precautionary principle, scenarios and risk management', *Journal of Risk Research*, vol 4, no 1, pp1–15

Rose, H. (2000) 'Science fiction's memory of the future', in N. Brown, B. Rappert and A. Webster (eds) *Contested Futures: A Sociology of Prospective Techno-Science*, Ashgate, Aldershot, UK, pp157–174

Rotmans, J. (1997) 'Indicators for sustainable development', in J. Rotmans and H. J. M. de Vries (eds) *Perspectives on Global Change: The TARGETS Approach*, Cambridge University Press, Cambridge, UK

Rotmans, J. and van Asselt, M. B. A. (1999) 'Perspectives on a sustainable future', *International Journal for Sustainable Development*, vol 2, no 2, pp201–230

Rotmans, J., van Asselt, M. B. A., Anastasi, C., Greeuw, S., Mellors, J., Peters, S., Rothman, D. and Rijkens, N. (2000) 'Visions for a sustainable Europe', *Futures*, vol 32, no 9–10, pp809–831

Sardar, Z. (1999a) 'The problem of futures studies', in Z. Sardar (ed) *Rescuing All Our Futures: The Future of Futures Studies*, Praeger, Westport, CT, US

Sardar, Z. (ed) (1999b) *Rescuing All Our Futures: The Future of Futures Studies*, Praeger, Westport, CT, US

Schmid, S.D. (2004) 'Transformation discourse: Nuclear risk as a strategic tool in late Soviet politics of expertise', *Science, Technology and Human Values*, vol 29, no 3, pp353–376

Schneider, S. H., Turner, B. L. and Morehouse Garriga, H. (1998) 'Imaginable surprise in global change science', *Journal of Risk Research*, vol 1, no 2, pp165–185

Schoemaker, P. J. H. (1991) 'When and how to use scenario planning: A heuristic approach with illustration', *Journal of Forecasting*, vol 10, no 6, pp549–564

Schoemaker, P. J. H. (1993) 'Multiple scenario development: Its contextual and behavioural foundation', *Strategic Management Journal*, vol 14, no3, pp193–213

Schön, D. A. (1983) *The Reflective Practitioner: How Professionals Think in Action*, Basic Books, US

Schooneboom, J. (2003) 'Toekomstscenario's en beleid', *Beleid en Maatschappij*, vol 30, no 4, pp212–218

Schwartz, P. and Ogilvy, J. (1998) 'Plotting your scenarios', in L. Fahey and M. Randall (eds) *Learning from the Future*, John Wiley and Sons, US, pp57–80

Schwartz, P. (1991) *The Art of the Long View: Planning for the Future in an Uncertain World*, Currency Doubleday, New York, US

Scott, A. (2002) '11 September, 2001', *Scenario and Strategy Planning*, vol 3, no 5, pp4–8

Seale, C. (ed) (2004) *Researching Society and Culture*, 2nd edition, Sage, Thousand Oaks, London, New Delhi, UK and India

Searle, J. R. (1995) *The Social Construction of Reality*, The Free Press, New York, US

Sharpe, B. and van der Heijden, K. (2007) 'Scenarios for success: Turning insights into action', *Oxfords Futures Forum*, John Wiley and Sons, Chichester, UK

Shell International (2002) *People and Connections: Global Scenarios to 2020 – Public Summary*, London, UK

Shell International (2008) *Scenarios: An Explorer's Guide*, Shell International BV, Amsterdam, The Netherlands

Shepherd, J. and Tsoukas, H. (2004) *Managing the Future: Strategic Foresight in the Knowledge Economy*, Blackwell Publishers, Oxford, UK

Slaughter, R. A. (1984) 'Towards a Critical Futurism parts 1, 2, 3', *World Future Society Bulletin,* July/August: pp19–25, Sept/Oct: pp11–16, Sept/Oct: pp17–21

Slaughter, R. A. (1999) *Futures for the Third Millennium: Enabling the Forward View*, Prospect Media, Australia

Slaughter, R. A. (2002) 'Where now for futures studies?', *Futures*, vol 34, no 3–4, pp229–233

Slaughter, R. A. (2004) 'Road testing a new model at the Australian Foresight Institute', *Futures*, vol 36, no 8, pp837–852

Smith, R. A., Vesga, D. R. A., Cadena, A. I., Boman, U., Larsen, E. and Dyner, I. (2005) 'Energy scenarios for Colombia: Process and content', *Futures*, vol 37, no 1, pp1–17

Stocking, S. H. (1999) 'How journalists deal with scientific uncertainty', in S. M. Friedman, S. Dunwoody and C. L. Rogers (eds) *Communicating Uncertainty: Media Coverage of New and Controversial Science*, Lawrence Erlbaum Associates, Mahwah, New Jersey, US

Stone, D.A. (1997) *Policy Paradox: The Art of Political Decision-Making*, Norton, New York, US

Svedin, U. and Aniansson, B. (eds) (1987) *Surprising Futures: Notes from an International Workshop on Long-Term World Development*, Swedish Council for Planning and Coordination of Research, Stockholm, Sweden

Swanborn, P. G. (1981/1994) *Methoden van sociaal-wetenschappelijk onderzoek*, 1994 edition, Boom, Meppel, The Netherlands

Tansey, J., M. Journeay, S. Talwar, J. Robinson and B. Brodaric (2004) 'Navigating pathways between policy and science', *Policy Research Initiative – Horizon*, vol 6, no 4, pp70–73

Thompson, M., Ellis, R. and Wildavsky, A. (1990) *Cultural Theory*, Westview Press, Boulder, CO, US

Tonn, B. E. (2003) 'The future of futures decision making', *Futures*, vol 35, no 6, pp673–688

Traweek, S. (1988) *Beamtimes and Lifetimes: The World of High Energy Physicists*, Harvard University Press, Cambridge, MA, UK and US

Uggla, Y. (2004) 'Risk and safety analysis in long–term perspective', *Futures*, vol 36, no 5, pp549–564

UNEP (United Nations Environment Programme) (1997) *Global Environment Outlook*, Oxford University Press, Oxford, UK

UNEP (1999) *Global Environment Outlook 2*, Earthscan, London, UK

UNEP (2002) *Global Environment Outlook 3*, Earthscan, London, UK

UNEP (2007) *Global Environment Outlook 4*, Earthscan, London, UK

van Asselt, M. B. A. (2000) *Perspectives on Uncertainty and Risk: The PRIMA Approach to Decision Support*, Kluwer Academic Publishers, Dordrecht, The Netherlands

van Asselt, M. B. A. (2004) 'Toekomstverkennen en de kunst van onzekerheidscommunicatie', *Beleidswetenschap*, vol 18, no 2, pp137–168

van Asselt, M. B. A. (2005) 'The complex significance of uncertainty in a risk era: Logics, manners and strategies in use', *International Journal for Risk Assessment and Management*, vol 5, no 2/3/4, pp125–158

van Asselt, M. B. A. and Rotmans, J. (2002) 'Uncertainty in integrated assessment modelling: From positivism to pluralism', *Climatic Change*, vol 54, no 1–2, pp75–105

van Asselt, M. B. A., Langendonck, R., van Asten, F., van der Giessen, A., Janssen, P., Heuberger, P. and Geuskens, I. (2001a) *Uncertainty and RIVM's Environmental Outlooks: Documenting a Learning Process*, ICIS/RIVM, Maastricht/Bilthoven, The Netherlands

van Asselt, M. B. A., Middelkoop, H., van 't Klooster, S. A., van Deursen, W. P. A., Haasnoot, M., Kwadijk, J. C. J., Buiteveld, H., Können, G. P., Rotmans, J., van Gemert, N. and Valkering, P. (2001b) *Integrated Water Management Strategies for the Rhine and Meuse Basins in a Changing Environment: Final Report of the NRP Project 0/958273/01*, ICIS, Maastricht/Utrecht, The Netherlands

van Asselt, M. B. A., Rotmans, J. and Rothman, D.S. (2005a) *Scenario Innovation: Experiences from a European Experimental Garden*, Taylor and Francis, Leiden, The Netherlands and New York, USA

van Asselt, M. B. A., van der Pas, J. W. and de Wilde, R. (2005b) *De toekomst begint vandaag: Inventarisatie toekomstverkenningen – onderzoeksrapport*, Universiteit Maastricht, The Netherlands

van Asselt, M. B. A., de Wilde, R., van der Pas, J. W., and Wolthuis, J. A. (2005c) *Houdbaarheid verstreken: Toekomstverkenning en beleid*, Ministerie van Binnenlandse Zaken en Koninkrijksrelaties, The Hague, The Netherlands

van Asselt, M. B. A., Mesman, J. and van 't Klooster, S. A. (2007a) 'Dealing with prognostic uncertainty', *Futures*, vol 39, no 6, pp669–684

van Asselt, M. B. A., Passchier, W. F. and Krayer von Kraus, M. P. (2007b) *Uncertainty Assessment: An Analysis of Regulatory Science on Wireless Communication*

Technology, RF EMF and Cancer Risks, Report for the IMBA project – work package 1, Maastricht University, The Netherlands

van de Kerkhof, M. (2006) 'A dialogue approach to enhance learning for sustainability: A Dutch experiment with two participatory methods in the field of climate change', *The Integrated Assessment Journal*, vol 6 no 4, pp7–34

van de Kerkhof, M., Hisschemöller, M. and Spanjersberg, M. (2002) 'Shaping diversity in participatory foresight studies. Experiences with interactive backcasting in a stakeholder dialogue on long-term climate policy in The Netherlands', *Greener Management International*, vol 37, no 1, pp95–99

van den Berg, H., Both, G. and Basset, P. (1993) *Het Centraal Planbureau in politieke zaken*, Scientific Office of the Green Left Party, Amsterdam, The Netherlands

van der Duin, P. A. (2006) *Qualitative Futures Research for Innovation*, PhD thesis, Eburon, Delft, The Netherlands

van der Duin, P. A., Hazeu, C. A., Rademaker, P. and Schooneboom, I. J. (eds) (2004) *Vijfentwing jaar later: De toekomstverkenning van de WRR uit 1977 als leerproces*, Amsterdam University Press, Amsterdam, The Netherlands

van der Duin, P., van Oirschot, R. and Kotey, H. (2008) *Regeren is vooruitzien. Een exploratief onderzoek naar het gebruik van toekomstverkenningen in strategie– en beleidsvormingsprocessen van ministeries*, Lenthe Publishers, Amstelveen, The Netherlands

van der Heijden, G. M. A. and Schrijver, J. F. (eds) (2002) *Representatief en participatief*, Eburon, Delft, The Netherlands

van der Heijden, K. (1996) *Scenarios: The Art of Strategic Conversation*, Wiley and Sons, Chichester, UK

van der Heijden, K., Bradfield, R., Burt, G., Cairns, G. and Wright, G. (2002) *The Sixth Sense: Accelerating Organisational Learning with Scenarios*, Wiley and Sons, Chichester, UK

van der Helm, R. (2007) 'Book review: Scenario Innovation: *Experiences from a European Experimental Garden*. M. B. A. van Asselt, J. Rotmans, D. S. Rothman, Taylor and Francis London', *Futures*, vol 39, no 9, pp1134–1139

van der Meulen, B. J. R. (2002) *Methodiek verkenningen: Naar een ontwerpbenadering voor het opzetten van verkenningen*, KNAW/Universiteit Twente, Amsterdam, The Netherlands

van der Sluijs, J. P. (1997) *Anchoring amid Uncertainty: On the Management of Uncertainties in Risk Assessment of Anthropogenic Climate Change*, PhD thesis, Utrecht University, The Netherlands

van der Sluijs, J. P., van Eijndhoven, J. C. M., Wynne, B. and Shackley, S. (1998) 'Anchoring devices in science for policy: The case of consensus around climate sensitivity', *Social Studies of Science*, vol 28, no 2, pp291–323

van der Staal, P. M. and van Vught, F. A. (1987a) 'Vijftien jaar toekomstonderzoek door de WRR: de uitgestelde methodologische reflectie Deel 1', *Beleidsanalyse*, vol 87, no 4, pp16–25

van der Staal, P. M. and van Vught, F. A. (1987b) 'Vijftien jaar toekomstonderzoek door de WRR: de uitgestelde methodologische reflectie Deel 2', *Beleidsanalyse*, vol 88, no 1, pp5–17

van der Steen, M. (2009) *Een sterk verhaal: een analyse van het discours over vergrijzing*, PhD thesis, Lemma, The Hague, The Netherlands

van Eeten, M. (1999) *Dialogues of the Deaf. Defining New Agendas for Environmental Deadlocks*, PhD thesis, Eburon Publishers, Delft, The Netherlands van Lente, H. (1993) *Promising Technology: The Dynamics of Expectations in Technological Developments*, PhD thesis, Twente University, Enschede, The Netherlands

van Lente, H. (2000) 'Forceful futures: From promise to requirement', in N. Brown, B. Rappert and A. Webster (eds) *Contested Futures: A Sociology of Prospective Techno-Science*, Ashgate, Aldershot, UK

van Notten, P. W. F. (2005) *Writing on the Wall: Scenario Development in Times of Discontinuity*, Thela Thesis and Dissertation.com, Amsterdam, The Netherlands

van Notten, P., Rotmans, J., van Asselt, M. B. A. and Rothman, D. S. (2003) 'An updated scenario typology', *Futures*, vol 35, no 5, pp423–443

van Notten, P. W. F., Sleegers, A. M. and van Asselt, M. B. A. (2005) 'The future shocks: On the role of discontinuity in scenario development', *Technological Forecasting and Social Change*, vol 72, no 2, pp175–194

van Steenbergen, B. (1996) 'Looking into the seeds of time', *Futures*, vol 28, no 6/7, pp679–683

van 't Klooster, S. A. (2007) *Toekomstverkenning: ambities en de praktijk. Een etnografische studie naar de productie van toekomstkennis bij het Ruimtelijk Planbureau (RPB)*, PhD thesis, Eburon, Delft, The Netherlands

van 't Klooster, S. A. and van Asselt, M. B. A. (2006) 'Practicing the scenario–axes technique', *Futures*, vol 38, no 1, pp15–30

van Twist, M. J. W., den Boer, M. C., van Mil, B. P. A. and Geut, L. (2002) *Beelden van bestuur: Berenschot trendstudie*, Berenschot/Uitgeverij Lemma, The Netherlands

van Vught, F. A. (1985) *Beter dan Nostradamus en Campanella? Over de wetenschappelijke status van de sociaal–wetenschappelijke toekomstkunde*, Rijksuniversiteit Leiden, The Netherlands

Vleugel, J. M. (2000) *Design of Transport and Land-Use Scenarios: Principles and Applications*, PhD thesis, Free University, Amsterdam, The Netherlands

VROM (1997) *Nederland 2030 Verkenning Ruimtelijk Perspectieven*, Ministry of Housing, Planning and the Environment (VROM), The Hague, The Netherlands

Wack, P. (1985a) 'Scenarios: Uncharted waters ahead', *Harvard Business Review*, vol 63, no 5, pp72–79

Wack, P. (1985b) 'Scenarios: Shooting the Rapids', *Harvard Business Review*, vol 63, no 6, pp139–50

Wardekker, J. A., van der Sluijs, J. P., Janssen, P. H. M., Kloprogge, P. and Petersen, A. C. (2008) 'Uncertainty communication in environmental assessments: Views from the Dutch science–policy interface', *Environmental Science and Policy*, vol 11, no 8, pp627–641

Weaver, P., Jansen, L., van Grootveld, G., van Spiegel, E. and Vergragt, P. (2000) *Sustainable Technology Development*, Greenleaf Publishing, Sheffield, UK

Weick, K. E. (1979) *The Social Psychology of Organizing*, 2nd edition, Addison-Wesley, New York, US

Weick, K. E. (1999) *Sensemaking in Organizations*, Sage, Newbury Park, CA, US

Wells Bedsworth, L., Lowenthal, M.D. and Kastenberg, W. E. (2004) 'Uncertainty and regulation: The rhetoric of risk in the California low-level radioactive waste debate', *Science, Technology and Human Values*, vol 29, no 3, pp406–427

Wells, H. G. (1902) 'The discovery of the future', *Nature*, vol 65, pp326–331

Wenger, E. (1998) *Communities of Practice: Learning, Meaning and Identity*, Cambridge University Press, Cambridge, UK

Western Australian Planning Commission (2000) *Future Perth: Scenarios of our Future: Challenges for Western Australian Society*, John Curtin International Institute, Perth, Australia

Wilkinson, A. and Eidinow, E. (2003) 'A brief introduction to building and using scenarios', *Journal of Risk Research*, vol 6, no 4–6, pp295–296

Wilkinson, A. and Eidinow, E. (2008) 'Evolving practices in environmental scenarios: A new scenario typology', *Environmental Research Letters*, vol 3, no October–December, pp1–11

Wilkinson, A., Elahi, S. and Eidinow, E. (2003) 'Riskworld scenarios', *Journal of Risk Research*, vol 6, no 4–6, pp297–334

Woolgar, S. (1988) *Science: The Very Idea*, Routledge/Ellis Horwood, London, UK

World Business Council for Sustainable Development (2000) *Biotechnology Scenarios*, Conches, Geneva, Switzerland

Wright, G., Heijden, K. van der, Burt, G., Bradfield, R. and Cairns, G. (2008) 'Scenario planning interventions in organizations: An analysis of the causes of success and failure', *Futures*, vol 40, no 3, pp218–236

WRR (2000) *Terugblik op toekomstverkenningen*, WRR – Stuurgroep Toekomstonderzoek en strategisch omgevingsbeleid, The Hague, The Netherlands

WRR (2009) *Uncertain Safety: Allocating Responsibilities for Safety*, The Scientific Council for Government Policy (WRR), The Hague, The Netherlands

Wynne, B. (1980) 'Technology, risk and participation: On the social treatment of uncertainty', in J. Conrad (ed) *Society, Technology and Risk Assessment*, Academic Press, London, UK

Wynne, B. (1982) *Rationality and Ritual: The Windscale Inquiry and Nuclear Decisions in Britain*, British Society for the History of Science, Chalfont St. Giles, UK

Wynne, B. (1992) 'Uncertainty and environmental learning: Reconceiving science and policy in the preventive paradigm', *Global Environmental Change*, vol 2, no 2, pp111–127

Zeisler, S. and Dyer, H. (2000) 'Order from chaos: Part two', *Scenario and Strategy Planning*, vol 2, no 2, pp14–17

Appendix

This is a compendium of the 25 studies used in Chapters 2 and 6.
Note: Studies with an asterisk (*) are only used in Chapter 6.

1 *Surprising Futures*
   Svedin, U. and Aniansson, B. (eds) (1987) *Surprising Futures: Notes from an International Workshop on Long-Term World Development*, Swedish Council for Planning and Coordination of Research, Stockholm, Sweden
2 *Beyond Hunger in Africa*
   Achebe, C., Hyden, G., Magadza, C. and Okeyo, A. P. (1990) *Beyond Hunger in Africa: Conventional Wisdom and an Alternative Vision*, Heinemann, Portsmouth, NH, US
3 *European Security beyond the Cold War*
   Hyde-Price, A. G. V. (1991) *European Security beyond the Cold War: Four Scenarios for the Year 2010*, SAGE, London, UK
4 *Mont Fleur*
   Le Roux, P. et al (1992) 'The Mont Fleur scenarios: What will South Africa be like in the year 2002?', *Deeper News*, July 1992, www.gbn.org
   Kahane, A. (1998) 'Imagining South Africa's future: How scenarios helped discover common ground', in L. Fahey and R. Randall (eds) *Learning From the Future: Competitive Foresight Scenarios*, John Wiley and Sons, New York, US
5 *British Airways**
   Moyer, K. (1996) 'Scenario planning at British Airways: A case study', *Long Range Planning*, pp172–181
   Ringland, G. (1998) *Scenario Planning: Managing for the Future*, Wiley and Sons, Chichester, UK
6 *ICL**
   Ringland, G. (1998) *Scenario Planning: Managing for the Future*, Wiley and Sons, Chichester, UK
7 *Port of Rotterdam*
   Global Business Network (1996) *Port of Rotterdam Scenario Workshop Report*, Global Business Network
   Jongman, P. J. (2002) Pers comm, 10 June 2002
8 *The Futures of Women*
   McCorduck, P. and Ramsey, N. (1996) *The Futures of Women: Scenarios for the 21st Century*, Warner Books, New York, US

9 *Destino Colombia*
   Global Business Network (1998) 'Destino Colombia', *Deeper News*, www.gbn.org
10 Questa
   Ministerie van Verkeer en Waterstaat (1998) *Verplaatsen in de toekomst: Project Questa* (in Dutch), Ministerie van Verkeer en Waterstaat, The Hague, The Netherlands
   WRR (2000) *Terugblik op toekomstverkenningen* (in Dutch), WRR - Stuurgroep Toekomstonderzoek en strategisch omgevingsbeleid, The Hague, The Netherlands
   Vleugel, J.M. (2000) 'Design of transport and land-use scenarios: Principles and applications', Free University, Amsterdam, The Netherlands
   Dobbinga, E. (2001) *Weerbarstigheid van organisatiecultuur: een organisatie-antropologische studie naar betekenisgeving aan moderne managementinstrumenten* (in Dutch), PhD thesis, Eburon, Delft, The Netherlands
11 *Scenarios Europe 2010*
   Bertrand, G., Michalski, A. and Pench, L. R. (1999) *Scenarios Europe 2010*, European Commission Forward Studies Unit, Brussels, Belgium
   Bertrand, G. and Michalski, A. (2001) 'Governance in a larger and more diverse European Union: Lessons from scenarios Europe 2010', in O. De Schutter, N. Lebessis and J. Paterson (eds) *Governance in the European Union*, Forward Studies Unit/ European Commission
   European Environment Agency and Alcamo, J. (2001) *Scenarios as Tools for International Environmental Assessments*, Environmental issue report no 24, European Environment Agency, Copenhagen, Denmark
12 *The European Environment at the Turn of the Century*
   European Environment Agency (1999) *Environment in the European Union at the Turn of the Century*, Report no 2, European Environment Agency, Copenhagen, Denmark
   European Environment Agency and DHV (2000) *Documentation and Evaluation of the EU98 Scenario Process*, Unpublished, DHV Environment and Infrastructure
13 *Which World?*
   Hammond, A. (1998) *Which World? Scenarios for the 21st Century: Global Destinies, Regional Choices*, Earthscan Publications Ltd, London, UK
14 *WBCSD Biotech Scenarios*
   World Business Council for Sustainable Development (2000) *Biotechnology Scenarios*, Conches, Geneva, Switzerland
15 *IPCC/SRES*
   IPCC (Intergovernmental Panel on Climate Change) (2000) *IPCC Special Report: Emission Scenarios*, Cambridge University Press, Cambridge, UK
   European Environment Agency and Alcamo, J. (2001) *Scenarios as Tools for International Environmental Assessments*, Environmental issue report no 24, European Environment Agency, Copenhagen, Denmark
16 *Norway 2030*
   Øverland, E. F., Neumann, I. B., Dokk Holm, E. and Høviskeland, T. (2000) *Norway 2030*, Royal Ministry of Labour and Government Administration, Oslo, Norway

17 *Possum*
Banister, D., Stead, D., Steen, P., Akerman, J., Dreborg, K., Nijkamp, P. and Schleicher-Tapeser, R. (2000) *European Transport Policy and Sustainable Mobility*, E. and F. N. Spon, London and New York
European Environment Agency and ICIS (2000) *Cloudy Crystal Balls: An Assessment of Recent European and Global Scenario Studies and Models*, Environmental series report no 17

18 *Schooling for Tomorrow*
OECD (Organisation for Economic Co-operation and Development) (2001) *Schooling for Tomorrow: What Schools for the Future?*, Paris, France
Miller, R. (2003) *The Future of the Tertiary Education Sector*, OECD-CERI, Paris, France

19 *Shell Global Scenarios**
Shell International (2002) *People and Connections: Global Scenarios to 2020 – Public Summary*, London, UK

20 *Finnish Aquaculture*
Bruun, H., Hukkinen, J. and Ekland, E. (2002) 'Scenarios for coping with contingency: The case of aquaculture in the Finnish Archipelago Sea', *Technological Forecasting and Social Change*, vol 69, pp107–127

21 *Foresight Futures*
Department of Trade and Industry (2002) *Foresight futures 2020: Revised Scenarios and Guidance*, Department of Trade and Industry, London, UK
Berkhout, F., Hertin, J. and Jordan, A. (1998) *Socio-Economic Futures in Climate Change Impact Assessment: Using Scenarios as 'Learning Machines'*, Science and Technology Policy Research, University of Sussex, Brighton, UK
Berkhout, F. and Hertin, J. (2002) 'Foresight futures scenarios: Developing and applying a participative strategic planning tool', *Futures*, vol 37, spring, pp37–52

22 *GEO-3*
UNEP (United Nations Environment and Development Programme) (2002) *Global Environment Outlook 3*, Earthscan, London, UK
Rothman, D. S. (2004) Pers comm, 18 March 2004

23 *The Shield of Achilles*
Bobbitt, P. (2002) *The Shield of Achilles: War, Peace and the Course of History*, Penguin, London, UK

24 *Tunis*
Barbanente, A., Khakee, A. and Puglisi, M. (2002) 'Scenario building for Metropolis Tunis', *Futures*, vol 34, pp583–596

25 *CPB Netherlands Bureau for Economic Policy Analysis*
de Mooij, R. and Tang, P. (2003) *Four Futures of Europe*, CPB, The Hague, The Netherlands
de Mooij , R. (2004) Pers comm, 6 February 2004

Index

abrupt discontinuity; *see* discontinuity
Achilles (scenario study) 31–32, 128
Adam, B. 2, 3, 8, 10, 107, 123, 124, 131, 132, 135, 142
Aligica, P. D. 24, 79
analytical scenarios; *see* scenario
anchor; *see* expertise as anchor
Aniansson, B.; *see* Svedin
anthropology 12, 15
apolitical preference 45–48
Armstrong, S. J. 23–24, 143
axes 62–68, 70–71, 73, 75, 80; *see also* scenario matrix
Ayres, R. U. 121, 135

backbone; *see* functional meaning
backcasting 27, 30
backstage 76, 142; *see also* front stage
back-to-the-basics family; *see* scenario families
baseline scenarios; *see* scenario
Behrens, W. W.; *see* Meadows
Bell, W. 2, 4, 7, 20, 105, 107–108, 113, 131, 135
BETER (scenario study) 73, 91
Berkhout, F. 2, 23, 61, 62, 63, 67, 108, 122, 125
Beyond Hunger in Africa (scenario study) 31–32, 128
bifurcation; *see* discontinuity-related concepts
Bijker, W. E. xi, 8, 21, 62, 76, 107, 114, 141–142
black-boxing uncertainty; *see* uncertainty
boundary work 18, 21
Bowker, G. xi, 61, 76

Bradfield, R.; *see* van der Heijden
Brier, D. J. 1, 106
British Airways (scenario study) 125, 135
Brooks, H. 108, 121, 131
Brown, N. 2, 10, 18, 21, 80
Bruun, H. 28, 128, 131
Burt, G. 4, 79, 99; *see also* van der Heijden
business-as-usual scenarios; *see* scenario
business foresight; *see* foresight

Cairns, G.; *see* van der Heijden
camouflage 84, 93–94, 98
causal tapestry 27
certainification 97–101, 105, 133–134, 139–141, 143–144
certainty; *see* scientific certainty
certainty connotation (of numbers) 84, 91–93, 98
certain uncertainties 99; *see also* known unknowns
chain scenarios; *see* scenario
civic scenario studies 26, 38
Clark, W. C. 121, 122, 128, 130
closure 62, 67, 71, 73–75, 89–90, 114, 138, 142
Club of Rome 2, 24, 85
communicating about uncertainty; *see* uncertainty information
communicating uncertainty; *see* uncertainty communication
communication habits; *see* uncertainty manners
complex scenarios; *see* scenario
concealing uncertainty; *see* uncertainty

construction of solidity; *see* uncertainty manners
constructivist thesis 8, 20, 65, 140–142; *see also* social constructivism
contextual scenarios; *see* scenario
contingent events; *see* discontinuity-related concepts
Cunha, M. P.; *see* Mendonça
cut-off times 106, 109; *see also* slicing time

Dammers, E. 2, 37, 70, 72, 91, 108, 122, 124, 131
de Jouvenel, B. 7,
delegation; *see* uncertainty manners
Destino Colombia (scenario study) 30–32, 129
de Wilde, R. xi, 4, 21
discontinuity 11, 25, 108–109, 118–135, 137, 139, 142–143
  abrupt 123, 127–129, 134
  economic 123, 128–129
  environmental 123, 128–129
  foresight literature on 121–124
  gradual 123, 125, 127–129, 134
  including 124, 127–131
  omitting 124–127, 130–132
  political 123, 128–129
  social 123,128–129
discontinuity-related concepts 122
  bifurcation 122
  contingent events 122, 131
  dislocations 122
  extreme events 122
  faites porteurs d'avenir 122, 135
  paradigm busters 122
  sideswipe 122
  surprises 32, 88, 108, 122, 125, 128, 130
  wild cards 122, 128, 130–131
discourse 107, 109, 116; *see also* uncertainty manners – numeric discourse
dislocations; *see* discontinuity-related concepts
disrupting events 123
Dobbinga, E. 12, 17, 76, 80, 99, 124, 126, 127

driving forces 42, 62–65, 67, 71, 73, 75, 80
Drucker, P. F., 121, 135

early warnings 122–123
Elahi, S.; *see* Wilkinson
Eidinow, E.; *see* Wilkinson
einzelgänger scenario; *see* scenario
enactment 62, 68, 71–73, 76–77
Energy Research Centre of the Netherlands (ECN); *see* foresight planning agencies (Dutch)
environmental outlooks 9–10, 30–32, 37, 80, 84–85, 88, 93–94, 129
environmental risk management 84
ethnography 12, 15–17, 20
  ethnographic moments 16
The European Environment at the Turn of the Century (scenario study) 31–32, 124
European Environment Agency (EEA) 10, 32, 124–125
European Security beyond the Cold War (scenario study) 31–32, 126
evolutionary paradigm 131
expert authority 85, 141
expert consultation 84, 88–90, 98
expertise 6, 18, 76, 84, 88–90, 92, 97–98, 101, 138, 141, 144
expertise as anchor; *see* uncertainty manners
expert judgment 84, 88–90, 98, 117
exploration 28–29, 31, 35
extrapolation; *see* policy extrapolation; trend extrapolation
extreme events; *see* discontinuity-related concepts

faites porteurs d'avenir; *see* discontinuity-related concepts
Finnish Aquaculture (scenario study) 31–32, 128
Flight of the Flamingos (scenario) 29–30; *see also* Mont Fleur (scenario study)
Fontela, E. 79
forecasting 23–25, 27, 38, 88, 91, 99, 137, 139, 143

foresight
  business 2, 20, 26, 38, 41, 58, 99, 135;
    see also foresight – organizational
  exploratory style 23–25
  organizational 20, 41–43; see also
    foresight – business
  predictive style 23–25
Foresight (academic journal) 1, 17
Foresight Futures (scenario study) 31–32,
    124–125
foresight planning agencies (Dutch)
  The Energy Research Centre of The
    Netherlands (ECN) 9–10, 37
  The Institute for Spatial Research
    (RPB) 8, 10, 33, 72
  The Netherlands Bureau for Economic
    Policy Analysis (CPB) 8–11, 25, 29,
    32–33, 37, 42
  The Netherlands Environmental
    Assessment Agency (former MNP,
    now PBL) 8–9, 11, 20, 37, 88
  The Netherlands Organization for
    Applied Scientific Research (TNO)
    9, 33
  The Scientific Council for Government
    Policy (WRR) xii, 2, 9, 25, 80, 101,
    124
  The Social and Cultural Planning
    Office (SCP) 8–9, 33
Forward Studies Unit (European
    Commission) 2
foundation; see functional meaning
Four Futures of Europe (scenario study)
    10, 29, 31–33, 37, 42
Fox, R. 84,
front stage 64, 71, 74–76, 142; see also
    backstage
functional meaning 62–77, 79–80, 83,
    138, 140–143
  backbone 62–8, 70–71, 73–75, 80,
    138, 140–141, 143
  foundation 62, 66–71, 73–75, 138,
    140
  scaffold 62, 69–71, 73–75, 138, 140
  showcase 62, 73–75, 138, 140
Funtowicz, S. O.; see Ravetz
future
  conceptualizing 1, 106–108, 133, 139
  delimiting 106

plausible 87, 115, 117
possible 4, 24, 29, 32, 42, 68, 84–86,
    98, 108, 110–111, 113–114,
    117–118, 134, 137
preferred 84–86, 98
probable 4, 84–86, 98, 110, 113–114,
    118, 120, 134
reference 88; see also trend extrapola-
    tion
short term 110, 113, 116, 118, 125
Futures (academic journal) 1, 17, 20, 25,
    96
The Futures of Women (scenario study)
    31–32, 128
futures studies 17–18, 20, 145
futuristic difference; see temporal reper-
    toires

Gallopín, G. 10, 122
Geertz, C. 2, 13, 20
Girod, B. 41
Global Business Network (GBN) 38,
    108, 122, 125, 126
*Global Environment Outlook 3
    (GEO-3)* (scenario study) 31–32,
    129
Goffman, E. 76
governmental scenario studies 25, 38
gradual discontinuity; see discontinuity
Groves, C; see Adam

Halffman, W. 21; see also Hoppe
Hammond, A. 28, 29, 30, 129; see also
    Gallopín
Hertin, J.; see Berkhout
heuristic 70, 75
Hilgartner, S. 21, 76, 141–142
Hine, A. 15
historians 4
historical knowledge; see past-based
    knowledge
historic determinism; see temporal reper-
    toires
Holling, C. S. 122
Hoppe, R. 8, 21, 102
Huitema, D. 45, 102
Hulme, M.; see Girod
hypothesis testing 145

ICL (scenario study) 135
ignore-ance (arrog*ance* to *ignore*) 126
Inayatullah, S. 20, 105
inscribe 2–3, 20, 62, 70, 74–75, 77, 133,
    138–139
Institute for Spatial Research (RPB); *see*
    foresight planning agencies (Dutch)
institutionalization (of Dutch
    foresight) 8, 10
Intergovernmental Panel on Climate
    Change (IPCC) 2, 10, 32, 35, 37–38,
    41, 62, 125
intergovernmental scenario studies
    25–26, 38
intuitive scenarios; *see* scenario
IPCC Emissions Scenarios (SRES)
    (scenario study) 31–32, 37, 125

Jasanoff, S. 21, 100
Journal of Forecasting (academic
    journal) 24
Journal of Risk Research (academic
    journal) 18
Jungermann, H. 26, 27, 123

Kahn, H. 2, 24, 43, 107
Kaivo-oja, J.; *see* Mendonça
Kates, R. W.; *see* Clark
Knorr-Cetina, K. 12, 15, 20
knowledge construction; *see*
    constructivist thesis; social construc-
    tivism
known unknowns 99; *see also* certain
    uncertainties
Koselleck, R. 7, 107

Latour, B. 8, 11–12, 15, 76, 102
legitimacy (production of) 76

managing uncertainty; *see* uncertainty
market family; *see* scenario families
Masini, E. B. 121
Meadows, D. H. 2, 24
Meadows, D. L.; *see* Meadows, D. H.
meantime 106, 133–134, 139
medical–sociological studies 84, 93–94
Mendonça, S. 122–124
Mesman, J. xi, 82, 84, 86, 93, 107, 114

metaphors 62, 64, 66, 70–71, 73, 76
Mieg, H., *see* Girod
minimally differentiated trend policy
    47–48, 51, 59
Ministry of Environment and Spatial
    Planning (VROM) 42, 44, 50, 52,
    91
modeling
    computer models 30, 91–93, 118
    mathematical models 91–93
Mol, A. 60, 62, 74, 76, 77
Mont Fleur (scenario study) 29–32, 39,
    129
Morgan, D. 3, 131
multi-method; *see* research approach
multiplicity (of functional meanings) 62,
    72, 74–75, 77, 79
Munn, R. E.; *see* Clark

native 14–17; *see also* participant obser-
    vation
negotiation of scientific facts 20, 65
Nekkers, J. 29, 42, 43
Netherlands Bureau for Economic Policy
    Analysis (CPB); *see* foresight
    planning agencies (Dutch)
Netherlands Environmental Assessment
    Agency (former MNP, now PBL); *see*
    foresight planning agencies (Dutch)
Netherlands Organization for Applied
    Scientific Research (TNO); *see*
    foresight planning agencies (Dutch)
Netherlands Polderland (scenario) 36;
    see also Questa (scenario study)

Noordegraaf, M. 82, 84, 102
non-intervention scenarios; *see* scenario
Norway 2030 (scenario study) 31–32,
    128, 130
no (significant) policy change principle
    47–50, 53–54, 56–57, 59, 61, 138,
    140, 142
Nota Ruimte (Dutch spatial policy plan)
    52–53
Nowotny, H. 3, 7, 80, 85, 102, 107, 141
numeric discourse; *see* uncertainty
    manners

objectivity (production of) 76
Old leaves us cold (scenario) 26
Organisation for Economic Co-operation and Development (OECD) 2, 31–32, 38, 125
organizational foresight; *see* foresight
out-of-the-box-thinking 28, 35

paradigm busters; *see* discontinuity-related concepts
participant observation 12–17, 21, 137
  insider 14–17
  observer style 16–17
  outsider 15–17
  participant style 16–17
past-based knowledge 107–108, 110–112, 114–118, 124, 132, 135, 141–142, 144
patients (and uncertainty) 84, 86–87
Petersen, A. C. 93, 102
Petersen, J. L. 122–124
planning agencies; *see* foresight planning agencies (Dutch)
plausible future(s); *see* future
Polak, F., 3, 122
policy extrapolation 47–50, 54–55
policy free principle 41–48, 53, 56–59, 61, 137–138, 140–143
policy poor/neutral scenarios; *see* scenario
Porter, T. M. 91
Port of Rotterdam (scenario study) 31–32, 125–126
positivism 8, 14, 20, 43, 74–75, 80, 102, 132, 138, 140–145
possibility space 23, 38, 68–69, 75
possible future(s); *see* future
Possum (scenario study) 30–32, 124, 126
prediction; *see* foresight – predictive; forecasting
preferred future; *see* future
pre-policy research 28–29, 31, 35
probabilities; *see* future – probable
probable future; *see* future
process (of foresight endeavor) 66, 71, 74–75
prospective uncertainty; *see* uncertainty
prudent formulations 93

quadrants 62–64, 66–69, 71; *see also* scenario matrix
quality improvement 3, 19
quantification 92
quasi-certainty 92, 101, 144
  statistics 92
Questa (scenario study) 31–33, 36, 124, 126

Ramírez, R. 43; *see also* van der Heijden
Randers, J.; see *Meadows*
Raskin, P. D. 10; *see also* Gallopín
Ravetz, J. R. xi, 102, 141
reference future; *see* future
reflection in action 3, 17, 21, 101, 134, 142–144
reflection on action 3, 17, 21, 134, 137–143
reflexive looping 17
reification (of functional meaning) 70, 74–76, 138, 140–141
repertoires; *see* temporal repertoires
representations (of the scenario matrix) 62, 67–72
research approach 12–17
  multi-method 14
  multi-sited 13
research questions 11
Ringland, G. 2, 20, 24–25, 42–43, 61–63, 122, 126, 129
Risk Analysis (academic journal) 18
risk research 18–19
Robinson, J. 27, 99
robustness testing 42–43, 53, 142, 144; *see also* wind tunneling
robust policies 42, 59, 90
robust trends 59, 135
Rose, H. 3, 21
Rotmans, J. xi, 21, 102, 122
Ruff, F.; *see* Mendonça

Sardar, Z. 1, 20
scaffold; *see* functional meaning
Scanning the Future (scenario study) 10, 29
scenario
  analytical 28, 30–31, 34
  baseline 124
  business-as-usual 124, 131

chain 26–27, 38
complex 28, 31, 34, 38
contextual 41; *see also* policy-free
   principle
einzelgänger 36, 38
intuitive 28, 30–31, 34
non-intervention 41
policy poor/neutral 47, 124
simple 28, 31, 38
snapshot 26–27, 38, 126
scenario approach 12, 18, 24, 34, 42, 118
scenario cartwheel 27–35
scenario families 35–36, 38
   back-to-the-basics 35–36, 38
   market 35, 38
   spring 35–36, 38
scenario matrix 3, 19, 61–77, 79–80, 83,
   101, 105, 107, 138, 140–143
   functional meanings; *see* functional
   meaning
Scenarios Europe 2010 (scenario study)
   31–32, 124
scenario theory 41
SCENE (scenario study) 37, 44, 49–50,
   65–73, 91, 117
Schneider, S. H. 121, 122
Schoemaker, P. J. H. 27, 102
Schön, D. A. 12, 17, 21, 80
Schooling for Tomorrow (scenario study)
   31–32, 125
Schooneboom, J. 8, 37, 99, 100; *see also*
   van der Duin
Schwartz, P. 20, 24, 41, 62–64, 102, 123,
   128, 135
science and technology studies (STS)
   18–19, 21, 64–65, 76, 107, 141
science fiction 3–4, 20–21, 106, 117, 130
scientific certainty 14, 82, 141
Scientific Council for Government Policy
   (WRR); *see* foresight planning
   agencies (Dutch)
seeds of change 122
seeds of time 122–123
self-accounts 3, 11–12, 15–17, 25, 28,
   30, 38, 80, 83, 98, 100, 118
Sharpe, B. 41, 42
Shell 2, 24, 37, 41, 62, 76, 126, 135
Shell Global Scenarios (scenario study)
   126, 135

short term future; *see* future
showcase; *see* functional meaning
sideswipe; *see* discontinuity-related
   concepts
signals of change 123–124
simple scenarios; *see* scenario
skeleton 64; *see also* functional meaning
   – backbone
Slaughter, R. A. 1, 20, 21
slicing time 109–110, 118–119,
   133–134, 139; *see also* time horizon
Smith, R. A. 62, 64
snapshot scenarios; *see* scenario
Social and Cultural Planning Office
   (SCP); *see* foresight planning
   agencies (Dutch)
social constructivism 7–8, 18, 20, 65, 67,
   74–75, 138, 140–143
sociology of science 76
spring family; *see* scenario families
stickiness (of functional meanings) 70,
   74
Strong Europe (scenario) 27
surprises; *see* discontinuity-related
   concepts
surprise free 124
Surprising Futures (scenario study)
   31–32, 128
Svedin, U. 121, 122, 128, 130

*Technological Forecasting & Social
   Change* (academic journal) 1, 17, 121
technology assessment 18
temporal continuity 23, 71, 107–108,
   110, 114, 118–119, 125, 133–134,
   139
temporal repertoires 106–122, 124–125,
   127, 130–134, 137, 139–140,
   142–144
   co-existence of 111–115, 120, 133,
   139
   historic determinism 107–120, 122,
   124–125, 130–134, 139–143
   futuristic difference 108–119, 124,
   127, 130–134, 139–140, 142–144
thick descriptions 2–3, 16
Thuring, M.; *see* Jungermann
time
   conceptualizing 105–107, 133, 139

time horizon 1, 24, 54, 106, 109–110, 125; *see also* meantime
time series 23, 81, 110
trend breaks 49, 120–121, 123, 126
trend extrapolation 23, 87–88, 91, 110, 112, 114, 119–120, 131
trend watching 4
triangulation 14
Tunis (scenario study) 31–32, 124
Turner II, B. L.; *see* Schneider
typical exemplars; *see* uncertainty manners

Uggla, Y. 82, 84, 96–97
UK Foresight Future Flooding Project (scenario study) 18
UK foresight programme 2, 32
uncertainty
    black-boxing 81–82, 92, 97–98, 101–102, 138
    concealing 81–82, 85, 91, 97–98, 138
    coping with 3, 97–98, 133, 138
    delegation of; *see* uncertainty manners
    disclosing 93
    managing 19, 79–80, 82–83, 93, 95–98, 100–101, 105, 134, 139–140
    prospective xi, 19, 58, 79–103, 105–106, 109–110, 112–114, 117–118, 133–134, 137–139
    wrestling with 97, 139
uncertainty awareness 80–84, 86, 92, 94, 97–101, 105, 133, 138–139
uncertainty communication 84, 92–95, 97–101, 103, 138
uncertainty evaluation
    expert judgment 84, 88–90, 98
    intuition 89
uncertainty expressions 93, 103
uncertainty information 93–95, 98
uncertainty intolerance 97–99, 101, 105, 133–134, 139, 141, 144–145
uncertainty manners 80, 82–98, 101, 105, 133, 138–140, 142–144
    communication habits 84, 93–95, 97–98, 101, 138
    construction of solidity 84–86, 93, 97–98, 100–102, 138
    delegation 84, 95–98, 101, 138
        to other persons 84, 95–96, 98

to the future 84, 95–98
    research questions 81–82, 96–97, 138
    expertise as anchor 84–85, 88–90, 92, 97–98, 101, 138
    numeric discourse 84, 91–93, 97–98, 101, 138
    typical exemplars 84, 86–88, 97–98, 101, 133, 138
uncertainty tolerance 101, 144
unchanged change 113–114, 131
United Nations Environment Programme (UNEP) 2, 30, 32, 38, 122, 129
unknowns 89, 96; *see also* known unknowns
utopian novels 3–4

vagueness 84, 93–94, 97–98, 101; *see also* uncertainty manners – communication habits
van der Duin, P. A. 1, 9, 20, 23, 25, 43
van der Heijden, K. 20, 24, 29, 41–43, 62–64, 76, 79, 99, 102, 106, 123
van der Sluijs, J. P. 88, 92, 102
van der Staal; *see* van Vught
van der Steen, M. 23, 105, 135
van Lente, H. 20, 21, 114
van Vught, F. A. 2, 8, 11
variation ambition 83
Verkenning van de Ruimte (VVR) (scenario study) 44, 55

Wack, P. 20, 62, 76
WBCSD Biotech (scenario study) 31–32, 128
weak signals 122–123
Wells, H. G. 1, 3
Welvaart en Leefomgeving (WLO) (scenario study) 37, 45, 47–48, 51–52, 57, 108–109, 117, 119–120, 125, 132
what-if analysis 24, 38, 110–111, 137
Which World? (scenario study) 30–32, 129
Wetenschappelijke Raad voor het Regeringsbeleid (WRR); *see* foresight planning agencies (Dutch)
Wiek, A. xii; *see also* Girod
Wiener, A.; *see* Kahn

wild card; *see* discontinuity-related concepts

Wilkinson, A. 18, 80, 99, 142

wind tunneling 42–43, 53, 142, 144; *see also* robustness testing

Woolgar, S. xi, 8, 11–12, 14–16, 21, 76, 102

World Business Council for Sustainable Development (WBCSD) 32, 127–128

World Resources Institute 30

Wright, G. 4, 20; *see also* van der Heijden

Wynne, B. 21, 102, 141; *see* also van der Sluijs